'An incredibly powerful memoir. The courage, fortitude and fire it takes to share a story of this magnitude is nothing short of miraculous'
**Diriye Osman, author of *Fairytales for Lost Children***

'Many gay men reading Richard Hall's brave, compelling, troubling and at times traumatic coming-of-age memoir will experience shivers down their spines as they recognise aspects of themselves, their lives and their behaviours. *I'm Fine* should be read by all gay men for its adamantine honesty and for the unflinching and often uncomfortable light it shines on masculinity, gay identity, sexuality and power. This is an important book'
**Neil McKenna, author of *Fanny & Stella***

'An exceptional coming-of-age story that manages to be both a joyous love letter to a time in our lives when everything seems possible and a damning exposé of those who seek to prey on us while we are learning who we are. *I'm Fine* is so charming and engaging and funny and sad and real that it's hard to believe this is Richard Hall's debut'
**Bethany Clift, author of *Last One at the Party***

'Hall captures what it means to be both seen and used — how predators can double as protectors, and how the lines blur when you're young, scared and already marked. He is funny, sharp-tongued, occasionally cruel — but never dishonest. Beneath the camp, there's something fierce and aching. This is the story of survival, told without apology'
**Ray Robinson, author of *The Mating Habits of Stags***

'Touching, honest, at times disturbing, but ultimately hopeful and heartening'
**John R. Gordon, author of *Drapetomania***

I'M FINE

# I'm fine

A true story of trust, betrayal
and criminal exploitation

Richard Hall

Published in 2025
by Eye Books Ltd
29A Barrow Street
Much Wenlock
Shropshire
TF13 6EN

www.eye-books.com

ISBN: 9781785634239

Copyright © Richard Hall 2025

Cover design by Nell Wood

Typeset in Garamond 3Lt Std and American Typewriter

The moral right of the author has been asserted. All rights reserved. No part of this publication may be reproduced, stored in a retrieval system, or transmitted, in any form or by any means without the prior written permission of the publisher, nor be otherwise circulated in any form of binding or cover other than that in which it is published and without a similar condition being imposed on the subsequent purchaser.

British Library Cataloguing in Publication Data

A catalogue record for this book is available from the British Library.

Our authorised representative in the EU for product safety is:
Logos Europe, 9 rue Nicolas Poussin, 17000, La Rochelle, France
contact@logoseurope.eu

The events in this book are true and accurate to the best of my recollection. Some names, locations and descriptions have been changed. Others have not.

To my mum.
She loved me from before I was born,
and I feel it every day of my life

In 1996, at the age of fourteen, I met a man who changed my life. In 2020, I called the police. On 28 March 2024, he was sentenced to twenty-two years in prison.

This is the story of what came before the police. How, isolated and alone, I walked into a world that I was too inexperienced to navigate.

# 1

My mum told me I was gay just before my tenth birthday. Well, she told me about gay people, when I inadvertently told her I was one. It was during a family holiday to Avignon in the south of France in 1991. The drive there was arduous. My older sister Jenny and I had been strapped into the back of the car all day, making each other squeal by poking and hitting each other, or issuing threats to do so. Each time we squealed, Mum sighed louder, and Dad frequently threatened to turn the car around and go home. Once, he even turned himself round to glare at us, which made Mum shout about watching the road, and Jenny and I screamed because if Mum was panicked, we were clearly all about to die.

I quickly learned that, in France, bread was life, so each day started with a walk to the bakery for baguettes. One particular morning, Mum and I left the house early, before it got too hot. Our house was on the edge of the village, and to nine-year-old me the walk seemed long. Our noses were filled with the scents of wild herbs, lavender and pine sap, which would fade later, as the day grew hotter.

'Mummy,' I said during this walk. 'Why am I different?'

She slowed her pace. 'What do you mean?'

'Well, all my boy friends like girls, and I like girls, but I think I like boys more.'

Mum nodded and started talking about friendships. Saying it was how a particular person made you feel that counted, not if they were a boy or a girl.

'No, Mummy, I mean, all my boy friends talk about *liking* girls, but I think I like *them* the way *they* like the girls.'

Our walk got slower still. Mum explained that while most boys like girls, sometimes boys like boys or girls like girls. 'For some people, it's just for part of their life,' she said, 'and for others it's their whole lives.'

'But how would two boys love each other?'

Mum came to an abrupt stop. She didn't answer.

'Mummy? We did babies at school last year, so how do two men do babies?'

Silence. Her face reddened.

'Mummy?'

We started to walk again. 'Did... Er... When they taught you about babies, did they tell you about where they come from?'

'Of course,' I said impatiently. 'Ladies have eggs you can't cook. And men have tadpoles that when added to the eggs make babies.'

'Erm, yeah, that's close. So they explained what sex is?'

'That's a bad word isn't it?'

'No. Well, it depends how you use it. Between you and me, just this morning, it's okay.'

We reached the village square where the bakery was, along with stalls selling vegetables and cheese, a butcher's and a café that seemed to only sell miniature cups of coffee. 'So they explained about vaginas and penises?' Mum asked.

'Vagina is definitely a bad word. Mrs Whitlaw said boys

can't say it because we don't have one.'

An old woman looked round from a vegetable stall because I'd said 'vagina' quite loudly.

'Good morning. Oh, I mean *bonjour*,' Mum said to the old lady, blushing. Then, to me: 'Let's get the bread and we can talk more on the way home.'

In the bakery Mum peeled my face away from the patisserie display case. 'So that's two baguettes and two – er, *deux* – *petites* strawberry tarts, um, *fraise, s'il vous plaît.*'

I didn't know what '*petites*' meant, but it was written in a decorative hand on a label by a tray of desserts small enough to fit in the palm of my hand. 'Do I get a whole one, or do we only get half each later?'

'If you keep your face off the glass, we get one each on the way home.'

Outside the bakery Mum passed me one of the tarts on a paper napkin. Underneath the shiny strawberries was the French custard that tasted so much better than its British equivalent.

'So, sex. They told you how it works?'

'The man puts himself in the woman when he wants a baby.'

'Well, sure, though maybe Mrs Whitlaw should do a lesson in equality.' She took a bite of her tart. 'But it's not always about babies. Sometimes, when adults want to, they have sex for fun.'

'Like playing a game?'

'Kind of. And when it's straight people there's a woman and a man. Gay people, there are two men.'

'And one of them has a vagina?'

'Not exactly. Two men, so two penises.'

'So one puts his penis in the other one's penis?'

'No. Just let me tell you and then we can have questions.

When two men want to have sex there are no babies.'

'Because two tadpoles?'

Mum blinked slowly. 'Well yes, kind of. Some men, if they want to, well,' – she was as red as the strawberries in the tart – 'they put their, erm, they put their penis in the other one's bottom.'

'With all the poop?'

'I...erm...I don't think so. Let's just say it's magic, okay?'

'So I should like bums then?'

'I said sometimes, and if they want to.'

'So I should like some bums?'

'That's closer.'

'Should I like my own bum?'

'It's not about the bums, okay; it's about adults being in love.'

'A LIZARD!' I ran towards the bright green creature that sat watching us in the middle of the path. But I tripped, and the remains of my tart landed where the lizard had been. I looked up at Mum. 'I only got to eat half.'

'Here; have mine. And let's not mention this conversation to Daddy or Jenny.'

We carried this secret together. I was alone, apart from Mum, and by the time I was fourteen, this was weighing on me.

One morning, at home in Wiltshire, I came downstairs to find Jenny lying on the sofa watching *Live & Kicking*, and Mum fixing breakfast in the kitchen. She was dressed for work, wearing the grey trousers that made her butt look even bigger, and already had a spot of margarine on her silk blouse. The sound of Dad lumbering around upstairs came through the ceiling as he got ready for work.

Just to be irritating, I took the remote from Jenny and

changed channels. Being older, she had a TV in her room. I didn't, which in my view meant I should get priority for the TV in the sitting room.

'I was watching that!' she shouted, jumping up and grabbing at the remote. 'Change it back now!'

I opened my dressing gown and stuck it down the front of my pants. 'You do it!'

'You're repulsive!' she bellowed, and stomped out of the room.

As I regally waved her away and dumped myself down on the sofa where the cat was asleep – she now woke and jumped away to safety – Mum appeared in the doorway. I assumed she was about to lecture me to be nicer to Jenny, so I pulled out the remote control and closed my dressing gown. Instead she held up a finger to show I should both wait and be quiet. A moment later the sound of *Live & Kicking* came from Jen's bedroom. Mum came and sat by me. She'd been going through the *Radio Times*, she said, and had seen a new show advertised: *Gaytime TV*. I said nothing as she explained it was a show for the lesbian and gay community. It had aired late last night and she'd managed to tape it without anyone knowing. She'd already watched it to check it was suitable for me. Did I want to watch it?

Of course I did. For the last five years it'd been just me, Mum and a dream there were more people like me out there. And now, it turned out, there were.

'You'll have to wait for the house to be empty.'

I begged, pleaded and promised to turn off the TV if Jenny came out of her room, but Mum wouldn't budge. 'I'll let you have the tape when you can watch on your own.'

Waiting was going to be torture, but Mum was right: I didn't want Jenny to know about me. If she told one of her friends, it would only be a matter of time before it got back to school. Worse would be her saying something to Dad. I didn't think he'd be able to support me 'choosing' a life that was sinful and might end with me dying young from AIDS. Even if he found a way to accept it, I could imagine the look I'd get every time a male friend came round.

The house was finally empty. Mum produced the VHS cassette. I eagerly pushed it into the VCR, pressed play and sat cross-legged in front of the TV, so close that I could only just see the whole screen.

For the first time in my life I was seeing people like me and listening to them talk about things I was thinking and feeling. A beautiful muscular man and a quick-witted, funny woman presented a current affairs programme. They talked about politics too much, but there they were, right in front of me: gay people being who they were with no apologies, no hiding, no fear. Living their lives the way I yearned to.

For weeks after that, Mum would record the show and watch it through by herself, then I would get to see it, and for that hour I'd lose myself in a world I could see but not touch. It was out there somewhere: a place where I didn't have to hide; with people who felt like I did. I hadn't known what I was missing until it was there in front of me.

A week came where there wasn't a tape for me, and Mum told me I'd have to wait until tomorrow. The next afternoon she stood in front of me with the video cassette in her hand, not offering it to me.

'There's about fifteen minutes of the test card towards the end,' she said. 'It was a segment that wasn't appropriate for you, so I taped over it.'

She wouldn't tell me what it was, which made me even more curious. I stuffed the tape in the VCR and hit play. I got lost in the show as usual, until the presenter was cut off mid-sentence and replaced by the test-card picture of the annoying girl and creepy clown, and the horrible high-pitched tone that went with it. I pressed fast-forward, watching the static lines rumble across the screen, then the show was back. I hit rewind and there was a skinny old man with a pencil-thin moustache who looked like a marionette. The shot opened up and Rhona Cameron, the female presenter, was holding her hand towards him saying, 'The amazing John Waters, everyone.'

I rewound and paused on the picture of the old guy, then pressed play again. There were only five minutes of the show left, and I spent all of them wondering what could be so transgressive about him.

Mum was sitting at the table in the breakfast room, her back to the door. Her shoulders jumped when I announced my presence by asking, 'Who's John Waters?'

She sighed. 'It's not so much him; it's some of his work.'

'Why?'

'He... He makes movies of a very adult genre.'

'You mean gay movies.'

'It's not that they're gay. They're just... in poor taste, even for adults.'

'You're straight. You don't get to say that gay people are in *poor taste.*'

'Don't twist my words.' She got up and moved towards the kitchen. 'I don't like the way he depicts people expressing their sexual nature. And I don't like him encouraging men to caricature women under the guise of drag.'

'What's drag?'

'I said you could watch the show *if* I thought it was appropriate. That bit wasn't. End of discussion.'

She plucked her teapot off the worktop and angrily shook the spent bags out into the sink. I turned on my heel, and made a point of stomping on each stair all the way up to my bedroom.

Two days later, however, she returned to the subject, saying, 'I think you may have been right.' She said I'd reached an age where I perhaps needed to speak to someone other than her, and for us to not carry my secret alone. She'd trawled through the *Yellow Pages*, got on the phone to support groups and helplines, and found a charity: the Swindon Gay Men's Health Project. One thing it offered was counselling. I didn't feel I needed counselling, but since this was a door into a world that I needed to be a part of, I meekly asked her to make an appointment for me.

My mind started creating elaborate fantasies about life if I wasn't alone. My hormones screamed *boyfriend*. Even the sight of a friend's underwear discarded on his bedroom floor would set my pulse throbbing. My heart, on the other hand, screamed *friend*: someone I could be honest with and not hide this huge part of myself that had been growing – or shrinking – in isolation for so long.

We lived in a town called Highworth, and Swindon was seven miles away. That would be over an hour on the bus, so I was glad when Mum said she'd drive me. On the day of the appointment, she pulled up outside an old Victorian building on the edge of town. My heart raced. Inside were people who would know I was gay, people to whom I would openly voice those words.

'Are you okay?' Mum asked.

'Yes,' I lied. My heart was hammering.

We went in. The receptionist, a plump woman with a crew cut, directed us upstairs with a friendly smile. Mum led the way. Her breathing was strained. Waiting at the top of the stairs was a man about her age. He was small-framed, maybe

5'8", dressed in clothes cut for someone bigger, and to my eyes he was a dork. I'd hoped for someone more handsome, like the host on *Gaytime TV*. This man's eyes flicked between Mum and me. On the upside, they had a warmth to them. Mum offered him her hand and he shook it, introducing himself as Tim, a key worker for Gay Men's Health Project. 'Can I get you a cup of tea?'

'I don't want to get in the way,' she said, then immediately began to do just that by asking questions: how long he'd been a social worker; whether he'd been to university and where; where he'd lived before Swindon. I stood there awkwardly, wishing she'd leave.

Eventually a voice with a strong American accent came up the stairs behind us and Tim introduced Chad, who'd be my counsellor. He was fat, wore a light-blue shirt and slacks, and held an A4 notebook with loose pages fanning out of it, and a mug of coffee. A pen in his breast pocket had leaked at some point, giving him an ink nipple, which I wanted to comment on, but didn't. Mum put a hand on my arm, looked deep into my eyes and asked, 'Are you okay with this?'

I quite enjoyed how protective she was being. 'I'm good,' I said.

'I'll wait outside in the car.'

Chad led me to a little room, sliding the brass slot on the door to 'In use' as he ushered me inside. Two small sofas faced each other informally across a low table. A vase held a single fake flower.

Chad led the conversation by telling me things about himself. He was Canadian, for instance, not American. As Highworth wasn't exactly a cosmopolitan place, his accent made me feel like I was in a TV show or film.

'We can talk about anything you want,' he said. 'It's all confidential. We won't tell anyone – not even your mother.'

'Okay.'

'How's school?'

'Good.'

'How are things at home? And your friends? Your family?'

All were good.

'Is there anything that *isn't* good?'

That question worked. Before, my brain had been in defensive mode. Now, suddenly I was talking about things I'd never said out loud before. The first time I said 'I'm gay' I whispered it, but the little smile it prompted in Chad gave me confidence.

After a while he asked about my sexual activity and what I knew about sexual health. I was anticipating the usual school crap: 'Don't have sex. When you do have sex use a condom. But don't have sex. Oh, and AIDS.' Instead, I realised, he was asking how I felt and if I was comfortable with myself.

All too soon the session was at an end and I was aware I hadn't made the most important point. 'What I want most is a friend my age,' I blurted out. The words were hard to say because it felt like I was saying I had no friends, but I saw that Chad understood.

'We can schedule an appointment for two weeks' time, if you'd like,' he said. 'I can see if one of the boys who lives with Tim can be here afterwards. Maybe we can find you that friend.'

The thought went through me like electricity. A friend who's a boy; a gay boy.

Back in the car I couldn't stop talking. The tension I'd been carrying rushed out of me like a tide, but my dreams of instant liberation soon beached on the shores of Mum's realism.

'It's just your first session,' she said. 'You're only fourteen. You've got a lot of growing-up to do.'

I didn't say anything. Chad had told me that counselling might change how I felt, and that others, like Mum, might not be as excited for those changes as I was.

I wondered if I should have told Chad about Stephen in my English class, or Charles' big brother with his jeans that fit so snugly around his butt and crotch. Or that, despite saying I had no gay friends, I was sort of dating Dan.

# 2

I'd been friends with Dan for about a year. It was one of those friendships that start because you both hang out at the same places, and continue because you live close to each other. He was in the year above me and had the wide shoulders of someone much older.

We didn't have much in common other than that we could both buy cigarettes, him because he looked older than he was, me because I had a fake ID – the result of a couple of hours in the school library with some Tippex, my birth certificate and the school photocopier. But he had an animal quality: a mane of wild hair and eyes that could fix you like prey and yet draw you in. Less appealingly, he had severe gingivitis. Inevitably his nickname was Shit Breath.

The day things moved to another level, we'd met up in the thin strip of dense woodland that ran along the side of his house, in the posher part of Highworth. It was a great place for teenagers to hide in, out of sight of the road, down an embankment. I watched the muscles in his back move under his t-shirt as he idly beat a tree with a fallen branch, bits of bark and leaves raining down around him.

We sat on a fallen tree in the centre of a clearing, staring out at nothing and sharing a single cigarette. After a while, and out of nowhere, Dan asked, 'Are you gay?'

Fear stopped me answering.

Thankfully he continued, 'Because I'm bi.' He said it like he was saying his name or the school he went to.

My eyes flicked to his crotch. 'I don't know what I am,' I lied. 'I'm just me.'

Could I have not been alone all this time? My mind flashed back to the time he got changed in front of me in his bedroom: his bulge large in his blue-check boxers, the two of us alone together.

'How does that work?' he asked. 'Do you like girls, boys, or both?'

My twisting nerves forced out a laugh. 'I guess both. I haven't had either yet.'

'Want to date then?'

The memory of him in his boxers, that little bit of hair running up to his belly button, burned in me. Was I about to get to look properly? To feel? Would it feel the same as mine? But burning just as bright was the terror of giving up my secret to the world. I had to answer him. 'Okay. We can try.'

'Great. Well, I'm going home. Catch you later.' And with a smile, he left. I stood there with the taste of fear still faintly metallic in the back of my mouth.

My thoughts swirled about. So, my secret was partially out in the world? I was dating a guy? Called Shit Breath? Who, five minutes ago, was a convenience friend? Who left without so much as a hug goodbye, never mind a kiss? The idea of my first kiss being with his breath… What if he let me see inside his boxers, but it smelled as bad as his breath? Did I even want to date him? I kicked some leaves about, and went home.

Dan and I hung out together a lot more often after that, but our 'relationship' wasn't much different from our friendship, though I soon told him I wasn't confused; I was gay.

Our primary activity was still smoking each other's cigarettes. We didn't kiss, we didn't cuddle, but we talked lots and lots about blowjobs and trying to find secluded spots to do them. Somehow the spots were never right: not private enough, too dirty, or else 'my parents may be home soon'.

None of these excuses were mine. It crossed my mind that Dan might not really be bi. Could he just be trying to be cool? But wouldn't that only work if he told people?

The two-week wait for my second counselling appointment sailed by, and Mum was comfortable enough to let me go on my own. Afraid I'd be late, I arrived far too early, but Tim was there and made me a cup of tea and let me sit in his office while I waited for Chad. Mostly he got on with his paperwork, but he asked me the odd question about how I was doing. I sensed that he was uncomfortable too, but then Chad arrived.

The second session was easier than the first. Dan came up. Though nothing had changed and I still hadn't done anything remotely physical with him, I talked it out with Chad and then we moved on to discuss what makes a good boyfriend. I managed to resist saying 'someone hotter than Dan' because I thought Chad would think I was shallow, and agreed on self-respect, self-worth and valuing what I had to offer. I didn't say what I actually wanted from a boyfriend, which was in his pants.

As Chad led me out through reception, Tim appeared in the office doorway. He smiled. 'Richard, there's someone I want you to meet.'

*Bollocks! The new friend! How could I have forgotten? Why*

*couldn't I have worn my Blur t-shirt, or my Spliffy jeans that Dad thinks are named after a band. And why do I even own tie-dye, let alone rainbow tie-dye?*

Tim stepped backwards into the office. I followed him.

'Richard, this is Alfie. Alfie, meet Richard.'

And there he was, draped over an office chair, a look on his face like he'd rather be anywhere else, but I was captivated nonetheless. Everything about him was perfect. His crisp white t-shirt and baggy blue jeans that matched his eyes. His blond hair gelled up in short spikes. He looked like an understudy for NSYNC. No, he looked like someone had taken NSYNC and Take That, squished all the best bits together, then sat back to admire their work. I was in love before he even spoke.

I sat on the chair Tim indicated, Alfie to my right, Tim on my left. The intensity of my attraction to Alfie meant I could barely make eye contact with him, never mind speak to him. Tim tried hard to keep the non-conversation going but soon enough it was time for me to get my bus.

As I stood up to leave, Alfie asked with apparent indifference, 'You want to come to the pub some time?'

'Yeah. I'd love to. Wait – you mean a gay pub?'

He laughed. 'Yeah, dummy. Of course.'

'Erm, yeah, that would be great. I'll need to ask my mum though.'

Tim passed me a bit of paper he'd been holding. 'Here's my number. Let us know what your mum says. You'll get to meet Ryan, too.'

I looked at the bit of paper to check it really was a phone number. 'Great, thanks. I'll ask her as soon as I get home.'

I slung my bag over my shoulder, took a last look at Alfie, and with a 'bye', I left. Could this really be happening, I wondered as I ran to the bus-stop; could I have made a cool gay friend? A cool gay friend who wants to take me to a gay pub with him? I was at the bus stop before I wondered who Ryan was. Would he be cute like Alfie, or old like Tim and Chad?

The entire bus ride home I rehearsed different ways to ask Mum for permission to go to the pub.

I was already allowed a glass of wine with dinner, and at the start of the summer holidays I'd even been allowed to go and drink with my friends in the park. I'd said it was just going to be cider, but Dad collected miniature bottles of spirits and I'd stolen half a dozen of them to make it more fun. After I was poured through the door by my friends at midnight and vomited on Skip, our bearded collie, while the cat watched the scene with disdain, that privilege had been revoked.

But there had to be a way to make the pub sound like something I should be allowed to do. I was almost fifteen, after all. Not a kid. If she said no, I could try and get Dan to lie for me and say I was at his house, although what would I say if he wanted to come with me? I didn't want to introduce him to Alfie. 'Hi Alfie, this is my not-exactly-boyfriend Shit Breath, who I don't have sex with.' I could imagine Alfie's nose wrinkling in judgement.

Maybe I could just sneak out, though Mum would be on high alert once I'd asked, so I probably couldn't get away with that.

By the time I got home, Mum was cooking, Dad was yet again discussing leaving Allied Dunbar to become a freelance contractor even if it would mean less money for a while, and Jenny was doing coursework at the dining table, periodically interrupting Dad's monologue to ask about the niceties of women's fashion in the '70s. 'What's a Farrah flick?'

I realised there would be no chance to speak to Mum privately till later. I went up to my room and checked the little bit of paper again. It was still a phone number.

During dinner, Dad said, 'You're uncharacteristically quiet.' He went on to ask if I was excited to be going back to school. The holidays were nearly over and I was about to start my GCSEs, and finally get to wear the dark uniform of the senior years. 'Are you going to apply to be a prefect?'

I managed not to snort shepherd's pie out of my nose. 'I've had two suspensions and six detentions. It's not exactly likely.'

'But one suspension was for shaving your head,' he said, looking hurt, as if my rebellious haircut – an attempt to look like Brian Harvey from East 17 – was a personal insult to him. 'And some of the detentions were for the whole class, weren't they?'

I'd forgotten I'd lied about the detentions. I was surprised he'd remembered. 'One suspension was for my hair, but the other was for the prank calls to Mr Samson.'

He exchanged a look with Mum. 'I've still no idea why you'd do that. You know about caller ID.'

Caller ID had been the last thing on my mind that day. I'd called Mr Samson to confess my undying love for him. He was my geography teacher and also covered some PE lessons. He had an adorable lisp that counteracted the sternness of his chiselled face. The days he taught PE, he wore running shorts cut so high that they left little to the imagination. Other kids made snarky remarks, but for me, one look at the smooth, pale, soft skin on the insides of his thighs and I'd spend the rest of the lesson wishing the swelling in my trousers would deflate.

I convinced myself that once he knew how I felt, we could live the rest of our lives happily together. We could adopt some cats, and obviously my grades in geography would improve. However, each time I heard my future husband's voice, I got scared and hung up. After the third hang-up he called back, and it was Dad who answered.

After dinner, without being asked, I did all the chores that I normally had to be harassed into doing. I cleared the table and wiped it down, I even rinsed the plates before loading them into the dishwasher, but I still couldn't get Mum on her own.

The next day I got up early, knowing there was a sweet spot of time after Dad went to work and before Mum went to McNally's, the local builder where she did the accounts and payroll. When my chance came, I jumped straight in: Tim's house, new friends, Alfie, young like me, this new guy Ryan, not too late, I won't get drunk, I probably won't even get served, I'll probably drink lime and soda, Tim will look after me...

'I'll think about it while I'm at work.'

'Thank you, thank you, thank you,' I said, bouncing with excitement.

'I haven't said yes. I've said I'll think about it.'

'Can I make you lunch for when you get back?'

'Stop it. I'll think about it and I'll talk to you later. And pick up the dog poo in the garden. It's been on your jobs list for days.'

Mum got home at lunchtime and found me in front of the TV. 'Where's your sister?'

'In her room.'

She sat down beside me and muted the TV. 'So, I've been thinking all morning, and it's a no. You're too young to be going to pubs. You can go to their house, but not the pub.'

My heart plummeted. How could I tell Alfie I was too much of a kid to be allowed out. 'But that's not fair. I've been hanging out in pubs in town for over a year.'

'Which pubs?!'

'That's not the important bit. The important bit is *this* pub, with my new friends, and being myself. This is *huge*.'

'It's a grown-up environment and you're only fourteen.'

'I'm fifteen in, like, two weeks! Call Tim. Please? Talk to him, then you'll feel better. Here, this is his number.' I pulled out the bit of paper I'd carried around in my pocket since I was given it.

She took it and sighed heavily. 'Okay.'

'Thank you, thank you, thank you, thank you.'

'I've already said no, and I haven't changed my mind yet.' She went through to use the extension in the breakfast room and closed the door. I could hear her voice but not the words. What felt like a lifetime later, she came back in.

'Tim's on the phone. He wants to talk to you. You can take it in the garage if you like.'

Taking the call in the garage was a big deal. The phone in the breakfast room had an over-long extension cord, the curly kind you could wrap round your fingers while talking. You could stretch it through to the garage, shut the door on it, and talk privately.

'Tim?' I said, dragging the phone through and closing the door on Mum.

'Hey matey, how are you?'

'I'm good. What did she say?'

'Well. She said yes, b—'

'OH MY GOD. Really? I can't be—'

'Quiet, mate. She said yes, but there are rules.'

'Don't care, I can come. Oh man, I can't believe this. What rules?'

Tim said Mum had agreed I could go out with him and

Alfie, but I had to be home by 11pm. Home meant Tim's. I was going to stay there overnight to avoid questions being asked by Dad or Jenny. Tim would be *in loco parentis*. He'd need to know where I was at all times, and preferably be able to see me. 'I have your mum's number and I'm not afraid to use it,' he warned.

'When can I come? I can have a drink, right?'

'No. No alcohol. If I catch you with alcohol, the night will be over and it won't be repeated. How does Friday sound?'

'Yes, yes please. What should I wear? When? Where do I meet you?'

'Your mum has my address. I'll see you Friday around four. As for what to wear...' He shouted for Alfie. 'He'll be better at this.' Tim said goodbye, and Alfie's gentle voice sounded in my ear, filling me with a warmth that tingled.

Because I couldn't see him, our conversation flowed more easily. Alfie told me white was the best colour, either for my shirt or my jeans or, even better, both. I didn't want to disappoint him by saying I didn't have anything white. His voice turned serious as he warned, 'And Richard? No tie-dye.'

By the time I was done learning all the things that were wrong with my fashion choices, Dad was home and Jenny was watching TV in the sitting room. I found Mum, wrapped my arms around her and we squeezed each other. She whispered, 'I'm trusting you. Remember the rules!'

# 3

Friday arrived, and I packed and repacked my bag with different outfit choices. Why didn't I own more white?

Time dribbled past. At around 3 pm Mum put me out of my misery. As she reversed down the drive I bounced in the passenger seat, then caught myself: I was acting like a little kid.

Tim's house was in a part of Swindon we didn't know. We drove past a low-rise block of flats with a discarded mattress in front of it and Mum made a face. I counted down the house-numbers on his street until we came to a semi-detached with a fake Cotswold stone frontage. A Ford saloon that had seen better days was parked in front of it. As Mum drew up, I jabbed excitedly at the catch for my seat belt and the buckle rewound with such speed I was lucky it didn't smack me in the face. I was out of the car the moment Mum put the handbrake on, marching up the garden path and rattling at the letter-box. Tim answered the door wearing a military green tee shirt tucked into blue jeans. He was still a dork but I jumped at him for a hug.

'Whoah there.' He peeled me off him, looking across at Mum, who was sorting out her handbag. As I tried to shove past him into a world where I could exist as myself, he added,

'There's no rush.'

As per our agreement, Mum came in for a cup of tea before leaving me. To make sure I was comfortable, she said. To make sure *she* was comfortable, she meant.

I went through to the front room, where Alfie was sprawled on a paisley sofa watching *Grange Hill*, a show I'd only been allowed to start watching that summer, as Mum didn't like the way it portrayed rampant bullying in schools as normal. God, Alfie was cool. I could never look that cool just watching TV.

The room was painted a tired magnolia, with an '80s electric fire, swirly carpet and mismatched furniture. I'd imagined the start of my new life would be glamorous like on *Gaytime TV*. Obviously not confetti cannons and dancers with pounding techno music, but something more than this. It didn't matter though. I was here; it was starting; we could add the sparkle and streamers later.

Mum and Tim followed me in.

'Put the kettle on, Alfie,' said Tim. Grudgingly Alfie got up and went through to the kitchen. I heard the rush of the tap as Tim said: 'How do you like it, Mandy?'

'Just milk please.'

'Richard?'

'Milk with two please.'

'You catch all that Alfie?'

Alfie had. Of course he had – he was brilliant.

Tim gestured for us to sit. I jumped in where Alfie had been sitting. I could feel his warmth on the cushions, and it stirred something in me. Mum and Tim made small talk. I looked at them: my real mum and what looked like my new gay dad. Alfie came in with the tea.

Tim tried to involve Alfie (now sprawled in an armchair) and me in the conversation, but Alfie wasn't interested, and I was too busy being interested in Alfie. He was watching the TV, now muted but with the subtitles on.

Eventually Mum said it was time for her to 'leave you boys to your night'. As she got up, she looked at Tim, her face tight. 'Look after him.' It wasn't a request; it was a warning.

'As if he was my own, Mandy.'

She turned to me and missed Tim winking at me over her shoulder. 'Show me out, please, Richard.' At the front door she said, 'This is a privilege and I'm trusting you. Don't let me down.'

I did my best to look innocent.

'Get a good night's sleep so you don't come home looking like you've been up all night, and say nothing to Dad or your sister.'

'I won't.'

'I love you, okay?'

'Mum, seriously! My friends are right there!' I waved in the direction of the front room.

'Tell your mother you love her!' Tim called, and I heard Alfie laughing.

I'd worried that, when faced by Alfie again, I'd clam up. But speaking on the phone with him had changed something. Until this point, apart from dully accepting Dan's repeated excuses for not having sex, I'd done nothing but lust after random boys at school. Searching every move they made or thing they said for a hidden code or hint they might be gay. But Alfie... I knew Alfie was gay. And he was so much hotter than Dan, and cooler.

After Alfie and I had chatted for a while about our coming night out, the conversation moved onto fashion, and things like how, although Alanis Morissette was cool, I should definitely not ask for her to be played at the pub. Tim sent us upstairs to get ready and let him watch the news. I followed Alfie eagerly, taking the chance to admire his butt as he pounded up the narrow stairs. On the landing a door opened, revealing a young boy with an inexpressive face. Wreathed in steam, his towel low on his hips, he roamed over me with his eyes. He looked younger than me: maybe thirteen. His skinny, hairless frame reminded me of the time my class turned up in the changing room for PE and found a first-year still there, looking tiny and scared. But this boy was definitely not scared.

'This is Ryan,' Alfie said, seemingly unfazed by the virtually naked child before us. 'Ryan: Richard.'

'Sorry I'm like this,' Ryan said coyly, gesturing at the towel. 'I didn't know you'd come so early.'

I didn't know how to react. It felt like this boy had some sort of power, at least here in this moment, and he wanted it known.

Holding the towel over his groin, he told me he couldn't wait to show me around 'his' pub. I was stunned by his confidence: holding a conversation with a stranger while basically naked. I still wore a t-shirt when I went swimming.

'You'll need to get dressed if you want to get into the pub,' Alfie said, leading me by the hand past Ryan and into his room. I couldn't believe he was actually touching me.

My heart raced as Alfie shut the door behind us. *I'm alone with a hot gay boy in his bedroom.* A double bed took up most of the floorspace and I couldn't help but wonder if Alfie's sheets smelled like him, sweet and manly. 'So do you and Ryan share?' I asked.

'Nah. He's Tim's boyfriend. They have the big room next door.'

'Oh wow. Okay,' I said, trying to sound casual. 'How old is he? He looks younger than me.'

Alfie laughed. 'He's a bit older than us, just turned sixteen.

But yeah, he looks like a kid. Acts it sometimes, too. It's always hard getting him served in pubs outside of Swindon.'

'Outside of Swindon?' I was as impressed as if he'd just said they got a private jet to New York for dinner.

'Mainly it's Bristol, but sometimes Tim takes us to London. Once the place knows us it's fine, but the first time can be tricky. Most are okay, as long as the young guys don't cause a problem. Tim told him to stay up here while your mum was around. Ryan can be...difficult.'

I was starting to really like Tim. He was the cool uncle who let you get away with things your parents wouldn't. And he was gay: he was one of us – just one of us that could drive. Tim, Alfie and now Ryan, had welcomed me into their home, and I felt comfortable there. Two gay friends my own age! I was winning.

'So you have a double bed all to yourself?' I asked Alfie, imagining sharing it with him.

'My boyfriend sometimes stays over if he's around.'

Of course he had a boyfriend. How could someone who looked like him be single? I didn't ask what the boyfriend was like.

Alfie pulled a t-shirt out of my bag and held it up critically. 'So, what's your look?'

'My look?'

'Yeah. Like, what's your thing?'

I shrugged awkwardly as he dropped the t-shirt next to my bag and picked up the next. 'I guess I have a lot of shirts with slogans on them.'

'Like brands? Brands could be your thing.'

'No, things like "I may ignore you" or "Parental Advisory". Is that a thing?'

He dropped the last shirt beside my bag, and searched inside for more. 'A thing is like, Ryan tries to be cute, but everyone knows he's a bitch. I don't really have a thing, but you should have one.'

I looked at him in his blue jeans and white t-shirt. His thing was clearly not knowing he had a thing.

'This one, then.' He held up my one white t-shirt. 'Do you only have those jeans?' he asked in a way that wasn't exactly rude but made my heart sink.

'Yeah, but they're okay, right?'

'They'll do. But maybe don't wear them next time. Underwear?'

It was like a line from a fantasy that started with, 'I'll show you mine if you show me yours.'

'Are they good? Doesn't matter I guess, if they're the only ones you have. Do you want a shower?'

I managed not to ask if he meant together. 'No thanks. I showered before I came round.'

'Get changed then. Tim will make us something to eat before we go out – line the stomach,' he said.

'My mum said I can't drink.'

'Your mum's not here.'

I'd eaten carefully so I didn't get food on the only item of clothing I owned that Alfie didn't hate. Now the vibrations of the car were making me want to burp. I held it in as Tim parked outside the community centre, which was also the overflow car park for the two local pubs – one gay, the other Irish. 'Right, we're here. The Cricketers Arms. Often called the Cricketers, or sometimes just the Cricks. Now remember, Richard, I need to see you at all times. And don't do anything these two do. They're a bad influence.'

'Bugger off,' Alfie said as he got out of the car.

Ryan turned to me. 'Do what I do and you'll be the second most popular here.'

'Do not do what he does!' Tim said. 'Not unless they offer you money.' He laughed.

'Second most popular?' I asked.

'I'm going nowhere, darling,' Ryan said. 'Second-best is all you can hope for.'

The thump of music was audible as soon as I got out of the car, growing in volume as we walked towards the nearer of the two pubs. There was also a hubbub of voices, one of which was so dominant, it must be artificially amplified. It was deep and gravelly but obviously gay.

The burp trapped in my stomach escaped, and the void it left behind was filled with butterflies. I suddenly needed to pee.

Ryan opened a side door and the noise within spilled through it. He went in, followed by Alfie and Tim – then me, keeping so close to Tim I was almost attached to him. His proximity was the only thing that got my nerves through the door.

The noise inside drowned out the scared voice in the back of my mind telling me to run. The room was full of energy, and heaving with people moving and mixing easily, not just sitting in tight groups like they do in straight pubs. I looked around warily. The instinct to not be seen eyeing other guys was so strong that even in this environment it ruled me. My eyes landed on an athletic guy in his early twenties standing chest to chest with a burly, bearded older man, their white t-shirts flat against each other as the younger guy kissed the bearded guy on the lips. The sight made my heart race and pine, but before I had time to understand how I was feeling, I made myself stop staring at what felt like a forbidden act.

Ryan and Alfie went through an arch that led to the main part of the bar, and the man on the mic said, 'Look out fellas, the chickens are here! And where's the chicken wrangler? Hiiii Timmm!' As I followed Tim, the voice went on, 'Ooh, you've got a new one in your flock. Would you look at yooou!'

The voice was now revealed to belong to a body, but voice and body didn't match. It was clearly a man – narrow hips, a bony face that, under the caked-on make-up, was almost gaunt; a large, angular jaw – but he was wearing a wig that would make Dolly Parton jealous and a gown that had so many sequins it made him look like a human mirror ball. Outsize costume jewellery sent laser reflections through the cigarette smoke that hung in the air. He reminded me of Dame Edna Everage on TV, though everything about him seemed bigger and more outrageous. Maybe this was a tranny. I'd seen one in an advert at the back of one of Dad's dirty magazines, which he kept hidden in his sock drawer.

The sparkling vision made its way towards me. Tim put his hands protectively on my shoulders and pushed me forward.

'This is Richard. Be kind to him. This is his first night out.'

'I don't know where you find them, Tim, but go back to where you got this one and find one for me! I'm Eartha, young man. Eartha Tits.' Eartha's voice blared from the speakers. I felt like I was meant to recognise the name in some way.

'Are you a tranny?' I asked.

Eartha choked dramatically. 'Oh god, baby. Am I a tranny?' The rest of the pub started laughing as this boomed out of the speakers. 'Kids say the funniest things, don't they?' He looked around at the audience. 'No dear, and that's a bad word. Don't say it again or I'll spank you.' One set of tarantula-leg eyelashes winked at me. 'No sweetie, I am a drag queen. I am not confused about my gender. I am not trapped in the wrong body. I, my dear, simply have too much fabulosity to present myself in the humdrum way the rest of these peasants do.'

Drag. A drag queen. This is what Mum didn't want me to see on *Gaytime TV*. But why? He thrust a microphone smelling of cigarettes and cloying perfume into my face. 'Tell us all about you dear, where have you been hiding?'

I mumbled into the mic, 'Erm...Highworth?'

For some reason this made everyone laugh too. 'Guess we're all going to Highworth tomorrow to see if there's more of him, am I right?' Eartha said. 'But we can't have anyone being funnier than me, so that's the last time you get my microphone, young man.' He turned and made his way back to the stage. 'Let's all welcome the Highworth chicken on his virgin night out.'

My face burned. He'd called me a virgin in front of everyone! He saw my mortified expression. 'Get this boy a drink, on me. Vodka tonic? You look like a vodka kind of boy. Goes down well, morning or night...'

'Beer please,' I shouted over the music and got a pretend slap round the back of my head from Tim.

'He'll have a Coke.'

'Ooh, Daddy's got this one on a short leash.'

Tim turned me around to face him. He was beaming with pride, though I couldn't see why. 'You did great. Did you hear them all laughing with you? Everyone likes you.' He gave me a sudden kiss on the lips, which felt weird and too personal, but seemed to be what everyone did here. Air kissing, blowing kisses across the room, the cute guy and the older man near the door full-on snogging.

Tim led me over to a table Alfie had found. Ryan glowered at me.

Something bubbled up in my mind as I took my seat. 'Why aren't you two upset about being called chickens?'

'Because it's what we are,' Ryan said, putting his straw in his mouth and sucking. 'You too.'

'I'm not a coward,' I said. I'd been scared going in the pub, but I *had* gone in, so—

'It's a compliment,' Ryan said. 'Take it. You probably won't get any more.'

'Chicken doesn't mean you're a coward,' Tim said. 'It means you're young and cute.' He took hold of my chin and squeezed it.

'So what are you if we're chickens?'

'Old,' said Alfie. I tried not to laugh but I couldn't help myself.

'I'm thirty-four,' Tim said pointedly to Alfie. 'A guy that's into chickens is called a chicken chaser or chicken hawk. But not many people say the latter any more.'

I glanced at Ryan, who clearly wasn't pleased by the attention I was getting. I didn't want him to hate me, but I also enjoyed seeing him sulk.

'So I'm a chicken,' I said. 'You're old, and Eartha is a drag queen. But what's a tranny?'

'I might be your daddy but I'm not old,' said Tim. 'I'll get you that beer.'

I was about to remind him he'd said no alcohol, but stopped myself just in time. If he was willing to provide it, who was I to argue?

Tim went off to the bar, leaving Ryan examining his fingernails, and Alfie and me shouting over the music about the guys in the room. Who was hot, who was looking at us, who was not hot, and shouldn't be looking at us. There were a pair of guys that kept looking over with expressions sourer than Ryan's. I asked Alfie about them. 'Some of the old ugly guys don't like us being here. "It's not a youth group," that bald one said to me once.'

'What did you say?'

'Just told him to get lost. It's not my fault they're old and I'm not.'

'All right, ladies,' Eartha's gruff tones filled the pub. 'It's that time of the night. Let's put on a good show for the new chicken.' The thudding club track was replaced by something gentle and atmospheric that brought a hush to the room. A smooth, intense, female vocal kicked in: 'I am what I am. I am my own special creation...'

I didn't know the Gloria Gaynor song, but the reaction to it could be felt in the air. One by one, each and every person in the place joined in. I was the only person who didn't know the words.

Tim leant into me and whispered, 'You'll catch it in the chorus.'

Actually there wasn't a chorus, but parts were repeated so much that there might as well have been. We sat or stood holding hands, or with arms round each other's shoulders like it was midnight on New Year's Eve. The whole congregation, joined in a single moment, affirming community.

The song ended.

'Right folks,' Eartha rasped. 'You don't have to go home, but you can't come to mine. Get out.'

And with that I said goodbye to new friends, everyone else said goodbye to old friends, and the four of us made our way back to the car.

Back at Tim's he gave us all beers and told Alfie to roll a joint. I was so wired with joy and excitement, I could barely sit still. Tim sparked up, inhaled, then passed me the joint. 'You could use this.'

I'd never had drugs before, but I eagerly took a massive drag.

My chest tightened and I started coughing like I was going to bring up a lung.

'Easy mate. Is this your first time?'

'No,' I lied, between coughs, my eyes watering. 'It's just strong.' They were all so experienced in life. I didn't want them to look at me as a kid that was a virgin to drugs as well as sex.

The hash softened the edges of my brain, and the beer blurred the centre. After a while Ryan went to bed. That left a spare seat on the sofa between Alfie and Tim, but I stayed on the floor looking up at Alfie. The weed had the two of us laughing and expressing any thought that crossed our minds, while Tim watched and laughed. Eventually, with a yawn, Alfie stood up and announced it was bedtime for him as well.

He left the room and Tim patted the sofa. 'Come sit up here. The floor can't be comfortable.'

I did as he said. He rolled another joint, and this time I went slow and smoked without coughing. After that it was mainly me doing the talking: the weed had opened doors in my mind and I felt full of insights.

Eventually Tim yawned and said, 'It's late; time we hit the hay. You have a shower, and I'll make up the camp bed in the kitchen for you. You'll find a towel in the airing cupboard.'

As I stood in the shower, my mind was clear and fuzzy at the same time. I tried to focus on the warm water caressing my body, and thought how the pungent smell of the hash must have soaked into my clothes. Hopefully Mum wouldn't know what it was.

After a shower long enough to drain the hot water tank and wrinkle my palms, I dried myself and put on my underwear. I wondered what Alfie thought wasn't good about them. It wasn't like Marky Mark would be modelling them, but they weren't *that* bad. I bundled up my jeans and top, and went downstairs.

It was strange moving around in someone else's house knowing everyone was asleep, like being a burglar. I checked the ashtray in the front room as I went past, in case there was any of the joint left. No such luck. I could see my camp bed set up in the dark kitchen, so I headed through.

'Hey matey, good shower?' Tim asked from the shadows.

His voice startled me and I dropped my bundle of clothes.

'Didn't mean to scare you. Want a cuppa, or a beer?' he asked. 'I fancied another brew before bed.'

'No, no, I'm okay,' I said, struggling back into my jeans, feeling stupid.

He smirked. 'Don't worry about your clothes,' he said. 'We're all boys here. Are you sure about that beer? Those other two would have the can open before it was out of my hand.'

'I'm just kinda tired.'

He put his mug down on the worktop and came towards me. I'd just about got my jeans pulled up and was fumbling with the lowest button as he reached me. 'You okay mate? You look like you've seen a ghost.' He put his hands on my shoulders like he had in the pub. There it had felt protective. Here, I didn't know what was going on. 'Did you not dry yourself properly, or are you sweating?' he asked, looking me over and rubbing my bare shoulders.

'I think it's just too much hash and beer,' I said, looking into his eyes, which were too close to mine. 'I should get some sleep.'

He smiled. 'Poor boy. Those two can hit it quite hard. I told you not to do what they do.' He hugged me, his hands sliding across my bare back, his arms pinning mine to my sides, hooking his chin over my shoulder. 'You'll be fine in the morning.'

I could feel the warmth of his breath on my neck. He relaxed his hug, moving his head so his face was once more in front of mine, but he didn't let me go. 'You had fun tonight, didn't you?' His face was so close now that each word had a physical impact. I nodded slightly. 'Don't tell Ryan I told you, but I could see how much he was hating the attention you got. You're a very attractive young man.' He closed his eyes and pressed his lips against mine. His tongue pushed into my mouth. I froze.

It felt alien. There was a denseness and roughness to it, not smooth and soft like I'd imagined a tongue to be. A taste of beer, tea and cigarettes. My first kiss.

I pulled away, trying to bring an end to it. 'I think I'm going to be sick.' Alarmed, he released me. I made for the back door. It was locked, but the key was in the lock. I turned it and swung the door open to gulp in the cool freedom.

I stood in the doorway staring out into the blackness of the garden. Tim came and stood so close to me I could feel his body heat. I flinched as he placed his hand in the small of my back, sliding it down to the top of my jeans and then, to my relief, back up again. I couldn't step out into the garden in my bare feet, I couldn't turn round.

'Can I have a cig?' I asked. 'I can't remember where I put mine.'

'Of course.' He stopped rubbing my back and went to get his cigarettes off the worktop. 'You look white as a sheet. Less hash for you next time,' he said with a chuckle, lighting two cigarettes in his mouth and handing one to me.

I desperately wanted not to be in that house, but I couldn't just leave. I could hardly wander about all night. Maybe I could get him to leave me alone, though. Looking out at the night I said, 'I'm so tired, but the air helped. I'll just have this and then crash out if that's okay?'

'You'll feel better in the morning. I'll take my tea to bed and leave you to it. Lock the door when you're done with your air.'

He left the room, shutting the door behind him. The taste of his tongue was still in my mouth.

The thought that he might return set off fireworks in my mind. *I can't move the bed to block the door, it opens the wrong way. I can't leave, because to leave is to admit – what?*

I got into the narrow camp bed still wearing my jeans, and tucked the top sheet tightly around me to form a cocoon.

# 4

I heard the click of the kettle, opened my eyes and turned my head to see Tim putting a teabag in a mug. The room was filled with light, so it had to be morning. My head was throbbing dully.

'Didn't mean to wake you. I just needed tea. Do you want one?'

I stretched. 'Milk with two, please.' As he turned to get another mug I grabbed my shirt off the floor so I could put it on before I got out of bed. He looked round as I swung my legs out and put my feet on the floor.

'You slept in your jeans?'

It was almost an accusation. I laughed awkwardly. 'It got cold in the middle of the night.'

He showed no sign of not believing me. 'Sorry about that. The door lets a lot of air through. But do you feel better this morning?'

'Much, thank you.'

I didn't know how I should behave. I'd seen the way adults acted when drunk, and how afterwards they seemed confused about their actions, even denied them. The one time I'd got super-drunk myself, great chunks of my memory were missing afterwards. Had Tim been drunk? He drove us home so he couldn't have been *that* drunk. But now he was acting like nothing had happened. Maybe he didn't remember.

He made some buttered toast and we went through to the sitting room. He was behaving like he always did: caring; supportive; one of us. *He must have just been drunk.* I glanced at the clock. It was nearly 10am. No sign of Alfie or Ryan. To be fair, I'd still be asleep if I'd not been woken. I wanted to talk to Alfie about Tim kissing me, so I didn't have this weird secret with Tim. Then I remembered Ryan was supposed to be Tim's boyfriend. What if Alfie told Ryan and Ryan blamed me and told Tim not to let me come round again? I saw that Tim was watching me. The desire to not be there crept back into my mind.

'What time are you taking me home?' I asked.

'Well, my tea tank is almost full,' he said. 'So any time after I brush my teeth.'

Yesterday, Tim's Ford Sierra had been a chariot conveying us to Elysium. Today it was taking me back to a life where I wore a mask and kept my true self locked away. The further we got from Tim's house, the quieter I became. He rubbed my knee and asked if I was okay. I was less comfortable with him touching me since that kiss, but there wasn't much I could do about it and I just shrugged in answer to his question. I didn't want to go into all the thoughts rattling around inside my head. Instead, to make conversation, I talked about school. He laughed as I moaned about all the homework I had to finish before the end of the holidays, in just over a week. I hadn't even started most of it.

'It's my birthday on Monday week, too,' I went on. 'I don't get a party though, as school starts on Tuesday.' Even I could hear the sulk in my voice.

'Well, that's crap,' Tim said. 'You should come out with us next weekend. I can make it extra special for you and we can have a proper celebration. We can go to the club after the pub. How does that sound?'

'There's a gay club too?' I said, marvelling at how much Swindon suddenly had to offer me.

'It's a bit of a hole in the wall, but it's fun.'

The Cricks had been brilliant, but a club would be even better. 'That would be amazing. Yes please, and thank you. I'll ask my mum as soon as I get in.'

Tim made a face. 'Don't tell her about the club. I only just got her to agree to the pub, and that was really hard work. Say it's another night out with us. That way you're not lying to her; you're just not telling her the full story. Secrets aren't always bad.' He signalled to make a turn. 'This is your street, right?'

'Yeah, this is me – that one on the corner.'

'Wow, nice place.' He pulled up in front of my house. 'Okay, hope you had a good time. I'll speak to you when you call Alfie. He should be up in a couple of hours.'

'Thanks for having me,' I said, getting my bag from the back seat.

He laughed. 'I didn't have you yet!'

I dutifully laughed back, but it wasn't funny.

I expected questions from Jenny or Dad about where I'd been, but there were none. It turned out Mum had said I was staying with my best friend Sarah, who was also in on the deception.

Sarah had transferred into the school the year before, and she was the only person except for Dan whom I'd told I was gay. She confused people with her confidence, wearing a boys' shirt 'because my boobs are too big', attractive without being conventionally pretty. I think it was because she was so much herself that I wanted to be my real self with her. Telling her had been terrifying, but she wasn't surprised, and after that we'd spent most of the summer talking about boys and other 'girl' stuff.

After lunch I went to see her to tell her all about the Cricketers. She lived in the nicest area of Highworth, where all the houses were big and detached, and curtains twitched if we stood in a group of more than two in the street. Her mum let me in and smiled indulgently as we scampered upstairs to Sarah's room. She was just as keen to hear everything as I was to tell it to her, but before I started, she had a gift for me.

I'd told her about this file I kept hidden in my room. I'd even shown it to her once. It was the kind with the rings you pull open so you can insert your papers in order. I'd decorated the front with letters cut out from different magazines to spell out 'boys boys boys'. It looked like a cross between graffiti and a sinister anonymous letter but I loved it. When I came across a picture of a cute boy in a magazine, or an underwear advert in a catalogue, or a naked tribesman in *National Geographic*, I'd carefully cut it out and glue it into a free space. Today Sarah had an addition for me: Shane Lynch from Boyzone. Recently he'd done a catwalk show and had modelled in just his underwear. My eyes went to his crotch. 'Wow!'

'I thought you'd like it,' she said. 'So tell me about last night.'

We sat on her bed and I tried to describe everything in order. When I got to the hash, she gasped. 'What was that like?'

I tried to describe how it felt, then went back to stories about the pub; the joy and freedom I'd felt now came back to me so clearly. I decided not to tell her about Tim kissing me. Instead I gushed about Alfie.

'What about Dan?' she asked, frowning.

'Ugh.' I fell backwards on the bed like I'd been shot. 'You know he still hasn't even kissed me?'

'Do you actually want him to? That breath!'

'How do I end it with him?' I asked the ceiling.

'Why don't you tell him you met someone last night? I mean, if he actually wanted you two to be a thing, then something would have happened by now, wouldn't it?'

I sat up. 'I could tell him I'm dating Alfie!'

'Why do you like Alfie so much?'

'Oh god. Well, for a start he smells god-like. Not of CK One like all the dorks at school. He's so cool! I could never be that cool.' I fell backwards again, this time flinging my arms out for added drama.

'You're an idiot,' she laughed. 'You *are* cool!'

Empowered by my conversation with Sarah, I decided there was no time like the present to speak to Dan. Besides, he lived three houses down from her, so it would save me having to go back later.

The confidence and certainty I'd felt while talking to Sarah ebbed with each step I took towards Dan's, but before I knew it, I was at his front door. I took a breath and rang the bell.

His mum answered and sent me up to his room. 'Good job Mum called up,' he said as I came in. 'I was just having a wank.'

I looked at the open copy of *Romeo and Juliet* beside him on the bed and snorted a chuckle at his lie. 'You don't want my help with it, then?'

'Not with my parents in the house,' he said, shuffling uncomfortably.

I nodded. There was always a reason for him to say no. I wasn't bothered this time though; it made it easier. We sat and talked about my night out, and he was interested, but in a distant way. I told him about Alfie. I lied about us dating. He hardly even blinked at the news. I was worried he was going to ask if we'd had sex. What would I have said? But he didn't even ask if we'd kissed. Something in me was disappointed.

Unfazed by the ending of our barely existent relationship, Dan moved the conversation on to hanging out during the week. We made vague plans before I made an excuse and went home.

It was Monday morning before I got to speak to Mum on her own. She wasn't working until the afternoon, so we could sit and talk properly. Having seen how happy I'd been when I came home, she'd been content to wait to hear the details.

Retelling the story didn't get old for me, and she smiled at my enthusiasm. I didn't mention the beer or the hash, of course. Part of me wanted to talk to her about the kiss, but I didn't. What if it meant she stopped me from going round to Tim's again? The worry must have shown on my face because she immediately asked me what was wrong. The only thing I could think of in the moment was to talk about Alfie's disapproval of my wardrobe. 'Can I get some white jeans for next time?'

'We'll see. I'm not made of money.'

After she'd left for work I called Alfie to tell him about dumping Dan, concluding, 'His vacant expression made him look like a surprised bowling ball.' Alfie laughed, so as an extra flourish I added that Dan had shown more interest in me the instant I told him it was over. 'You've lost your chance mate,' I told Alfie I'd said. He laughed again.

'We're taking you to Rear Entry for your birthday, I hear,' he said.

'Taking me to what?'

I could hear his eyes roll over the phone. 'The club. It's called Rear Entry 'cos it's round the back of the Flag and Whistle.'

I was dimly aware of the Flag and Whistle, a straight pub over the road from the train station. I'd had no idea there was anything so interesting behind it. 'Oh right! Yeah, I can't wait. What's it like? Is it like the Cricks?'

'Nothing like it. We'll have a blast. You have other jeans, right?'

Kill me now! 'Yeah, of course.'

After an hour, the conversation started to dry up. I was slightly scared at how he'd react, but tentatively I said, 'Alfie?'

'Yeah?'

'Next time. On Saturday... Can you, erm, can you not go to bed until I do?'

There was silence at the other end of the line that made me regret bringing it up. When Alfie did speak, his voice was hushed. 'We can go at the same time. Make Tim take his last cup of tea to bed with him.'

# 5

The rest of the week dragged by at a glacial pace. I spent a lot of time on the phone with Alfie, annoying my sister, who was used to monopolising the line gossiping with her girlfriends. Alfie got me to describe, in detail, every item of clothing I owned. We decided which t-shirt I should wear – a green one with 'You'll Do' in large letters across the chest. For my jeans we decided on black Levi's. Alfie said rips were cool.

'Where do you think I should rip them?' I asked, imagining Mum and Dad's disapproving sighs. 'The right thigh, and the left knee?'

'You have underwear that isn't baggy, right?'

'Yeah,' I said, pinning the phone to my shoulder with my chin while using both hands to rummage through my underwear drawer. 'I've got black, blue and red.' I didn't mention the ones with teddy bears on.

'Wear red. Then when you rip your jeans, do a rip high enough up the leg that your underwear can be seen.'

I laughed. 'Yeah, right.'

But he insisted he was serious. As soon as we were off the phone I got Mum's fabric scissors, put the red underwear and black jeans on to work out how high to make the rip, then went round to Sarah's because I needed the denim held tight while I cut it.

'You'll look like Daisy from Dukes of Hazzard,' she said.

'Alfie says it will look cool.'

For the rest of the week, I distracted myself by finally starting on the mountain of summer homework, making a reasonable dent in it. Otherwise I hung out with friends, though I felt like I was pretending to be someone I wasn't any more.

Saturday finally came round. Mum dropped me off at Tim's, sending me in with a kiss and a 'Mind your Ps and Qs' as I shut the car door on her.

Alfie and I were in his room when Ryan came in without knocking, bare-chested and barefoot, wearing jeans with strategic rips in them, up the thighs and just under his arse. He climbed onto the bed and leant into me, telling me to smell his neck. He was trying a new perfume, he said. He smelt like laundry left wet for too long, but I wasn't going to say that.

'This bit smells good, but here,' I said, touching his extended neck and trying to be tactful, 'I think it's mixed with something you already had on and the scents are clashing.'

'No! I smell? I need to shower again! Then one of you can help me with my nails.' He flounced out. Alfie rolled his eyes so hard it must have hurt. A minute later we heard the rush of water from the bathroom.

Once Ryan was out of the shower and no longer smelled like old laundry, he got half-dressed again and came back in with a selection of nail varnishes.

'Are you any good at nails, Richard?'

'I've done my friend Sarah's in art class. It was acrylic paint, but our teacher said I'd done a good job.'

He looked at me like he was weighing up a big decision. 'I'll let you try. But do not get varnish on my cuticles.'

'What's a cuticle?'

Alfie laughed. 'You're screwed, Ryan.'

Ryan curled his lip. 'If I'm lucky.'

'If someone has forty pounds in their pocket,' said Alfie as he left the room.

I was enjoying the way everyone talked to each other: grown-up, comedic, brazen. In the non-gay world, you could never speak to someone that way – not unless you wanted to be nasty. But in the gay world, I was discovering that the better you knew someone, the worse you spoke to them. All the years of verbally sparring with my sister were about to come in very useful.

'What colour?' I asked Ryan, studying the labels. Sunshine Sparkle, Pearl Grey, Espresso Your Style, Lilac. 'Is this one gold?'

'I don't know,' Ryan sighed. 'I've worn them all so much. I need Tim to get me some new ones.'

'And you just use one colour at a time?'

He looked like he'd just tasted something nasty. 'If you think I'm going out with each finger a different colour, this will be the end of our friendship right here, right now.'

'No, you plum.' Calling him a plum was as close to insulting as I was willing to get. 'I mean, what about these two as halves?' I held up Sunshine Sparkle and the one I thought was gold. 'Your little finger with a vertical divide. This one on the right and this one on the left. Next finger the same, but in reverse.'

'I love it. Do it. But in these.' He picked up Thai Ocean Blue and Espresso Your Style. 'They match my eyes and my pants.' I checked his eyes to make sure his underwear wasn't brown. Turquoise peeped through.

I sat chatting and giggling with Ryan, painting my very first set of nails, and learned far more than I ever had from reading my sister's copies of *Cosmopolitan*.

'It's all in the lips and the hips,' Ryan said, after I'd asked what giving a blowjob was like.

By this time Alfie was back. 'It's got nothing to do with hips,' he said. 'Ryan just likes waving his arse around.'

We all laughed at that, and finally it felt like Ryan and I had bonded enough to become friends.

As we drove to the pub, I looked around the car and smiled to myself. I was really part of the group now. Alfie was fast becoming my best friend, and now that I was getting on with Ryan, we felt like a little tribe. It was so good to be back in my world, and Tim had been his normal caring self, so my concerns about him kissing me had faded. He was our protective leader.

Going into the Cricks, my nerves were back in my bladder, but at least I was feeling more secure as part of my clan. I didn't even skulk in last: Tim followed the pack this time, Ryan leading the way.

Soon I was learning from Ryan how to 'act cute'. Done right, it made guys react like I needed looking after and want to buy me drinks.

I'd graduated from beer to alcopops. Hooch was my favourite, and that evening I discovered Martini Rosso and lemonade, both of which had enough sugar in them to give me a buzz, never mind the alcohol. I quickly worked out that if I hung around the bar with the dregs of a drink, looking forlorn, some guy would usually buy me another.

Shepherding the three of us from the Cricks to the club, a walk of about ten minutes – by then it was a bit after 10pm – Tim was having trouble asserting control. We were all tipsy and being rather loud. He singled me out, which felt unfair as I didn't think I'd been drinking more than the others; it had just been so easy getting drinks, and the alcopops had such great flavours that I wanted to try them all.

'Maybe have some water or a Coke every now and then,' Tim said. 'Last thing I want is to be holding your hair back while you puke.'

'What can I say? Guys like me, and I have an excellent teacher,' I said, boldly taking Ryan's arm and slipping mine through it.

Tim's voice was suddenly low and intense. 'Easy, boys. You know not to do that round here. Keep it for indoors.'

His tone cut through my drunken haze. I'd forgotten that the world I was falling in love with wasn't the real world. The one we hurried through now was the real one. Ours was behind closed doors; outside it was their world and it could be dangerous.

Tim had explained it to me last weekend: 'You are loved, you are right to be who you are, but we get attacked and we get killed.' He'd warned, 'Don't expect anyone to help you. The calls of queer, poof and faggot will stop any assistance. And once it's over, there'll be no help from the police. They have an unwritten rule: we leave them alone and they leave us alone. Most importantly...if you're stopped, even just to be asked the time, if it doesn't feel right, you run!'

Attacks, or bashings, were, I was to learn, all too routine. People would disappear for a couple of weeks while the bruises and cuts healed, or come out still wearing them, as a middle-finger to those who wanted to stop them from being themselves.

'Sorry Tim,' I now said, letting go of Ryan's arm.

'Next lesson,' Ryan said in a loud, upbeat tone. 'How to get them to pay for more than drinks!'

Alfie and Tim laughed.

'Do you really get paid for sex?' The alcohol in me asked the question.

Ryan gave me a look. 'Seeing as I've had so many compliments on my nails tonight, I'm choosing to let that go. I am not now, nor have I ever been, a prossie. No matter what anyone tells you.' He looked at Alfie and Tim, who were sniggering. 'Anyone can sell their body. It takes skill to get them to give you things for doing nothing.'

'Or in exchange for your old underwear,' said Alfie.

'Shut ya face!' Ryan snapped, then turned to me. 'So, are you ready for some Rear Entry?'

We were standing near the Flag and Whistle, and I could hear music thudding somewhere but... 'This is just a pub car park,' I objected.

'It's over there,' Tim said, pointing at a long, squat building with blacked-out windows, a bit like the tarpaper-roofed cabins my school used for religious and personal studies, only more permanent-looking. 'It's the function room for the Flag. Or at least it was, until they converted it into a den of iniquity. Go in with Alfie. If you go in with Ryan, you'll have a reputation from the get-go.'

'Again. Shut ya face!' Ryan said, leading the way in the direction the noise was coming from.

Tim pulled one of the club's black double-doors open for me and I stepped into the presence of two mountain-sized men in black dress shirts. Tattoos were visible beyond their cuffs and collars, and they had military-style crewcuts and more piercings than I would have guessed was possible. I stopped mid-step, expecting to be turned away. The feeling of hands on my shoulders made me jump, then I heard Tim's voice behind me:

'Graham, Eddie, this is Richard.'

They looked me over dispassionately, then the scarier of the two said, 'Evening, gents.' Gents! Excitement rushed through me. 'Free entry is over, but it's quiet, so just go in.'

Just then a tall, broad man with cropped blond hair walked backwards through the inner swing doors that kept some of the music out of the lobby. 'It's working now,' he shouted at someone, 'and Stella's only 10p more a pint.' He turned round, almost colliding with Eddie. 'Christ on a bike, I need to put a bell on you.'

Eddie, having made no attempt to get out of the way, said, 'This still okay, right, Phil?' He gestured at me as he spoke.

Phil looked me up and down, and my pulse quickened. 'This is my club, so it's my rules,' he said, looking serious. 'I don't want this place turning into a creche.' But then he smiled. 'I'll tell you all the rest of what I don't want later.' At the main doors he stopped. 'Oh. Name?' When I hesitated he added, 'Today, sweetie. I can't just call you skinny kid.'

'I'm Richard. Nice to meet you.'

'Voice like bloody royalty. What could possibly go wrong?' The door swung shut behind him.

Feeling like I was on the headmaster's naughty list already, I let Tim push me past the well-dressed ogres. He explained that he'd had to talk Phil into letting another underage person into the club, and that it was free entry before 10pm, a policy designed to get people in and paying for drinks before closing time at the Cricketers. After that it was £2, which was about the cost of a drink. I thought of my pocket money and made a mental note to always get there before ten.

It was less than a month since I'd met Chad the counsellor, my first real-life gay person, and now I was standing in an actual gay club with my gay friends. The club wasn't the hole in the wall I'd expected; in fact, to my eyes, it was glamorous.

Past the bar, marble-effect tables and chairs upholstered in a rich red lined one wall of a narrow space; beyond, I glimpsed a large dance floor, which was empty even though music thudded from the speakers. There were only a handful of people dotted around the place, mostly pairs of men nursing their drinks. One guy was on his own; alert, hungry, trying to look casual. Close by him a table of three: a loud, animated woman with an attentive man on either side of her.

'I'd offer to show you around, but this is it,' said Tim.

'You getting them in then?' Ryan asked him.

'What are you all having? Are you off the beer for good now, princess?' Tim asked me.

'Hooch please. Lemon or orange. Surprise me.' I showed off my best cute smile. I was surprised how quickly I felt comfortable here. The behemoths hadn't welcomed me, but Phil had, sort of, and with them guarding the entrance and Tim guarding us inside, it already felt like home.

'Bloody hell! You're getting more like Ryan with every hour,' Tim said with an eye roll.

'Don't say that like it's a bad thing,' Ryan said. 'I'm amazing!'

'You're something all right,' Tim said, turning to the barman. 'A Hooch lemon, two pints, and whatever this one wants in a large glass, so his hands look smaller.' Tim and Alfie both laughed, but I didn't understand why.

'Twat!' said Ryan. He turned to me. 'We can do movie night and get you caught up on all the references and jokes. I'm assuming you haven't seen *Priscilla*?'

'Who?'

Once the Cricketers closed, the club quickly filled with faces that were becoming familiar to me. In the Cricks there was chatting, maybe some dancing, lots of laughing, but here there was touching too. The music was so much louder, we needed to lean into each other's ears to hear and be heard. Guys would rub my arm as they shouted compliments. Someone would pat my butt as he walked past, and the dancing...could get very close indeed.

It started with Alfie and me running to the dance floor when Gina G came on. He could do what I couldn't; get his feet and arms to move in unison. But I was new, I was young, and it wasn't long before we got invited to dance with other people. I say invited – it was more them dancing closer and closer to us until we were dancing with them. Alfie's new partner had a matching white t-shirt, and mine had a moustache that belonged on Freddie Mercury, which I thought looked unhygienic. He must have been nearly thirty, but he did have the deepest green eyes and a substantial chest.

I was awkward at first. It felt strange for a grown man to put his hand on my arm or shoulder while looking longingly into my eyes, but it felt right too: natural. As my confidence grew I touched him back, running my hand up his arms, feeling the warmth of his skin and the flex of his muscles.

Then I was dancing with a twenty-something who draped his arms over my shoulders and pulled me closer. I put mine round his waist and nestled my head into his shoulder, the scent of his woody aftershave filling my nostrils, and the experience felt like what I'd been missing my whole life. It was hard not to let the attention go to my head. I was popular, wanted, desired, and when wrapped in a guy's arms, I was home.

I was loitering at the bar waiting for someone to buy me a drink when a flushed, beaming face appeared beside me. It was the woman from the table of three I'd noticed earlier on. Short, plump, mid-twenties, an energetic smile.

'Drink?' she asked me, waving a banknote at the barman.

I wasn't expecting an offer from a woman, but a free drink was a free drink. 'If you're buying?'

'I am,' she said, 'but Martin is paying.' She gestured towards the two guys she'd been sitting with, one of whom had long black hair and was watching me with an expression that I couldn't work out – sullen, or maybe playful.

'Is it okay if I accept the drink even though long hair is a deal-breaker for me?'

'No, silly, that one's mine. Martin is the one beside him.'

I should have guessed: the guy with the long hair was wearing the same top as the woman talking to me – some band logo that looked like a heavy-metal album cover. The guy beside him was small, older than my dad, with thick glasses that made his eyes look unnaturally big. I smiled falsely in their direction.

'Is it okay if I accept even though that is never going to happen?'

'Of course, babe.' She frowned. 'He doesn't get out much. In fact, this is his first time here. Can you come and talk with us? I'll tell him you aren't interested, so it won't be uncomfortable.'

The way I'd been treated like a star all night made me feel like it was my responsibility to talk to my people. I completely forgot it was actually my first time there too. 'Sure, but double Martini Rosso and lemonade?'

She laughed and ordered. 'I'm Jo. What's your name?'

'I'm Richard.'

Carrying our drinks, we joined Martin and not-Martin, whose name turned out to be Wayne.

'Pleasure to meet you both, and thank you for the drink, Martin,' I said, sitting down beside him, adding, 'I got a double' as Jo gave him his change. Now I was close to him, his thick round glasses and wrinkled face made him look like a mole.

With a thick Irish accent and a would-be charming smile, Martin told me it was a small price to pay to get to speak to the prettiest boy in the club. I managed to not cringe as he took my hand and kissed it. When he let go, I got out and lit a cigarette, so I no longer had free hands to be held or kissed.

Watching me, Jo said, 'Wayne, tell Richard how you described the place when we came in. It was so perfect.'

I turned to Wayne as Jo leant into Martin's ear. Wayne said, 'Like Marilyn Manson designed a wake for *My Little Pony*.'

I cackled. It reminded me of when I used to pull the heads off my sister's My Little Ponies and wait to hear her scream. But then I saw the smile slide off Martin's face. He rallied quickly, though. His accent and the noise around us made him hard to understand, but the conversation flowed all right. He made no further moves on me, and said he was shocked to find out I didn't turn fifteen until Monday.

'Oh god,' he groaned. 'I bought a fourteen-year-old a drink?'

'And a double to boot,' I said, holding my glass up and rattling the ice cubes. 'But strictly speaking, you didn't. She did.' I looked at Jo. We'd been making small-talk for twenty minutes, so I stood up and said, 'I should get back to my friends. You've all been so much fun though.'

I looked around for Tim and realised there was a wobble to the room.

'Here, take our number,' Jo said, searching in her bag to find something to write on. 'Let's do this again.'

'Call any time,' said Martin. 'If you ever need anything, call us.'

'You all live together?'

'Me and Wayne rent a room from Martin,' Jo said. 'He has a house in Gorse Hill.' This was a depressed area mainly consisting of Victorian rail-workers' terraces, betting shops, tattoo parlours and pubs where fights spilled out onto the pavement every weekend.

'The third room is going if you ever need somewhere to stay,' Martin said, with a hint of drunken desperation.

The idea of hanging out with Jo again appealed to me, so I took the old receipt she'd scribbled their number on. 'How about next weekend?' I said, not wanting to miss the opportunity to have a private space to myself. 'Could I bring a guy back if I meet someone?' I added, to emphasise that didn't mean I was interested in Martin.

Jo laughed, but Martin, with a thoughtful expression, said I could.

As I staggered my way back to Tim, Alfie and Ryan, I saw a guy getting shots lined up in front of him at the bar. He'd bought me a drink earlier, and though he wasn't one bit handsome, I had to let my swelling confidence push the boundaries. I went up to him, put my hand on his butt and asked, 'One of these for me?' Despite the shock on his face, and before he could answer, I downed it. It tasted of liquorice and was so strong it made me close my eyes and shake my head in disgust. I was expecting vodka.

'These cost a kiss each,' he said. I leant in obediently, but just before our lips touched, a hand slipped between them.

'You've had enough for the night. Time for home.' It was Tim. Behind him were Ryan and Alfie. Tim moved me away from the would-be kisser, then led me unsteadily to the exit. I didn't resist. I knew I was being a brat, and Tim was an authority.

As we stepped out of the club, I stumbled. Alfie stopped me from falling. I laughed to try and hide the realisation of how drunk I was. While downing all the drinks I'd felt so grown-up and in control, but now I couldn't even control my feet.

'You two stay here and look after him,' Tim said. 'I'll fetch the car.'

Alfie helped me to a bench. 'Should have stuck to beer,' he said.

I looked up into his perfect blue eyes. 'You're so...' I was about to say beautiful, but instead my stomach rose and I spewed everywhere.

# 6

A loud 'MORNING!' ripped me from my sleep. As I blearily came to, I realised I was on the camp bed in Tim's kitchen, and he was looking at me over a steaming mug of tea, his eyes twinkling mischievously.

'Well, some would call this lunchtime,' Tim added.

I squirmed round in my narrow, rickety bed, trying to hide from the daylight.

'I'm about to tell you about everything you did last night. I'm guessing you were too drunk to remember. Want a brew?'

'Yes please. And I remember everything. You got nothing on me.' I sat up. 'Where are my cigs at?'

'Get your drunken arse out of bed before you smoke – that's how fires get started. You remember doing a striptease on the bar then offering the barman a blowjob for an apple Hooch? You remember stumbling out the club telling Eddie that you loved him and then puking all over Alfie? You reme—'

'I puked on Alfie? Oh my god!' I collapsed back onto the bed and pulled the duvet up over my head.

'That's the bit you question, eh? Not the rest of what I just made up? You've fallen for him hard.'

I flapped the duvet off my face. 'I haven't fallen for Alfie, you tosser. He's a friend.'

Tim snorted. 'Well, you only nearly puked on him – he got out of the way in time. But you were a mess, mate. You need to learn to pace yourself. Do you even remember the guy you almost kissed?'

'I kissed someone? Was he hot?'

'I said almost. I stopped you. It was the same guy you said a few hours earlier – and I quote – was a fugly creep. If you can't learn to manage your alcohol, I'll tell the bar staff to manage it for you.' He had a stern look on his face but a cheeky glint in his eyes.

'Sod off. You can't do that,' I said, getting out of the camp bed and pulling my jeans on.

'You guys only get to be in the club because of me. The state you were in last night, anyone could have taken you home and done anything to you.'

'And that's a bad thing, right?' I said, laughing, lighting up and nearly choking on a lungful of smoke.

'Cheeky twat. Next time take it slower, okay?' He took our teas through to the sitting room. I pulled on last night's t-shirt and followed him. At least I didn't seem to have puked on myself. 'We ended up having to carry you home. Next weekend—'

'Oh, next weekend I can stay with Jo,' I said airily. 'In a real bed. Not here in your kitchen. I can even take a guy back there if I want to.'

'Oh my god. Do you listen to a word I say? Who's Joe? I don't think I know a Joe. I'm not sure I like the idea of you staying at some random guy's place, especially if you get yourself into the same state you were in last night.'

'Jo is amazing and not a guy. I was sat with her and her boyfriend last night. They were the heavy-metal-looking couple.

They live with that Martin guy.'

'Who?'

'The other one, Mole Man.'

Tim snorted his tea.

'They have a place in Gorse Hill and a spare room, so I can crash there next weekend, and then I won't get woken up horribly early because you need your morning tea.'

'It's lunchtime!'

'I'm a teenager. This is still early for young people.'

'When did you become so chopsy? Just because you're flavour of the month *this month* doesn't mean you have to be an arse.'

He had a point, but not one I was willing to admit right then. 'As long as people remember me!'

'Oh, they remember you, mate. Half of them will spend the next few days trying to forget! Anyway, what time do you need to go home? You still have homework to do, don't you?'

I rolled my head. The joints in my neck clicked. 'I need toast first. You want some?'

'It's my toast you're offering me!' Tim said as I went through to the kitchen. 'Did you move in when I wasn't looking?'

I stuck my head back out of the kitchen. 'Can I?'

'No! And marmalade on mine, please. Use the spoon. Don't just dig in with the knife.'

Monday morning was my birthday. I lay on my bed staring up at the graffiti and marker-pen notes that had been inscribed over the years on the wooden slats of the upper bunk, some by friends, some by me. Words, doodles, quite a good sketch of a duck by Sarah. My eyes fell on a stack of numbers ranging from 1:13 to 2:47. It was the first day of my fifteenth year and I smiled to myself, thinking about twelve-year-old me timing how long it took to climax, as if getting it done quickly was some kind of achievement that needed recording.

I looked over at my brand-new TV on its wall bracket. From now on there'd be no fighting over what channel to watch. There were still people to tell me I'd been watching for too long or late, but it was a step in the right direction. I reached for the remote and the screen flickered into life. I didn't care what was on, just that I could choose.

Mum was at work and Jenny was at a friend's, so I called Alfie and we dished our weekend. Then I called Jo, a little nervously, but we talked like we'd been friends forever and made plans for the coming weekend. We decided to meet up on Saturday night, as she had to work Saturday daytime and didn't want to be out late on the Friday. I immediately started scheming how I could get permission to go. I thought Mum would like Jo, and I reckoned Jo was too cool to mention me getting drunk to Mum if they spoke, but what if she mentioned we'd met in a club?

Dad came home in the early evening, carrying an enormous box from Jade Palace takeaway. Because it was my birthday he'd got all the things I liked, with extras of prawn toast and prawn crackers. Then it was time for more gifts. My main present was the TV, but I got a few small things from Mum and Dad on top of that. There were cards from older relatives, along with cash and vouchers – the cash always more welcome than the vouchers, which were sometimes for really boring shops like Boots. A few postal gifts from uncles and aunts. Mum took notes as I opened each one, so I knew I'd be nagged to write thank-you letters. Then Jenny excitedly gave me hers: two singles on cassette and a really big Blur poster.

Like her, I was on the side of Blur in the Blur vs Oasis war. They were more fun, they had clever lyrics, much better hair and, most importantly, they had Alex, the bass guitar player. He was just a dream. If I hadn't been gay before seeing him, then after watching him on *Top of the Pops*, cigarette hanging out his mouth, hair flopping over his eyes, I certainly would have been. But how many Alexes had I seen last weekend? Not playing guitar, obviously, but gorgeous men with great hair dancing to good music... I was one of them now.

I put the poster up on my wall and sat on my bed, contemplating it. It was cool, and yeah, six months ago I'd probably have kissed it goodnight – kissed Alex goodnight, that is. But now? Jenny looked proud when she gave it to me. It wasn't her fault she didn't know who I was any more.

Tuesday was the first day of the new school year. I grabbed my bag from the chair in the hall, spine-wreckingly heavy with a full week's worth of books. I called goodbye to Mum through the piece of toast clenched between my teeth, and was out the door, off to meet my friend John to walk to school. He'd made an impression on me the first time I saw him with a shocking stripe of dark brown hair right down the top of his mousy-brown head. Not in a cool Mohawk kind of a way; rather, he'd taken his mum's spray-on hair dye and made his head look like a two-tone skunk. He claimed he'd done it for a dare, but I suspected he just liked being weird. Either way, it was enough for us to be friends from day one.

We strolled through the back gate just in time to make it to registration.

'Nearly late boys – and on the first day, too,' said a nerdy prefect.

'Boys? Shit. You're the same age as me!'

He shifted his feet awkwardly, suddenly less confident. His prefect badge was too shiny. Not just new: he'd polished it. 'I can report you for swearing, you know.'

I pointed at his badge. 'I could have had one of those, if I hadn't chosen to have a life instead.'

'We are actually going to be late,' John said. His mum was the school nurse, so he was better behaved than me, at least in public.

As we hurried to registration, John pointed out that I hadn't needed to engage. So now that was two people – Tim and John – saying my behaviour was the problem. If people stopped treating me like a kid, maybe I wouldn't react.

I ate my lunch out on the cricket strip with Sarah and a few others who brought sandwiches because school meals were disgusting. We spent most of our lunch hour bitching about how it sucked to be back. That our new classes were crap because all our sets had changed and, as we covertly smoked and watched Mrs Chewelah setting up some track and field equipment, we bitched about having to do PE again after a lazy summer.

As we ambled back from the pitches, something felt different. We were getting more attention than normal. The group I was with – misfits that fit everywhere – was cool, so it must be our senior-colour jumpers, I thought. Cool, plus jumpers, equalled extra attention.

Back in the quad we were about to split off in different directions when a small, slightly scared-looking first-year pushed into our circle. He fidgeted with the strap of his bag, looked at me, said 'Queer!' and ducked just before Sarah backhanded him. 'Sod off,' she said, 'or you won't find out what it's like to grow up to normal size.'

At mid-afternoon break, it felt like we were getting whispering too. 'One crowd has to get all the attention – why not us?' said John lightly as we colonised one of the picnic tables.

Then Sarah appeared, looking worried.

'Richard, come talk to me.'

I left the table and followed her. 'What's up? People will think we're dating,' I said through a laugh.

'That would be good, actually. Have you not heard? No one's said anything to you yet?'

'Heard what?'

'About what Holly's telling people?' The bell went. 'Shit. Meet me back here this afternoon.' She turned and ran for her class.

'Sarah, wait. What the fuck?'

'MISTER HALL! First day of the year and you're out here cursing like you're in the merchant navy. And at a girl, no less.' It was Mr Foxton, standing there like he thought he was still in the military. He always wore the same blue suit, all the buttons done up, even on the hottest day of the year.

His beady little eyes fixed on me gleefully. 'Detention for you young man – my first of the year. Why am I not surprised it's you? Thursday lunchtime. You know where it is.'

I had bigger things to think about. Holly? Holly wasn't one of the cool girls. She wasn't sexy, sporty or nerdy; she wasn't anything except a bigmouth with lots of blonde hair who enjoyed being a dick. What had she said about me and why? I ran for class, and made it with seconds to spare.

When the final bell rang out, I wiped my stuff off the table into my bag and was out of the classroom like there was a fire alarm.

Sarah stood waiting at the picnic tables looking around, slightly out of breath. She pulled me to a table.

'Richard, you still haven't heard?'

'What the hell are you going on about?'

'Holly's been telling people about you.'

'Telling people what?'

'She knows Dan.'

My heart stopped. He couldn't have! He wouldn't have! How could she be telling people about Dan and me, but I'm the only one in the news? He's in the year above me. He should be more of a story than I am.

'He told her after you dumped him and she's been telling everyone, all day.'

Around us other students were catching up with friends, making plans for the evening, heading home, or to after-school clubs. I looked down.

'Is she...is she telling them I'm—'

'She's telling people that you and Dan dated over the summer. She's telling people he's bi and you're gay. She's telling everyone.'

My world crumbled around me. 'He's confirming it? Or saying she's just making up lies?' I still had the tiniest hope that I could brush this off as fake gossip.

'I was saying it wasn't true, but then they told me he's out there telling people too. Don't cry – not here. Don't let them see you cry.' My hands were a knotted ball in front of me. She gently wrapped hers around mine and held them.

'Can we just stay here? Until they all go?' I asked, unable to look at her. I knew if I saw the pity on her face I wouldn't be able to hold the tears back.

'We can stay here as long as you want.'

My house was further from the school than Sarah's, but she walked me home. To my relief no one was in. After an awkward goodbye on the step, I went up to my room and collapsed in a ball on my bed.

In the solitude of my room, my face half-buried in the duvet, the tears flowed. Not sobbing, not wailing – just crying continuously. I wasn't ready for this. I was still learning who I was, and now everyone knew I was a faggot. A dirty, shirt-lifting, ring-raiding, doughnut-punching, knob-jockeying, filthy, little queer!

# 7

I couldn't bring myself to tell anyone – not even Mum. I thought about calling Tim, but short of him coming and rescuing me, like he had Alfie, there wasn't anything he could do. And I would still have to go to school, wouldn't I?

I came down from my room when I was called for dinner and ate in silence.

'You know you can still watch TV with us?' Dad said amiably as I cleared the table and he commandeered the remote. 'It's *Peak Practice* tonight.' I smiled wanly and went back to my room.

I got some sleep, but not much. I kept waking up and going over everything. The next morning, dazed, I went round to John's. Unusually, his mum answered the door. She looked surprised to see me. He'd told her he'd needed to go in early, she said.

John never went in early.

'He told me he'd called you.' Her eyes were saucers of pity: she knew.

He couldn't walk in with me any more because he didn't want people thinking he was a disgusting queer too. Everyone knew, and I had to walk on my own.

\*

I walked slowly. Better to be late than have to deal with hordes of people watching, pointing, whispering. Today would be worse than yesterday: they'd had a whole evening to call each other and tell anyone who hadn't heard. But my feet took their orders from my subconscious, and that was working at speed. As I got closer to school my fears became reality. Everyone was staring, whispering behind hands, giggling. I kept my head up, my eyes straight ahead. Yesterday you all thought I was cool, some of you thought I was to be feared; there had to be some residue of that still floating around. The only person who had a smile for me was Nerdy Prefect. Was that out of fear, or sympathy?

Once I was on school grounds a few people talked to me, if I talked to them first. But those were short conversations, quickly ended. They didn't want to be seen with me, or was it because they didn't want to get close enough to catch gayness from me?

Eventually Sarah found me. I was so busy trying not to acknowledge anyone else's existence, I didn't even see her coming.

She had a forced cheeriness to her. 'What's up, buttercup?'

She kept me company until the bell rang and we had to go in different directions.

Sarah wasn't the only person to talk to me. Mel, in my form, still had time for me – more than usual, in fact. The boys, though – that was a desert. All the people who were my friends yesterday couldn't get far enough away from me today.

The day dragged slower than one of the classics we were forced to read in English. It felt as though everyone was talking about me and no one was talking to me. Some weren't even trying to hide it, pointing at me as they spoke. I spent the whole day counting down the minutes. In my penultimate class I got out my new schedule to remind myself what the next lesson was. PE! No. I'm not doing that. I'm not going in the bloody changing rooms.

I hurried to the gym and through to the teachers' office. *Please don't let it be Mr Foxton.* I knocked on and opened the door, and was relieved to see it wasn't Foxton, but Mr Reynolds. Mr Reynolds was a good one; young with a kind face.

'I forgot my kit, Mr Reynolds. Can I go to the library and study instead?'

'There's lost property in the corner there. Find stuff that fits.'

'I can't.' There was a whining edge to my voice. 'I just need to go to the library. Please, sir.'

He looked at me more closely. 'Are you okay, Richard?'

'I'm fine, I just can't... I just forgot my kit.' I looked at the floor. *Please, for the love of god, just let me leave.*

His fingers drummed on the desk, then he said, 'It's easy to do, especially at this time of year. Get off to the library. Quickly. I don't want to be seen dishing out favours.'

'Thank you. I mean it. Thank you,' I said, heading out as fast as I could.

To my dismay the library was filled with a class of first-years, being supervised by Mrs Fitzpatrick, a colourless, elderly teacher with a perpetual sniffle who wore over-large homemade cardigans. I took a seat at a desk away from them and tried to bury myself in my books, but soon enough they were whispering and staring. I got up and wandered into the stacks, pretending to look for something. They'd be going back to their class soon enough, then with any luck I'd have the place to myself.

A voice broke in on my thoughts. 'You're Richard, aren't

you?' I turned from the book I was pretending to be interested in and found myself faced by a skinny little boy with a bold smirk on his face.

'That's me. Who are you?' I said, putting the book back and continuing to let my eyes roam the shelves.

'I'm Aaron.'

'That's nice for you.'

'Give me your cigarettes.'

I turned and looked at his squirrelly little face. 'Why don't you sod off back to Snow White and the other dwarves?'

'Give me your cigarettes, or I'm going to tell people you touched me. Everyone knows you're a queer.'

Mrs Fitzpatrick appeared at the end of the aisle.

'Aaron, leave the seniors alone. If they're in here during lessons, they have a project to work on. Back to your own work please. Quick quick.'

'Faggot,' Aaron mouthed as he backed away.

I had to remember that Snow White line to tell Alfie.

Finally, the last bell of the day rang out the end to my hell. I grabbed my bag and made my way to the back gate and out into the street. About a hundred metres along, a grating voice with poor-enough diction to mean it was one of the rough boys, shouted behind me, 'Queer!'

I kept walking.

'Queer, I'm bloody talking to you!'

Tim's advice was screaming inside my head. *Run. Doesn't matter if they think you're crazy, just fucking run!* But if I run today, they'll know I'm weak, and they'll come for me again tomorrow.

'Richard the faggot! I'm talking to YOU!'

I turned back to face the voice. 'I'm not a faggot!'

'Not what my little brother says. He says you touched him.'

I saw Aaron hiding behind his brother, but more importantly he was also hiding behind his brother's friends.

'He's talking shit.' I turned and started walking again. I heard the slapping of shoes on the pavement behind me, and I still didn't run. My arm was grabbed and I was spun around. He got two handfuls of my jumper and slammed me against a high garden wall.

'You put your dirty queer hands on my brother – now I'm going to bloody deck you.' His friends closed in behind him. Behind them, a semi-circle of onlookers was forming and starting a chant of, 'Fight, fight, fight.'

'I didn't touch your brother 'cos I ain't a bloody faggot.'

A teacher's whistle blew from the direction of the school gates, and a shout came from the direction of the whistle. 'Hey! What's going on?'

'Over the wall with him.' The others grabbed my clothing, my arms, one of my legs. 'Put the pansy with the flowers.'

In a move too quick to understand, I was going up in the air. A shooting pain rolled down my back as I was tipped backwards over the wall. I tried to turn as I fell, and only succeeded in landing face-first amidst ornamental rocks and border plants in the garden on the other side. I could hear my attackers laughing as the clatter of their shoes on the pavement receded.

# 8

The commotion on the other side of the wall died down as a teacherly male voice called for the running boys to come back. They didn't, but I cringed as the voice asked if someone had gone over the wall. It sounded like Mr Reynolds. Turning my head, I saw the gate opening and then a pair of trainers stood in front of me. The right side of my face was burning from the ornamental boulder on which I'd landed face-first; the rest of me was scraped and sore, and my left wrist hurt.

'Richard? Bloody hell, you're bleeding. Are you okay?' The trainers became a pair of knees as their owner knelt beside me. I looked up and saw the distress on Mr Reynold's face. Had he heard what they were saying about me?

'I'm fine,' I said, pushing myself up into a sitting position amid the broken plants. A sharp pain shot through my wrist. He caught my hand when I reached for my face.

'Don't touch it. Let me look. Who were those boys?'

'I don't know, sir. I don't know them.'

He gave me a sceptical look. 'Stop moving. You have some dirt in the wound. Just your luck to land in a rockery, not on a nice soft lawn.' He smiled wryly.

'Richard?' I turned from Mr Reynolds' kind eyes and saw

Vicky, a friend of my sister's from the year above me, hovering uncertainly at the garden gate. 'Are you okay?'

'I'm fine.'

'You need to get the wound cleaned properly,' Mr Reynolds said. 'I'll take you to Mrs McBride.'

'No!' Mrs McBride was John's mum. 'Vicky can take me home, then I'll go to the doctor's.'

Vicky stood doing the 'I need a wee' dance.

'Well, let's see if you can even walk first.' Mr Reynolds stood up and took a step back.

I tried to stand. 'Shit.' My ankle gave way. I caught his arm, steadied myself and straightened up. 'I'm fine.'

'You're saying that a lot, and I believe you less now than I did the first time. I want you to come back into school, but I can't force you to.'

'I'm—'

He turned to Vicky. 'Are you okay to walk him home?'

'Yes, of course. Are you okay, Richard?'

I limped towards her. 'Is my bag out there?'

'I brought it in. You're bleeding,' she said in a meek voice.

'He told me.'

'I'm going to have to report this,' Mr Reynolds said. 'I'll call your parents when I get back inside.'

I turned on him. 'You think they won't fucking notice when I come home with blood all over my face?'

'Watch your language. They need to be told.'

I stared at him. I could see the concern in his face, but all I could manage was, 'Sorry. Let's go, Vicky.'

'Richard!' he called after me. 'Come and see me tomorrow. I want to help you sort whatever this is out.'

I didn't look back.

It was a long, slow walk home, me hobbling with my damaged ankle and Vicky struggling with my school bag, which must have weighed as much as she did. When we arrived at my house, she said, 'I won't say anything to Jenny.'

I looked at her. 'You don't think she'll spot the rocks sticking out the side of my face?'

'You know what I mean,' she said.

She didn't want to let me out of her sight until she knew I was safe, so we went in together. Mr Reynolds had already called Mum. She was waiting in the kitchen, looking scared. She thanked Vicky, and waited in silence until she'd left. Then she spoke to me in a tone I'd not heard before. It wavered between authoritative and angry. It wasn't anger at me though; I could see that. She'd already called the doctor's, she said, and I needed to get changed quickly so that we were in time for the appointment.

Coming out of my room after changing, I caught my reflection in the mirror and saw a face that wasn't mine. This one looked raw, rough, like it belonged to someone who hangs out in the park with a skateboard and a scowl. From the way everyone had gone on about it, though, I had expected more blood. My right cheek and eye, up to my temple, were red, but in a dull way. Not that the swelling was dull: it was already going puffy, and once I'd seen it, I could feel the throbbing of more blood being pushed into the puddle accumulating under my skin.

On the drive to the surgery I gave in to Mum's endless questions, but I shorthanded it and told her that everyone knew I was gay, and that was why I'd been attacked. Her questioning was replaced with a weighty silence that I felt no need to break.

She came into the doctor's office with me. She didn't ask if I wanted her to, just stood up when my name was called and led the way in. Like Vicky, she clearly didn't want to let me out of her sight. The doctor, a young woman with a mane of dark curly hair, cleaned up my face then checked the rest of me over. My ankle had a mild sprain, and while bandaging it, she asked if I had injuries anywhere else. I told her about my wrist and that my back hurt, and she lifted my shirt. I twisted my neck and craned to see the damage. The bruise from scraping over the wall was already forming.

One of the stone-chips I'd fallen onto was embedded in my cheek, and she said she was unwilling to forcibly remove it. Instead I was told to keep the area clean and dry, cover it with a light bandage, and if the stone didn't work its way out naturally in a few days, then to go back. I looked at Mum. There were tears in her eyes. I looked away.

On the way home, Mum couldn't stop talking – about everything but the attack.

'Have you thought about what you want to do this weekend?' After she got no response from me she started going on about what she might cook for dinner. 'Does that sound good to you?' Each time I didn't respond, her topics of conversations got more random. 'I remember when you were little, we were always in and out of the doctors with one injury or another. Do you remember the time you—'

With Tim's words about how gay people were treated ringing in my head, I interrupted her. 'This isn't going to stop, is it? This is my life now.'

She swallowed hard. When she spoke again, there was a shake to her voice. 'This isn't your life; it's an incident in your life. I'll call the school once we're home. You're not going back until they can assure me you'll be safe there.'

Once home I went straight to my room and snapped the

blinds closed to shut out the world. I turned on my TV, hoping that numbing my brain would ease the throbbing in my body. There was a knock at my door. I muted the TV with the remote as Mum came in. She closed the door behind her and told me that the school hadn't answered the phone but she'd try again in the morning. That meant I got the next day off, as she wanted to speak to them before I went back.

'We can tell Dad and Jenny it was just a fight for now. Your life is complicated enough at the moment.'

Later in the evening, there was another knock on my door. Jenny peeped in. 'It's Vicky,' she said, holding up the cordless phone. 'She's worried about you and wants to talk to you. Is that okay?'

'Yeah,' I said, reaching for the phone. Pain shot through my back muscles as I took it and Jenny backed out, closing the door behind her. 'Hello?'

'I didn't tell her,' Vicki babbled. 'I was just talking to her, telling her I found you and we walked home together, and that you said the f-word to Mr Reynolds.' The last bit got a small laugh from me, as Vicky *never* swore.

'Thank you, and thank you for walking me home, too.'

'I was so worried about you. I wasn't going to leave you alone. I'll come and pick you up tomorrow morning and then we can walk home together after school.'

'Mum is keeping me home tomorrow.'

'Okay then, Friday. I've told Jenny I'll look after you, but no swearing at teachers, okay?'

'I'll try my best.'

Knowing I wouldn't have to go to school the next day, I slept quite well, only waking when I rolled over onto the right side of my face or my back twinged. Dad and Jenny left before I got up, so that morning it was just Mum and me. She fussed over me, which was both annoying and nice. She'd called the school before I got up and was waiting for them to call back. When they did, she shooed me out and shut the kitchen door to stop me from hearing. I didn't care. I just wanted her to say I never had to go back there ever again. I could hear her raised angry tones through the door.

Eventually she came through to the sitting room, moving with purpose. 'Okay. Move your feet,' she said, sitting beside me. 'That was Mr Bole. He sends his regards and was very complimentary about you as a student.'

Mr Bole was head of my year. He was one of the teachers who could see I was bright, not disruptive. That was hopeful.

'We've agreed that you'll go back in tomorrow. Jenny said Vicky will pick you up – hopefully she won't arrive too early – and if anything happens, you can go to Mr Bole's office. The other teachers are being made aware of the situation, and that you're allowed in the waiting area. He's suggested that as your PE lessons are both last period, you'll be excused and can leave early on those days, and we'll keep a close eye on everything and see how it all goes.'

All I heard was, I had to go back, and now all the teachers were talking about me too. Plus, they were keeping The Gay away from the changing rooms.

'So, I have to go back?'

'You have to go to school. Only one day left this week. I can't just keep you home forever, and you can't just watch TV for the rest of your life.'

'Okay,' I said, deflated.

'How are you feeling? Is your back okay?'

'It's just sore. The stone is still firmly in place.'

'Let me take a look.' She peeled the bandage off and probed

my face tentatively.

'Shit! OW!'

'I need to check it. It looks okay – no infection. You're going to have a big black eye though.'

Friday arrived all too quickly. Vicky walked me into school, and as much as I appreciated it, I wondered what help she'd be if anything happened. At least her cheerful wittering was some distraction from the looks I was getting. They were different today. No longer the looks of laughter and fascination. Now they were of pity, and that odd fear that comes from seeing something different. Nerdy Prefect had a smile for me again. It made me feel guilty for being so nasty to him on the first day.

I paused. 'What's your name?' I asked him.

'He's Oliver,' Vicky said. 'He's in charge of the science club.'

I looked from Vicky back to Oliver. 'Hi Oliver. I'm Richard.'

'Everyone knows you,' he said.

His words felt at first like a dig, like he was taking my olive branch and trying to hit me with it. But when I saw how small and shy he looked, almost apologising for being there, I realised it wasn't that. 'Laters, Olly.'

As I turned to leave, he called out, 'Please don't call me Olly.'

And as much as I wanted to be nice to him, that comment still stung, so I flicked him a V sign and called out 'Peace' just in case a teacher saw.

That day most people avoided me, looking on from a distance. Come one, come all, come see the freak in your midst. First person to come out in the school. Well, I hadn't actually come out yet, I'd still not said the words – just been accused. I now had to deal with a new nickname: Bumboy. Last year most people wouldn't have dared call me anything like that, but now they took glee in it.

That day half my year had a health-and-safety class in the main hall. We filed in through the double doors as I listened out for whispers about me, or to me. All the insults seemed to be sex-based: sucker, licker, lifter, bum, dick, bender... Was that all I was in their eyes, someone who liked weird sex?

The class focused on first aid. There was a talk, then a demonstration of how to check someone who'd fallen, fainted or had a seizure.

'Now it's your turn to practise,' the instructor said. 'Pair up please. If you can't find a pair, I'll give you one. Boys with boys and girls with girls.'

Every boy near me vanished into the crowd in the blink of an eye.

The instructor called out, 'Chris, Richard is the only other one without a partner. You two can work together over here.' Chris was an acquaintance from chess club – somewhere I'd only started going because it had been raining one break-time.

There was an eruption of, 'Oooh, partners!', some wolf whistles and sly comments about boyfriends.

One partner was to lie on their back on a mat, and the other would check them over. Chris lay down. I looked at him, expecting to see fear on his face, or hatred, or for him to whisper a threat, but somehow, only using his eyes he conveyed calm, support, caring, disinterest. The look told me it's okay. He's okay. I'm okay.

I shut my eyes when it was my turn to be frisked. It was soon over. I was left with emotions I couldn't pin down. I looked at Chris, and tried to get as much sincerity into two words as I possibly could: 'Thank you.' I wanted to say so much more, but that was all I could manage.

The bell went. After break it was PE, so my day was done. Oh god, had anyone told Vicky I was leaving early? I couldn't have her thinking I'd disappeared; she'd worry and think the worst. I found her and told her, then went to the back gate and escaped.

Mum was at work when I got home, so I called Jo and we made plans for our night out. It was good to step back into my real world.

# 9

I breathed in the silence of the empty house and had a long shower. I closed my eyes and listened to the hiss of the water. It needled and stung my bruised skin, but I didn't mind.

Enveloping myself in a big fluffy towel, I stood in front of the mirror and checked out the black eye developing in my reflection. Purple and green, it wasn't as swollen as I'd expected from the tightness in the muscles around my eye. Part of me wished it was bigger: if this was my war wound, it hardly reflected the viciousness of the battle.

I touched the stone embedded crustily in my cheek. It came loose and fell, making a *plink* sound as it hit the side of the sink. It bounced around the bowl a few times like the world's most screwed-up roulette wheel, then it was gone down the plughole. I hadn't wanted to keep it, but to have the choice would have been nice. On the bright side, at least I wouldn't have a stone in my face on Saturday night – just the cuts and bruises.

When Mum got home I told her I was going to stay at Tim's again that weekend. Her face tightened. Picking her words carefully, she told me she wanted me to stay home where she could look after me. I told her I needed to be with my people, in my world. I needed to feel normal again and I couldn't do that in her world. She tried, but couldn't put up a fight for long.

On Saturday morning Mum pulled me aside and told me she'd drive me to Tim's. I had to refuse, as I wasn't going to Tim's. I told her I'd rather take the bus. A long discussion ensued that basically boiled down to:
 'I'll take you.'
 'I'll take the bus.'
 'I'll take you.'
 'I'll take the bus.'
Round and round we went until I ended up giving in. Then, once I'd showered and dressed, and when she wasn't looking, I grabbed my bag and left.

I got off the bus at the Co-op on Cricklade Road. Jo had told me to look for the house with the fish tank in the window, and I had no doubt I had the right one when I saw a Victorian mid-terrace with a bay window entirely taken up by a tropical fish tank. She answered the door and gawped like one of the fish in the window. I should have warned her about my appearance.

I shrugged in what I hoped was a cool way. 'You should see the other guys.'

'Yeah? You mess them up?'

'Not unless my foot hit one of them as I went backwards over the wall.' Being around Jo again gave me enough distance from the attack to be light-hearted.

'Wait. What? You went over a wall?'

'Not by choice,' I said. 'You gonna invite me in?'

The house reminded me of an old country pub: textured wallpaper yellowed with age, ornaments on all the surfaces and the occasional mini-shelf crowded with knick-knacks. Jo led me through to a large, ramshackle kitchen. Beyond was an overgrown garden. Stairs went up from a corner of the room. I pulled out an ornately carved chair from the dark-varnished kitchen table and sat down. Jo put a vodka and Coke in front of me and turned back to grab a beer for herself. The bubbles fizzed a welcome song.

Martin appeared on the stairs wearing a dressing gown M&S would have been proud of. He froze, then said, 'What happened to your beautiful face?'

'I got tired of being beautiful,' I said. Then, more sincerely: 'Thank you for letting me stay. I so badly need this night out.'

He cast his eyes down. 'Let me show you your room. My mam always said guests should be treated like kings, so I've made up my room for you, as it's nicer.' I swallowed the rest of my vodka and Coke and followed him up the stairs, praying he wasn't planning to sleep there too.

It was like a homely hotel room, though all the cupboards were crowded with his stuff, as I discovered when I snooped later. I put my bag on the bed. A double bed! I began to feel vaguely excited. Martin got more lively as he showed me around the house. I got the feeling he was trying to impress me. The way he was looking at me – sad but attentive – made me hope my black eye wasn't going to make him try and comfort me. I didn't know what Jo had said to him last week to tell him I wasn't interested: maybe she'd been vague. It was bad enough that I'd had Tim kissing me; if Jo hadn't been firm enough, then I could end up with an even older man trying it on. I went back up to the bedroom to see if there was a chair I could put up against the door later, but no such luck.

Jo led the way as we walked to the club, in matt black Dr Martens with tartan laces and yellow stitching. I walked beside her, with Wayne and Martin following. The evening was warm and the route we took showed me areas of Swindon I'd never seen. The conversation was refreshingly light. Wayne told me my music taste sucked. Part of me felt the need to pretend I liked his music, but death metal was lost on me, and it didn't matter like it did with Alfie or Ryan. I really liked him and Jo, despite their dress sense. Martin tried to ask me about school, but thankfully Jo changed the subject, saying how much she loved the club and was excited to go back tonight.

By the time we arrived, Martin was leading us, but dropped back to let me go in first. My heart raced as I pulled the door open to find Eddie standing there. Was he going to let me in without Tim? If I was refused entry with my friends standing behind me, I'd die of embarrassment. And where the hell would I go? It wasn't like I could go back to their house without them and watch *Blind Date*. Eddie stood there with as much expression as the wall behind him. He took a few seconds to let his eyes roam over me, while my hands went sweaty. 'Interesting look,' he said.

*He wouldn't be commenting on my appearance if he was going to turn me away*. My confidence flowed back. Despite the gruff façade, there was a warmth to his tone.

'Cheers!' I blew him a kiss and led the group in.

'You come here a lot, then?' Martin asked me.

'More and more each week,' I said, laughing at a joke no one else got. 'First round's on me. What you all having?' I hoped none of them wanted anything too expensive: I had £8.75 in my wallet. I'd guessed Wayne would want lager, Martin probably that black Irish beer which was more expensive. As long as Jo didn't want something pricey I could still get a Hooch and have enough left for a second drink. I'd just have to get my drinks bought for me after that – although the prospect was less fun when I knew it was either that or go without.

Just after placing the drinks order, I heard Phil's voice booming over the music. A career in the pub trade and a passion for performing meant he could really make himself heard when he wanted to. 'Richard! Do you know how long I was in that car park cleaning up your puke last week? Too chuffing long, that's how long. One night here and th—' He stopped as I turned round. 'Jesus!' He kissed me hello. 'You okay?'

When I'd first met Phil, I was scared; then, by the end of the short conversation, confused as to whether he liked me or hated me. He'd found me later on and had me laughing, telling me about his club and the rules that I had to follow to be allowed to be there. He did it in such a way that I wasn't sure if he was serious or doing a comedy routine, but by the end of it I knew that, although he was concerned about his licence, he cared. A bit like a big brother letting you join in his party, but giving you a slap when you crossed a line after too many vodka shots.

'I'm okay,' I told him now. And this time I meant it. The events of the week already felt distant.

Phil was big, too. Taller than me, with a broad, powerful chest, kinda hot actually, now I was looking at him almost sober.

The dribble of people coming into the club became a stream. Most of them gave me a knowing look, some talking about my bashing as an initiation. 'You're close to graduating the university of gay, dear.' Others hugged me, some I knew, some just to show support. It should have made me feel sad that everyone just assumed what had happened to me was a bashing; or maybe embarrassed that I didn't run like I'd been told to. But it was more a feeling of pride. I was really one of them now, worthy of being there.

Something pulled my attention towards the entrance. I saw

Tim mouthing my name, but he was too far away from me to be heard. He hurried up to me, looking concerned. He reached a hand up to my face, but didn't touch me, then gently took hold of my right wrist with both hands and lifted it, studying the scabs on the back of my forearm. 'Why didn't you run like I told you to?'

I shrugged and hung my head as the pride I had felt a moment ago came crashing back down onto me.

Looking straight into my eyes, his edges softened. 'Come with me, buddy. You don't want to cry out here.'

He led me through a door marked 'staff only'. The room beyond was brightly lit and radiated cold: this was where they stored the beer barrels and bottles for the bar. It surprised me how much the temperature bit into my bare arms as the door closed, cutting out the noise beyond. Tim wrapped his arms around me. As he held me, all the emotions I'd been hiding spilled out of me. The mental and physical pain, the isolation. No words, just waves of tears. Tim sat us down on a barrel and I held onto him for fear of losing myself.

'It's all right, you're safe with me. Let it out.'

In that refrigerated room I lost track of time. My sobs slowed. Tim said, 'How are you doing, matey? Other than cold? You're shaking.'

'I'm okay. Am I a mess?' I asked, coming back into my body.

'You mean, apart from the puffy red eyes?' He pointed a finger around my face.

I wiped the tears from my cheeks with my t-shirt, making myself wince as I pushed on my bruised eye. 'Oh god, I can't go back out there looking like I've been crying.'

'You can't stay in here either. You're turning blue, and if we're in here much longer, everyone will think we're screwing.' That made me laugh. 'Let's go to the toilet and wash you up a bit. The ladies is always quiet, and has a nicer sink. Come on, a quick dash through the lobby. No one will see you.'

Tim was right: the ladies' toilet was much nicer, and being a sweet young guy with tear-stained eyes and a mashed-up face, I made a few friends there too. I also learned that if I wanted someone hurt, then all I had to do was ask a lesbian to do it for me. I had a lot of offers that night to sort out the guys who'd done this to me. What with my unburdening to Tim in the beer cellar and now being mothered by lesbians, a lot of time had passed, and when I emerged from the ladies', the club was heaving. Tim bought me a drink. Ryan and Alfie couldn't get over how I looked. Alfie was almost fearful while Ryan seemed to be enjoying the drama of it, as if getting attacked had been an achievement for me. Then Jo found me. I'd been gone so long they were all thinking I'd left.

For a while it felt like I was holding court at the corner of the bar. But as much as I loved all the support I was getting, I needed a break from talking about these things, and the dance floor was calling me.

Going from social pariah and punching-bag at school, to hot twink *du jour* at the club, I let the attention go to my head. There was an endless supply of people for me to dance with that night, and after the week I'd had, it was liberating. Guy after guy in front of me, or behind me, interspersed with Alfie and Jo, even Martin at one point, whose shameless dad dancing made me laugh.

As the night progressed, the weight of the week lifted and I got more and more drunk, then Ryan and me put on what was more or less a simulated sex show on the middle of the dance floor, kissing, touching, grinding on each other. I got lost in it, forgetting where I was. I wasn't attracted to Ryan, but I could see why he was attractive to others, or at least would be when he was older. But in that moment I found something. All the times my friends had spoken of school discos or first dates and first kisses, and here I was experiencing it, years after they did. There was something just right about it, even though it was Ryan, and he was probably judging not only my dancing but how my kiss tasted like orange Hooch. But we were two hot boys together, and it felt good.

We were brought back to reality when others tried to join in, and we had to push their hands away. I looked around and saw one of the few guys I hadn't danced with watching me from the edge of the floor, leaning against a partition wall. Probably in his early twenties, he had an interesting look: not hot, but somehow appealing. Thick dark blond hair, with a tight, distressed white t-shirt to accent his slim body, looking like at any moment he could roll a packet of cigarettes up in his sleeve like a character from *Grease*, but with a thoughtful expression, like he'd be a good person to ask where the library was. The enormous bunch of keys clipped to his belt wasn't the best accessory, but for some reason it suited him. Now we'd made eye contact, he grinned. My money long spent, I needed a drink, so I went over and said with a cheeky grin, 'Enjoying the view?'

'Parts of it.'

'Okay.' I'd expected more. 'Fancy getting me a drink?'

He lit the roll-up he'd just made. 'I'm about to head home.'

'That's a shame. You don't want to stay out for one more?'

He fumbled past the bunch of keys and pulled out his wallet. I was thinking he was going to give me a fiver and tell me to buy my own, but he pulled out a business card, handed it to me, said, 'Call me,' and left.

I looked at the card. Oscar. The name didn't fit the man, but what was in a name? At least now I didn't have to call him Key

Guy when talking about him.

Looking around, I sighed. This club, this world, these people all just living their lives. No one hating me, judging me, wanting to jump me, because we were all the same. We'd all suffered the same, and when we stepped back through the doors of one of our places, out into the world that was 'theirs', we hid the same. We knew each other, even if we didn't. This was our world; my world.

I siphoned the mood of the room into myself. I rounded its edges, formed it, made it into something tangible. It became a free drink, and I went to find Jo, Martin and Wayne. Martin complimented my dancing. 'I thought you might never stop,' he said, his eyes bright behind the thick puddles that were his glasses.

'Oh! My! God!' The words burst from me.

'What?'

I realised I'd grabbed Martin's thigh. I let it go and hastened to explain. 'That boy. He used to go to my school, but left as I went into the second year.'

'Which one?' Martin asked, looking round.

'Grey top; no neck.'

There had been rumours spread about the boy in question after he went to college, whispers when he walked down the street or got off the bus. I'd assumed it was all just gossip. Now I realised I'd known someone like me, that far back in my history.

'Missed your chance there,' Martin said.

'Have I? We'll see about that.'

He stood with two friends, both around the same age as him and all dressed like Jarvis Cocker in skinny jeans and polo shirts. I burst in on them. 'James, right? You went to Warneford?' My sudden appearance and mention of our school jolted him out of the fun he was having. He did what most other people did that night, staring at my bruises before noticing who they were attached to.

'Wow. What happened to you?' he asked. He didn't seem to recognise me.

'This is what coming out at Warneford gets you this week.'

'You came out? Congratulations,' he said, raising his bottle, seemingly wanting to move on from talk of school. 'What you drinking? This needs to be celebrated.'

'More like I was outed.' I said, trying to shrug it off.

'Congratulations anyway. Things only get better once you're able to be yourself.'

It wasn't long before his friends wandered off and we went into a huddle of two. He told me about how much better college was than school. I told him about how horrible Warneford still was. James was getting more attractive the more we spoke. At first glance his head was so square it could have been made of Lego, but when he smiled it made his jaw solid and strong, and his whole face was held in place with cheekbones a sculptor would be proud of. Martin came over, trying to get my attention, but not wanting to interrupt us. Eventually he touched my arm and said he was thinking of going, and asked if I was ready.

'Martin, this is James. He escaped my school with less visible injuries than me.' I whispered to Martin, 'It's still okay for me to bring someone back, right?'

'Yes, if you want.'

I turned back to James and said, 'You want to come back with us? I have my own room.' My words hiding behind a laugh, in the hope I could play it off as a joke if he said no.

'Great idea.' He downed his drink, smacking the empty bottle down on the bar with a smile.

We were crossing the car park when the doors of the Flag crashed open to reveal Phil. 'You can't leave yet, upchucker. You still owe me a drink.'

My smile turned into a chuckle while I struggled to come up with a response. I wanted to match his spontaneity and humour, but I just wasn't free enough. 'Next time, babe. I need to go now.'

'Babe? When the hell did I become your babe?'

I went over to him for a hug. 'I'm getting lucky!'

'Not with the old one, I hope,' he whispered in my ear as we embraced.

'Sod off, and no. See you next week and I really will get you that drink,' I said, walking away.

'I'll believe it when I'm drinking it.'

'Love you too, arsehole!'

As we neared Jo's, talking and laughing noisily, the curtains twitched in the neighbours' houses and first-floor lights came on. She briskly herded us all indoors. Inside she made drinks for everyone and handed them round, but the bedroom was calling me. As we stood around in the kitchen chatting, James took my hand in his and squeezed it. It was the first time another boy had done that. I met his eyes, smiled, then broke eye contact with him as I started feeling silly.

We didn't announce anything or try to say goodnight. We just left the kitchen and went upstairs, my heart beating faster with each step. Then we were alone. Me, in a bedroom, with another gay guy. I wanted to tear every item of clothing off both of us, but I also wanted to put everything I owned on and hide in the wardrobe.

James took me in his arms. Our noses were so close they touched. I was giggling on the inside: it didn't feel real. It felt like the things I'd dreamed about for so many years. The warmth of his lips against mine flowed through my body and melted my nerves. The tender way the tip of his tongue swept across my upper lip, made me want to kiss him forever.

Breathlessly he asked, 'What do you like to do?'

'What do you mean?'

'In bed. What do you like? Kissing? Sucking? I don't do anal on the first date.'

'Yeah, all that sounds good.' I had no idea what I liked to do, but everything he listed I'd spent countless hours daydreaming about. I hadn't been undressed by someone since I was a toddler, and I'd never undressed anyone else. Once I got his polo shirt over his head I managed to get his arms stuck in it, and then repeated the problem when he tugged my shirt off. We kissed again, his warm, bare chest pressed against mine feeling like nothing I'd ever felt before. He started fumbling with my belt. My jeans fell to my ankles but I couldn't step out of them, they were tangled round my trainers. My fear of falling over faded as he crouched down and his face came level with my now tented crotch. He tugged my underwear down, and the rush of what happened next went through my whole body, electricity flowing and tickling every nerve ending.

'Don't stop,' I begged, but it came out as a demand.

He laughed, 'You like that, then?' He came back up and we kissed more. 'Are you cold? You're shivering.'

It was true. But not from being cold.

We continued exploring each other and exchanging pleasure until he straddled me as he stroked himself. He closed his eyes and looked up like it was a spiritual experience, biting his bottom lip as his hand moved faster. Afterwards we lay there in silence, our breathing slowing to normal levels.

A short time later he rolled off the bed and said he had to

go home. It felt odd. I'd just had this series of amazing new firsts, intimate and personal, yet shared with him. Now he was getting dressed and talking about what he had to do in the morning, like we'd just shaken hands. I don't want to say I felt cheap, because I didn't; just that it was no longer special; more something routine.

Martin had put a bath towel and a hand towel on the corner of the bed for me. Now I reached for the hand towel to wipe off my stomach and chest. By the time I'd done that James was standing by the door looking impatient, so I grabbed Martin's dressing gown off the back of the door, put it on and went downstairs to show James out.

I went back to bed, turned onto my side to get out of the wet patch, and slept like a baby.

# 10

When I woke up, I was momentarily confused as to where I was. Once I realised, I lay there for a bit with my thoughts and a smile, then got up. I pulled on last night's clothes and staggered downstairs to find Jo at the kitchen table in a dressing gown. She looked at me expectantly.

'You want tea? Tell me all the details.'

'Milk with two, please. What time is it?'

'Eleven thirty. I was wondering if you'd ever wake up.'

'Bugger. I'll have this and then get going. My mum will start wondering where I got to.'

'So how was the school reunion?'

After waiting for what felt like an eternity to touch and be with a guy, I was still on a high from the experience. But having someone so eager to hear the details made me clam up. Other than with Alfie, Tim and Ryan, I'd never really spoken about gay sex. With Ryan it was mostly me listening to what he said I should do. And Tim tried to make things a joke: 'Always use a condom; I have them delivered by the gross.' Which sounded gross, and made me feel uneasy – that his humour was a mask for something. With Alfie it was different – more mates chatting and sharing, even though I tried to steer the conversation into flirting, which never worked. But Jo seemed excited, like we were in a scene from a movie where two girls dish their week over cocktails in a bar. I tried to relax and told her the bits I was comfortable with. She probed for more, and I eventually gave in once I realised she seemed to see sex – any sex – as simply an aspect of life.

Then Martin joined us and his questions – 'Was his cock big? Did he fuck you?' – made me uncomfortable again. Both because of the way he licked his lips, and because Martin made me feel like I hadn't done what I was supposed to. Once the conversation went back to regular topics I got myself together and was ready to leave. Martin told me I was welcome to come back any time, even if it was only to drop by for a cup of tea.

I got home after everyone had finished their lunch and found Mum waiting for me. Her jaw was set and her body was tense. I immediately regretted not having phoned her when I got up. Quietly she said, 'Go to your room and wait for me there.'

I went upstairs and put my TV on. About twenty minutes later, she walked in without knocking, closed the door quietly behind her, marched across the room, turned the TV off and sat down angrily at my desk.

'Anything you want to tell me?'

I'd had time to think about how to apologise and had it all planned and ready. 'I'm sorry, I shouldn't have left like that. I just didn't want a lift. The idea of the quiet time on the bus seemed like a nice break from the week I'd had, but it was rude, and I'm sorry.'

'Nice try, but try again.' She had me locked in a death stare. 'I called Tim this morning. Does that help jog your memory?'

Crap!

'I wondered what time he'd bring you back. He said you

weren't there!'

I tried to speak, but she cut me off.

'I trusted you and you lied to me. How do you think that makes me feel?'

'I just fancied staying somewhere else, and Jo is so much fun.'

'So you think lying to me, going out to a pub and staying at some strange guy's house is okay? You're barely fifteen. What part of that don't you understand?'

'Jo is short for Joanne. She's not a guy, actually.' I almost added 'she's nearly the same age as you', but thought better of it.

'It doesn't matter. You're fifteen and I'm your mother. I have a right to know where you are. And take that tone with me again and I'll ground you for a month!'

'Mum, seriously, you're making too much out of this. I was fine. I am fine.'

'That's it. You're not going out again. This little experiment is over.'

'NO! You can't take this away from me. It's the only place I can be myself.'

'Keep your voice down! No one else knows what's been going on, and I *can* take this away from you. You are a child. My child. If you can't be trusted, how can I let this continue?'

It wasn't a question that expected an answer, but I found words for one all the same. 'You have to let it continue. I have friends; I can be myself there; I can be free. This is my world you're taking away from me. I don't fit in your world.'

'Don't be so dramatic! Tim says there's a youth group that meets at the Health Project. You can be yourself there. That can be your world. He's not happy about being dragged into your little lie, by the way. This little escapade of yours has burned that bridge too.'

'Oh my god, a youth group? That's not the same thing. You're killing me!'

'My bloody heart stopped this morning when I heard you weren't at Tim's. Have you any idea how scared I was after the week we've just had?'

'*We? We* had? *I* had, Mum! I was the one being tortured and attacked. Not you. It was me.'

'Keep your damn voice down! The decision is made. Sulk all you want, but I'm not changing my mind.' She got up to leave.

'Mum, please, you can't do this to me.'

'I've done it. Stay up here. I don't want to see you for a while. I'm too angry that you could betray me like this.'

The door closed and I heard her go downstairs. I collapsed backwards onto my bed. This couldn't be happening. I couldn't spend all week in hell at school and only get to go to a crappy youth group. I needed to dance. I needed to see my friends. I needed to be in my world. If that was taken away from me, I had nothing.

I grabbed the remote and turned on the TV. I wasn't really watching, though. My mind's eye was seeing everything I was losing. I tried doing some homework but couldn't concentrate. Eventually, I sneaked downstairs, got the cordless phone, went back upstairs with it and called Tim's number.

'Hello?'

'Alfie, it's Richard. Is Tim there?'

'He's not happy with you. I'll go see if he wants to talk to you.'

A little time passed, then I heard the rustle of the handset being picked up, followed by Tim's voice. 'Mate! Are you kidding me with this shit?'

'Tim, you can't be angry with me too. You just can't. She's

taking my life away.'

'She was so quiet earlier when I told her you weren't here. I had a feeling you were for it.'

'But you're not angry with me, are you? She says I've burned my bridges with you.'

'No, mate. Well yes, I'm annoyed. That's a hell of a situation you put me in. Why didn't you tell me what was going on? You know I would have covered for you.'

'She says I can't go out any more. Not ever! My life is over.'

'Did she tell you about the youth group?'

'Shut up. That's not remotely the same thing, is it?'

'Well, you have to take what you can get. If that's all that you're allowed, then that's what it has to be.'

'Can I come and live with you? I can be myself at yours. I can get a job and pay rent or whatever you need me to do.'

'You're fifteen. You can't get a job – no one will employ you. You have a home. You may not like it at the moment, but you're loved and safe there. You're still welcome here. You may just have to sneak over, as I don't know if your mum will let you come.'

'I can just tell her I'm coming for a movie night and then we can go out anyway.'

'She ain't stupid. What if she calls to check, and there's no answer because we're all out?'

'Oh for Christ's sake, my life is over,' I whined.

'It's not over, it's just beginning, and from what I hear, it got more interesting last night. You were seen leaving with a guy...'

'Yeah, but now I can't even do that again. Now I'm just a kid getting tortured all week at school and then coming home to my prison.'

'Stop – you're making me sad. We'll find a way. We need to

let your mum calm down before we try, though. Even if it is only movie night, I still want you to come over here for beers, TV, or a bit of hash, your little bed in the kitchen. After the shock of this, she may calm down and let you come out properly again. We'll just have to wait and see.'

'It feels like it's over,' I said, determined to be miserable. 'Now I've nothing to look forward to. I'm just supposed to drag through the week with nothing at the weekend except a roast on Sunday.'

'Hey, a roast ain't nothing to be knocked, especially a spit roast.'

'The one with the pig going round?'

Tim laughed. 'Bless ya. Let me get Alfie. He can explain, and you can tell him all about your new boyfriend too.'

'Hardly a boyfriend. He left before I'd even wiped the cum off my chest.'

'Now there's an image I'll save for later. Here's Alfie.'

Alfie was excited to hear about my first sex, but he cut me off saying, 'Ryan wants to talk to you.'

Ryan's excited voice burst into my ear. 'Hey, slut!' He paused like he thought I was going to respond to that. 'So now you're a real gay, you need to take precautions.'

'I know. Condoms, condoms, condoms.'

'Yes, but also regular testing, because sometimes guys won't wear them. Tim takes me every three months. You can come too, like an outing. It's just piss in a cup, a thing put down your willy. Ow!'

There was a rustling on the line and then Ryan's voice sounded further away as he said, 'What have I told you about hitting?'

Alfie clearly had the handset back. 'What have I told you about being a whore? Ryan needs an MOT. Every three months or fifty guys – whichever comes first.'

'You're just jealous,' Ryan said.

I heard a door slam and Alfie and I got back to our conversation. I went into detail about everything. This was the conversation I wanted to have, not the one with Jo, and then Martin, prying and leering. With Alfie I could be truly open about it and how I felt. I even confessed that I thought I gave shit blowjobs. He said it was just practice and that I'd get better. Which was a bit dismissive, but he was probably right.

Ryan and me grinding on each other and kissing on the dance floor had apparently been a big deal. People were talking about it all night, Alfie said. Ryan had told him I was a good kisser, so at least I was getting something right.

Then Alfie asked about school. I'd been enjoying not thinking about it, which made it less real. But today was Sunday, so it would be real again tomorrow morning.

Eventually the smells and sounds of Dad basting a leg of lamb and turning the roast potatoes crept under the door of my room and lured me downstairs. He enjoyed cooking and was good at it; I enjoyed eating and was good at it, so it was an ideal combination. He'd stopped doing a double-take every time he saw my facial injuries, but I never worked out if he was disappointed that his son was fighting, or proud that I was being manly. Mum was still angry with me but doing her best not to show it. After I finished my second helping, I offered to clear the plates and load the dishwasher to get some points back in the good column. Dad looked happy with this and settled in front of the TV.

When I was done, I found Mum in the breakfast room on her PlayStation. I was never sure if I was proud or mortified when a friend asked about the games console. On one hand my mum was cooler than their mum; on the other, I wasn't as cool as them as I didn't play on it myself. Mum liked to play sitting on a dining chair to support her back. I sat behind her on the sofa and watched. After a while I said, 'Can you not be angry with me any more?'

She paused the game. 'Let me close the door.' She got up and when she came back, she looked troubled. 'I'm not angry. I don't think I was angry earlier. I was scared. I know this week has been hard for you, but it's not been a picnic for me either. I've had to see you come home with blood all over your face, and there is so little I can do. I can't come to school with you and protect you. I can't walk you there and back. That would only make things worse. I can't find the boys that did this to you and knock their heads together. My baby boy is hurting and I'm helpless.'

My eyes burned with tears. Her pain was my fault. 'I don't know what to do either. I don't want to go in tomorrow.'

'Here's a tissue.' She produced one from a sleeve, the magic trick they taught at mother school. 'We can talk about school when we've talked about last night.' She paused to think. 'Mostly today I'm hurt; deeply hurt. It hasn't been easy for me on this journey that we're on – and it is a "we", not just a "you". I'm the one with sleepless nights hoping you're okay. Worrying if I've done the right thing and made the right choices for you. I left you with a stranger and you went to a pub. Your sister isn't even allowed to do that and she's older than you. I trusted you, and then this morning I find out you've lied to me. I'm not angry; I'm hurt.'

'I didn't mean to hurt you. I just love it there so much. I wanted my own bed and not a camp bed in a kitchen. I need you to forgive me.'

'Of course I forgive you. But we have to have trust and

respect, or we have nothing.' She sat next to me on the sofa and hugged me.

I snorted back a tear. 'I don't want to go to school tomorrow. They all think I'm a freak.'

'You're not a freak. You know that. That's what matters, but you have to go to school. I've spoken to a few teachers and given one of them a piece of my mind. You will be supported while there. You aren't in this alone.'

'Which teachers did you tell off?' I said with hope.

'Mr Foxton. Does that matter?'

'Good. He's a twat.'

'Language!' she said, but she was smiling.

'I'll try. But I'm not saying I'll stay there the whole day.'

'But you will try to?'

'I'll give it a go.'

# 11

The second week of term started out almost as bad as the first had been. The bell for lunch rang, announcing freedom for everyone but me. I was shoved and bounced around like a human pinball. I'd told Mum I'd try, but now I was done with this circus and the shit-slinging monkeys that performed in it.

I found Vicky, who was with her friends. The looks they gave me tightened the ball of darkness inside me. Ignoring them as best I could, I told Vicky I was leaving so she wouldn't need to walk me home. She tried to talk me out of it, but my decision was made.

Nerdy Prefect Oliver was on the back gate again and said something about permission slips.

'Look. You know what's going on, the whole world knows what's going on. Report me if you want to, but I'm leaving. It can be with a smile and a thank you, or I can vent some of my anger on you.'

'Your smile is a lot nicer than your anger,' he said.

I felt a stab of guilt. 'Sorry about last Tuesday; it was a bad day. Well, I thought it was a bad day. Look how the rest of the week went.'

'Okay, one more smile and then I didn't see you, I didn't hear you, you never used this egress.'

There was something oddly charming about him. 'Egress? You're a riot. How about that? You even got a laugh to go with the smile.'

He stood aside.

'Thank you,' I said as I passed him.

'Hey?' He called after me. I turned back. 'Maybe I'll see you out one night?'

The penny dropped. 'Come down the Cricketers some time,' I said. 'I'll teach you how to get old guys to buy you drinks.' The relief of talking to one of my people so unexpectedly let out some of my darkness, but his face flushed, and he looked around nervously to make sure no one was near enough to hear. 'Laters.' I tossed him another smile and left.

I spent the afternoon in the strip of woodland where I used to hang out with Dan, sitting smoking and trying not to think. Then, when it would have been the end of the school day, I went home.

The next day I talked inside my head as I forced my feet to walk towards school. Today couldn't be worse than yesterday, right? Someone must have done something to take the heat off me by now.

The pep talk got me there, but only proved how stupid I was. I was still only referred to as Bumboy, but now they'd learned a new trick, throwing themselves at walls to protect their rears and their virtues saying, 'Don't bum me, Bumboy.' The voice inside me screamed that they were ugly, that they were dumb. It begged them to leave me alone, but I pushed it down, and avoided people's eyes.

As I neared a set of fire doors in a corridor, they swung open to reveal Aaron's big brother, and I was slammed into the wall. This time I didn't fight. I let them play with their little faggy rag-doll. 'I'll get you again after school, but this time properly, you disgusting queer,' he said. I stared at him and felt his breath drying out my eyes.

In geography, bony-faced Matthew announced to the class, 'Sir, I need a new chair. Richard touched this one; it's got gay on it.' I got a sharp look from the teacher, who told Matthew to sit down and be quiet, then glanced back at me before continuing with the class.

*I'm alone. I'm going to be attacked again after school, and the teachers don't care.*

My knuckles went white as I held onto the seat of my chair. If I let go, I wouldn't even wait for the bell. My fingers were an anchor stopping me from walking, or screaming, or picking up the gay chair and throwing it at Matthew's head.

I made it through the lesson but now I was done. I was marching though the school corridors when I heard, 'Mr Hall!'

It was Foxton, deputy 'dick' head.

'You were absent on Thursday. You missed your detention. I happen to be hosting it today. You can come with me and make it up.'

I turned to face him, looking at his beady little eyes and the smug grin nestled under his ridiculous moustache, and the dam inside me burst. 'Did you not get the memo?'

'Excuse me, young man, what exactl—'

'No, I won't excuse you! I *am* a young man, a young man under your care while here and you let this happen to me.' I gestured to my face. 'That's why I missed your poxy detention. So NO! I will not be coming with you.'

Foxton's moustache started dancing. 'How dare you speak to me like that!'

'How dare *you*! You act like you're in charge of this school, yet your crappy teachers are standing by while these arseholes ridicule and abuse me.' I waved a hand at everyone now clustering in the corridor, drawn there by my raised voice. They watched, fascinated, excited, maybe even a little afraid. 'Fuck you! Go to your detention and put yourself in there for being such a cunt!'

I turned to go. *Don't run*. Behind me, I could hear Foxton spluttering in outrage. The corridor was full of kids, but also full of silence. People moved out of my way as I walked towards them. Then two hands slapped together. The sound became a clap. The clap become a slow rhythm. A whoop joined it.

The indignation holding Foxton in place broke. 'Stop that clapping! Mr Hall, get back here! You will respect me!'

I reached the exit, my head held higher than it had been all week. The applause was increasing, and it was for me! I'm still me, I thought; I'm still one of the kids you used to envy or fear, and I'm not done yet. At the double doors I turned back, shouting loudly: 'Who the hell would respect a dickless little Nazi like you!' And with that I threw the doors open and was outside in the sunshine. I could hear the cheering, screaming and clapping from within all the way to the back gate. I knew I was so screwed when he called Dad, but fuck me, that felt good.

That evening I sat at the dining table watching Dad's nostrils flare as he stood looking down on me.

'You called the deputy head a c—' He stopped himself. 'You called him the C-word. What on earth…?'

I let out a little sigh. I didn't feel I needed to justify my actions. 'Not like everyone else wasn't thinking it. He is a cunt.'

'Do not use words like that in this house! You will go in tomorrow and apologise to Mr Foxton. Do you understand me?'

If it hadn't been for the tremble on his lip, his act of intimidation might have worked. I moved one side of my hair off my forehead, and stared back at him.

'Don't add ignoring me to your list. You are not too old to be put over my knee.'

The back legs of my chair caught on the carpet as I stood up and the chair clattered against the wall. I was an inch and a half taller than him.

'I will not be apologising to him; I have no intention of ever speaking to him again.' I turned and made for the stairs.

'Don't you walk away from me,' he shouted. 'Get back here.'

I looked back from the bottom step. 'Make me.'

'That's it. You're grounded for a month, and the TV is coming out your room the first chance I get.'

I shut my bedroom door and paced my room, stepping over the clothes, books and general crap littering the floor. I was done being everyone's victim, I told myself. I would not be bullied or threatened by anyone any more. I would take control of my life. People felt they could put their hands on me, call me whatever they wanted, control me, and I was supposed to just sit and take it. Fuck them, and fuck that.

I kicked my school bag and hurt my ankle. I dragged the bag to a clearing on the floor and yanked on the zip to open it. The books spilled onto the floor and I tossed the empty bag across the room. Sitting down in front of the pile, I picked up the first one: maths. I gripped it in both hands but didn't have the strength to tear it in half, which was harder than it looked on TV. Instead I opened it up and tore it down the spine, then tore a chunk of the pages in half. Rip by satisfying rip, the entire book became one-inch squares of my hate. I reached for the next one: history. The clump of pages I ripped out was still too big to be torn. By English, I was getting the hang of it: rip, rip, rip. At science, I paused; Mr Bole was a good one, so larger pieces, but still pieces. German, I wiped a tear from my cheek and the book went the way of the others. One by one, rip by satisfying rip, every single book turned into confetti of my pain.

Mum knocked and walked in.

I looked up from my nest of paper, tears running down my face. 'If I haven't got books, I can't go to school,' I said, like it was a rational conclusion. My voice didn't break or wobble.

She came over, knelt in the pile of former schoolbooks and pulled me into her. I could feel her body shake as she started to cry, too.

After a while her chest shook less. She loosened her hug and wiped a tear from underneath the rim of her glasses, then wiped one from my cheek and took a deep breath. She said I didn't have to go to school tomorrow. She'd demand to talk to Mr Bole, and we could talk when she was back from work.

The next morning, I felt an eerie peace. I'd decided what I was going to do before I went to sleep. It was time. I got up, washed and picked out a nice outfit. It was a big day, after all. I could and would take control of my life. I wrote a note to Mum. She'd be back first, so it didn't need to be to all of them. Besides, she was the only member of the family I wanted to address.

*I can't do this any more.*
*It's too much, and I know you will have to send me back to school.*
*I just can't go.*
*This will be hard for you, I know, but it's what I have to do.*
*I will be fine.*
*If I'm not here, they can't blame you any more.*
*Lots of love*
*Richard*

I turned, looked around the dining room and hall, taking in every little detail one last time, grabbed my key, and left.

# 12

Since it was mid-morning, there were only a few other passengers on the bus, but I used my bag to block off the seat next to me all the same. I wasn't in the mood for strangers to come close, or worse, to talk to me. My mind kept going back to the note I'd left. Had I said I loved her? Already I couldn't remember.

I stepped off into the crowds at Swindon bus station. I'd have to walk the rest of the way.

As I got closer to my destination, my neck and shoulders began to bunch and ache with nerves. By the time I turned the last corner, my heart was pounding. I reached the house, where the fish swam back and forth in the window. Jo answered the door, dishevelled in her PJs. It must be her day off, which was a relief as I'd had no back-up plan if she was out.

'Hey honey, why aren't you in school?'

'Can I come in?' I'd hoped not to, but immediately burst into tears.

'Oh my god, what's happened? Come in, come in.'

She led me through to the kitchen. After flicking the kettle on, she gave me a hug, then pulled out a chair for me, and over a mug of tea I gave her the unabridged version of what had been happening, jumping backwards and forwards as I remembered different elements of the story. She listened, unusually quietly for her, only interjecting when I wasn't being clear. Eventually I finished with, 'Can I live here?'

After a moment of thought, she said, 'Of course you can, honey. We'll need to ask Martin, but I'm sure he'll be happy to take you in. We can ask him when he gets home from work.'

'Thank you so much. I just can't be at home any more. My parents want to stop me from going out and force me to go to school, and at school they want to kill me.' I left out the part about me lying to Mum when I stayed there last weekend.

'I'm sure they're doing what they think is best. It's hard being a parent. Maybe they just don't understand what you're going through.'

'I'm going through hell. I've died, and school is actual hell. That's what I'm going through.'

'Well, in the meantime, how about some breakfast?'

I hadn't realised how hungry I was, but as soon as she mentioned food my stomach reminded me.

After eating we spent the day getting to know each other better. Wayne joined us once he got up. In a quiet environment, he was a lot chattier. He and Jo had met at an Iron Maiden concert in Wolverhampton. She'd been knocked to the floor in the mosh pit, and he'd rescued her from being trampled. It was love at first sight, he said: her combination of defiance and helplessness.

'I punched you on the arm,' she reminisced.

'You thought I was trying to steal your bag.'

'But you were just being a gentleman.' She smiled.

Martin got home and was surprised to see me, then pleased.

'You know how you said if I need anything?' I said, trying to look appealing. 'Well…'

He seemed almost excited by the idea of me staying. 'You'll have to take the spare room, though,' he said. Then, apologetically, 'It's a work in progress.'

He wasn't kidding. Bare walls, a single, unmade bed, a dark wood wardrobe that had seen better days. Chunks of plaster were missing from one wall, exposing the brick. Martin said the plaster had come off with the wallpaper when he started stripping it because it was blown due to age and damp.

'I can put posters up to hide the holes,' I enthused. 'There's more than enough room for my stuff in here,' I added, opening the wardrobe. 'Thank you.'

'We don't have time to wash the sheets and have them dry for tonight,' Martin said, 'but I only slept in them that one night.'

'Not a problem. I love it. Thank you again.'

I gave him a big hug and then began to take some stuff out of my bag to put away.

'I'll get dinner on. You look hungry,' he said, leaving me to it.

Alone in my new room, I could breathe for the first time in what felt like weeks. How could it only have been a week and half since school started? I sat on the bed and stared at the bare plaster wall. It had a kind of beauty to it, the holes and cracks a map of its history. I didn't know what would come next, but finally I had some control. No more arseholes at school, no more having to get up early. My life was mine once more.

I woke the next morning to an empty house. It was odd being there on my own, but nice to have some head space and not have to talk to anyone. In the living room I found a note on the coffee table and a packet of cigarettes. 'I thought you might need these. Royals, not B&H. They're cheaper and you get more in the pack. Love Martin.' I smiled at the unexpected kindness, but it did make me think about money, and how quickly my meagre amount would run out. What then?

The next couple of days blurred into each other. I had no routine other than watching TV, talking with whoever was around, eating what was cooked for me or brought back from a takeaway, and sleeping. As the weekend approached, I was ready to engage with my life again. I called Alfie. Tim answered. When he heard my voice, he was frenzied. It brought me some comfort knowing he cared that much for me. He said he needed the names of who I was staying with, the address, the telephone number. He checked a dozen times that I was safe and had my own room, and told me that Mum had been calling repeatedly. She'd even been round there twice to check he wasn't lying about me not being at his.

'You need to let her know you're safe,' he said. 'It's not fair on her, she's going out of her mind.'

As much as I wanted to speak to her, I wasn't ready yet. She'd focus on taking me home and making me go back to school, which would be even worse since I'd vanished. The rumour mill would have been going at full speed in my absence. Tim wasn't happy about this but agreed not to give my phone number or address to Mum. Then, after checking I was okay again, he let me speak to Alfie, who sounded hurt that I hadn't told him right away. We found things to laugh about, though, and agreed to meet at the Cricketers later for a proper catch-up.

Less than an hour after we hung up, there was a knock at the front door. I recognised Mum's silhouette through the frosted glass. *Tim, you're a dick!*

I backed away from the door, hoping it was dark enough inside for her not to have seen me. She knocked again. Guilt stabbed through me. I couldn't leave her standing there, so I opened the door. I found her looking down the street, and when she turned her expression went from distraught to relieved.

'Your note made it sound like you were going to kill yourself. I haven't slept in days. I love you, but you're a shit.' No smile, and to be fair, she wasn't wrong.

'Come in, I'll put the kettle on.'

Once she'd had the tour and seen my room, I made some tea and we sat down to talk. She said a hundred times that she wanted me to come home, and I explained again and again that I couldn't. She told me that Dad and Jenny knew about me and everything that had been going on. She'd had to explain why I'd left.

I didn't like it, but everyone else knew, so why not them? I wasn't brave enough to ask how they'd reacted. She told me how she'd not only seen Mr Bole face to face, she'd also demanded to see Mr Foxton and had read him the riot act. Apparently, faced by a wild mother bear, he'd decided his best option was to just stay quiet.

'I reserve the right to turn up here at any point,' she said. 'I could call the police, you know? Have them bring you home right now. But I won't. I want the number for here and I want to meet this Jo and anyone else that lives here.'

I agreed to it all. We arranged for her to come back the next night to meet Jo and Martin. I wrote down the phone number for her, then asked if I could have some money. Scowling at me, she reluctantly got her purse out. We hugged for an uncomfortably long time, until I wriggled and made her let go.

'I really do love you. Remember that,' she said as she got ready to leave. 'You're my boy and I love you.'

'I know, and I love you too.' I could see the pain she was in, and I knew it was caused by me.

When I told Martin about Mum's visit, he was worried.

Would she come back, but this time with the police, to question him and drag me out?

'Don't you close your curtains at night,' he said. Instead, he would go into my room and close them for me, just in case my parents hired a private detective to watch us.

'How would that look better?' I said, trying to laugh it off. 'They'd then see you closing the curtains in my room.' I looked at my watch. 'Shit, I'm going to be late to meet Alfie. Don't wait up.'

I grabbed my jacket and rushed out, heading for the Cricks.

I got there on time but Alfie was late. Though my bruises had faded, my cuts were still enough to get me my first drink. Thursday nights were a lot quieter than Fridays, so I was relieved when Alfie finally showed up, bringing with him a £20 note. He said the drinks were on Tim, as an apology for calling my mum.

As the evening went on and the drinks went down, Alfie asked if I was missing my friends from school, and I guiltily remembered Sarah. I checked my wallet for coins and went outside to the payphone. It was past 9pm, a bit late, but I called her anyway. No one in school knew what had happened, and she seemed like a good person to let them all know.

'Hello!' A male voice, presumably her dad.

'Hi, is Sarah there?'

'Do you know what time it is? Who's this?'

'It's Richard, her friend from school and the amateur dramatic society.'

There was a pause. 'Okay. Let me check if she's awake...'

Sarah came on the phone, sounding excited. 'Dude! You're bloody famous, calling Foxton a Nazi. Where are you?'

'I called him a *dickless* Nazi. People are talking about it still?'

'Oh my god,' she said, 'it's all anyone is talking about. Well, the boys are still talking about you being gay, but I told them to shut the hell up. Who cares if you're gay? Be proud of it. When are you coming back?'

'I'm not. I've left home and I'm not coming back to school. I can't.'

'You're joking, right?'

I quickly filled her in on all my news and my (very vague) plans for the future, which did not involve Highworth Warneford School.

'I'm done with school, I'll just go straight to college when I'm old enough and do catch-up classes.'

'Babe, come back. We all miss you.'

'Tell them I've died because of how they treated me,' I said cheerily. 'Okay, the beeps are going and I'm out of change. Love you.'

'Love you t—' She got cut off as the last of my money ran out.

# 13

Mum visited several times over the next week. She never turned up unannounced as she'd threatened, but invited herself round, sometimes twice a day. Our conversations became less stilted, but she still kept asking me to come home. Then it was Friday – party night, and the first where I felt like a free man. The others didn't want to come out, but Martin gave me £10 for drinks, and off I went. When I got to the Cricks, I made my way through the crowd, stroking my hand across the backs of anyone I thought was hot. I found Tim, who had the look of a dog that'd just been told off.

'I had to call her. You understand, right?'

I nodded. He hugged me, bought me a drink, and I joined him and Ryan. Ryan was very impressed with my dramatic exit from school. With mock pride, he said, 'My boy is learning so fast. Don't take no shit from no one.'

'Anyone,' Tim corrected him primly. 'You sound like a pleb.'

We arrived at the club later than usual and it was busy, so I should've had to pay, but Eddie let me in for free anyway. Now I knew this was my world, my life, and no one could take it away from me. I was not just a free man, I was a prince among men and the dance floor was my kingdom.

While working up a sweat, I saw Oscar standing on his own again, watching.

I went over wearing a cheeky smile. 'Going to buy me that drink tonight?'

'You didn't call. I'm starting to think you're just after drinks.'

'What would I say when I call? "Hi, it's that boy you like to watch dance"?'

'Who said I like to watch you dance?'

'You did, the way you watched me. Now how about that drink or – I don't know – asking me what my name is?'

'What's your name then, dancing boy?'

'I'm Richard. Pleasure to meet you, and I drink Hooch or Martini and lemonade.'

'Good to meet you, Richard,' he said, extending a hand for me to shake. 'Call me and I'll take you out for that drink.' He dropped the remains of his roll-up onto the floor and ground it out with his shoe. 'I look forward to hearing from you.'

Then he left. I didn't know what to make of it: was he interested or not?

Time passed, and Alfie, Ryan and Tim left too. Eventually the music ended, leaving a hubbub of happy and dejected voices, and a minute later the club was suddenly bathed in harsh white light. Shortly afterwards, people began to trail out.

I was sitting with Phil and a friend of his I'd not met before, Finlay, watching the exodus, not wanting to leave. I was smitten with Finlay from the moment I saw him. He was in his mid-twenties and had cheekbones you could cut diamonds with. The way he dressed, the way he moved, he just oozed understated cool. It was like everything he did was for himself alone and I wanted to be like that. I spent so much time worrying about what other people would think of my outfit, my hair, if what I said would be funny, but Finlay wore a baggy white t-shirt with a cream silk shirt over it, and made the look work because he was comfortable and confident.

'End of the night already?' I said, disappointed.

'Stay for the lock-in,' Phil said.

'What's a lock-in?'

'It's when they kick the riff-raff out and we all drink for free,' Finlay said.

'You know it's being a twat that makes me love you,' Phil said to Finlay as he got up to help his staff close the bar.

The harsh lights stripped the club of some of its mystique, but it was still my haven; now I just knew what it looked like the morning after. Phil and the security team took the cash over to the pub, and when he came back, he bolted the doors. Now I got it: a lock-in, 'cos you got locked in.

Phil put some music on, saying it was a group called Shakespeare's Sister – 'you know, with the non-crap one from Bananarama' – and then he and Finlay ganged up on me in a gently comedic way, making jokes about how only a couple of weeks ago I was shy and innocent. I told them about meeting Eartha Tits for the first time, wanting them to know I'd made the whole pub laugh, adding in more laughter to make myself look better.

Finlay raised an eyebrow. 'You don't recognise me, do you?'

While I was trying to figure out where I would know him from, he stood up and threw his left arm out dramatically. He held his right fist to his face, dropped his voice to accentuate the gravel hiding in it, and said, 'Let's all welcome the Highworth chicken to his first night.' It was Eartha's voice.

I couldn't speak. Finlay, or possibly Eartha, sat down again, patted my leg and said, 'The terror all over your face that night. Priceless.'

'But look at him now,' Phil said. 'Working the guys like he's been at it all his life. Even when he looked like he'd dragged his face down the side of a wall.'

With my friends at school, this would have been bullying. But here with these two, it was fraternity. Eventually Finlay said it was time for him to go and Phil asked me how I was getting home. 'There won't be any taxis at this time of night,' he warned – not that I could have afforded one.

'I'll walk. It's not that far.' Actually it was miles and miles, but I'd been walking so much recently, what did one more trudge matter? 'I can cut through Manchester Road.'

'At this time of night? You've only just got your face looking half-normal again... Finlay, are you going his way? Or you can stay in the Flag with me and walk home in the morning.'

'I can stay in your pub?' I asked excitedly, not waiting for Finlay's response.

'Before you and your liver get any ideas, the alcohol is all locked away. You drink more than a haddock with a bladder infection.'

Phil and I waved Finlay off from the entrance to the Flag. As if to remind me who he really was, he twirled the way Eartha did when lip-syncing on her little stage. I was still chattering excitedly away, but Phil shushed me as he bolted the pub doors. 'Don't want to wake the ghosts of drinkers past.'

I'd never been in a pub when it was shut before, with towels over the taps and no sound coming from any direction. It was so big, now it was empty.

'You want something to eat? Baked potato?' asked Phil, heading towards the kitchen.

'What are the other choices?' I said, following him.

'Starvation or bin scavenging.' He opened one of the large metal catering fridges and peered inside. 'I can additionally offer you cheese, beans or – well, that's about it actually, unless you want some sliced lemon.'

'Both please, but without the lemon.'

Phil took two potatoes out of the fridge and tossed them in the microwave.

'You can bake a potato in the microwave?' I asked in disbelief.

'You can do loads of things in a microwave. Fish, broccoli, rice. You can even dry your pants. Not that I would, of course,' he said with a wink.

We carried our plates through a labyrinth of back rooms and doors and up some stairs, the smell of the melting cheese teasing my nostrils and stomach. Phil flung open a door and, with an expansive gesture, said, 'Welcome to the palace. Please don't touch the dust. It's been here longer than you've been alive.' He pointed back through the door we'd entered by. 'Don't go out there at night. If you need to, then wake me up. That room is alarmed.'

We ate sitting on a flabby cream leather sofa, watching an old movie that Phil talked over, telling me about camera angles, directing, lapses in continuity and something called post-production. Then it was time for bed.

His bedroom was large, with room for another sofa, which was currently piled with clothes. A desk was strewn with ideas for song lyrics, and he even had a barbell and dumbbells, heavier than I could lift.

'This is my side,' he said, making an attempt to straighten the duvet. 'If you roll around during the night, I'll push you back onto yours. I'm old and need my beauty sleep.'

'So you don't love me?' I teased. 'I'm just another cheap floozie?'

'You ain't cheap! I've had to pay for drinks for you, now I find myself feeding you. You're like a stray cat. You feed it because you feel sorry for how sad it looks, and now it won't sod off and your house smells of cat piss.'

I cuddled into him, laughing. His big chest was a great pillow, and it felt so nice having his arm around me.

'You know I won't be able to sleep with all this bloody hair in my face?' he said.

Softly I said, 'I wasn't planning on sleeping yet.'

'Don't go getting ideas. You're here to sleep – and stop playing with my bloody nipple!'

'But it's a cute nipple.'

'Of course it's a cute nipple; it's attached to me, but that doesn't mean you can play with it.'

'You're enjoying it, though.'

'How do you know what I'm enjoying?'

I boldly moved my hand from his chest to his groin. 'You're enjoying it.'

'Owhowwho. No. No touching the penis.' He was flapping around like a fish out of water, half trapped by me lying on his arm. 'You're a child.'

'A hot child, though.'

'There is so much wrong with that sentence I don't know where to start. There will be no sex for you here, boy!'

'All the other guys want it.'

'All the other guys aren't in this bed. Now, you can cuddle, or you can get the fuck off my side of the bed, but those are your only options.'

'Kiss goodnight?'

He gently pressed his lips against my forehead. 'Now go to sleep. Jesus, you're a lot of work.'

'Night, Dad.'

'Oh, don't start that shit with me. I'm not old enough to be your dad.'

'How old are you?'
'Fuck off and go to sleep.'

I got back to Martin's place after lunch, wearing the clothes I went out in, which didn't go unnoticed by Jo.

'Ohhh, the dirty little stop-out returns, and he's doing the walk of shame without the slightest hint of shame.'

'I stayed for the lock-in. Afterwards Phil said it wasn't safe to walk home.'

Martin told me he'd been worried when he got up and saw I wasn't in my room. He had two sides. This one I liked: morning Martin, filled with gentle concern. Night-time Martin, after he'd had one drink too many, had an edge, and he could get handsy and domineering, but I was used to seeing a change in Dad when he was drunk, so this was nothing new. I thanked Martin for caring and assured him I'd always be fine.

After a sandwich and shower, I went for a nap. The night before had been the first time I'd shared a bed with anyone, and it had badly disrupted my sleep. I'd had friends take the top bunk in my room, or I'd slept on the floor in theirs, of course. But being in the same bed as someone, especially someone I knew was gay... All night I'd been alert to the slightest movement and the thought of where that movement might lead.

When I woke from my nap, it was time to eat, shower, and head out again, this time with Jo. Life was good.

# 14

I got up after lunch on Sunday and, while reflecting that I needed to get a handle on my sleep pattern before I became entirely nocturnal, I decided to call Oscar. I'd made him wait long enough, he hadn't been in the Cricks or club last night, and his aloofness had piqued my interest.

An uptight-sounding woman answered and summoned him to the phone.

'Hey,' I said. 'It's dancing boy.'

'Good to finally hear from you. How are you?'

'Great weekend thanks, so I'm a bit tired today,' I said. 'Is that your mum that answered or something?'

'Or something, yeah. So, this drink you want,' he said, changing the subject. 'How about Wednesday? We can make a proper date of it.'

A date? I wasn't expecting that. I awkwardly asked if I should come to his. But he said definitively that he'd pick me up around seven.

'Okay,' I said.

'Great. What's your address?'

I told him. That was it then; my first date booked. I'd been thinking more bedroom fun than boyfriend. Getting to expand on my experience with James, only this time better. So I wasn't sure how I felt about it. And how should I dress for a date? I called Alfie for help.

'Hey, call me back. I'm on Martin's phone.'

'Okay, one sec.'

We hung up. I grabbed the receiver on the first ring. 'Hey, so what should I wear for a date?'

'You got a date? With who?'

'Oscar – the guy with the big bunch of keys clipped to his belt.'

'Okay.' A pause. 'Don't you think he's creepy, just standing and watching you all the time?'

'He's unique, not creepy! So, should I just dress like I do when we go to the club, or more casual, like I don't care?'

'Where's he taking you?'

'Don't know. He's picking me up, so I don't think it will be at his.'

'Don't get in his car, okay?' I could almost see the finger he pointed at me when he spoke.

I heard Tim's voice in the background. 'Is that Richard? Whose car is he getting into?' Now he'd taken the receiver from Alfie. 'Who are you dating and why do you need to be in his car?'

'Calm down, grandad. It's Oscar.'

'Who?'

'The guy with the keys.' So he did become Key Guy after all.

'I know who you're talking about. Tell him I can track him down if I need to.'

'Oh, that will be a great opening line.'

'Cheeky arse. I'm being serious.'

'Put Alfie back on. We're talking about what I should wear.'

Alfie came back on the phone. 'You're stressing Daddy

out.' We laughed while Tim shouted 'Fuck you both!' in the background.

'So, what should I wear?'

'Good underwear,' Alfie replied.

Later, Mum called. Nowadays when we talked there was usually a hint of equality in our discussions. But today she was hesitant. I asked what was wrong. 'Nothing's wrong. We want to come and see you tomorrow.'

'We? Like, all of you?' I pictured Mum and Dad sitting on the sofa with Jenny squeezed between them, all staring at me.

'Myself and your father. After work. Probably at around seven-thirty. You'll be in, I assume?'

'Yes. I'll arrange it so we can have the place to ourselves.'

I said this more to protect Jo, Wayne and Martin from having to deal with Dad, since Mum had already met them. That first time, I'd mostly watched rather than talked, but as Mum only glanced at me to check my expression after someone else said something, I think she liked that I was being quiet.

Martin had dressed up a bit in a button-down shirt and carefully ironed trousers. I was used to seeing him in jeans and a t-shirt, or his work jumper and stiff cargo trousers. Seeing them together, I realised he must be about ten years older than my mother.

But watching Jo natter on at Mum was the most unnerving part of the visit. I was thinking more and more of Jo as someone my own age, but I guess I'd aged myself up in that equation. Looking at them sitting next to each other, I became aware that the age gap between Mum and Jo wasn't that big.

It went well though, with Jo thankfully not dropping any bombs about clubbing with me. Martin looked so nervous he was practically robotic, which I think actually benefitted him.

I poured a vodka as soon as Mum left. The whole encounter had left me feeling very young, and a little out of place.

On Monday morning it was just Jo and me at home, and we were getting on like sisters. We sat with tea and talked, mainly about my upcoming date. Then she awkwardly changed the subject and said, 'You're so confident, and know everyone on the scene, but I was wondering…'

It was unlike her to not just say whatever was on her mind. 'Spit it out, the suspense is sending me to sleep.'

'The other week… James, was that your first time?'

I felt my face get hot. 'How did you know?'

'It was how you were afterwards. How you talked about him and what you did.'

'I'm so embarrassed,' I said with feigned drama. I didn't know what else to say.

'We all have to start somewhere. Tell me the real details, then; tell me what it was like. Not as the Richard that you project, but as the Richard that just did it for the first time.'

We knew each other so much better than the last time she'd asked, so it felt less like prying and more comfortable to talk about. Although I was still slightly uncomfortable telling her about 'gay things', I went over everything again. How excited I was. How it took me ages to get him to moan when I was sucking him. Now and again she stopped me and gave me advice on how to make it feel good. I felt like I should take notes. Considering how easy it was to make myself feel pleasure, there were so many things I had to do to give a good blowjob. Lips, tongue, pressure, hands, fingers, tickling, gripping; no wonder they called it a job.

As my account of my first sexual experience drew to a close, she said, 'Then Wednesday – that's your first date?'

'Kinda. There was Dan, who I dated in the school holidays. He was the guy that opened his stinky mouth and told everyone about me. Sorta dated. It was complicated. He was strange, we said we were dating, but we never kissed, not even a hug. So yeah, I guess this is my first date.'

'Oh my god, I'm so excited. I'm going to stay up until you get home so I can hear everything about it. I want absolutely every detail the moment you get back.'

She was far more excited than I was, but the idea of having someone to talk to about the date as soon as it was over was appealing. With Alfie I'd have to keep up a front if it was crap; with Jo I could tell the truth.

I couldn't seem to sit still: the apprehension of seeing Dad that evening was building up in me. He was always supportive of me in areas he felt comfortable with. If I showed the slightest interest in any sport, he'd get me all the equipment I needed, then help me practise. But things like this... He was coming with Mum, so it wasn't going to be finger-in-the-face shouting; he never did that in front of her. But my fear of what he might say grew more and more intense.

Eventually the time came, and there was a knock at the door. My heart pounding, I opened it, and it was just Mum standing there. I was both relieved and disappointed.

'Where's Dad?'

'He can't come to the house; he doesn't want to see it. He's waiting in the car park by the shops.' She looked back along the street as she spoke.

I got my shoes and followed her down the street. 'He's struggling,' she said, 'but he's trying his best. Okay? Remember that, please. Be nice.'

'Of course I'll be nice,' I said. But then the memory came

back of the last conversation we had: me swearing at him and walking off.

We reached the end of the street and I saw Dad across the road. He was standing by the car under a streetlight with his hands stuffed in his coat pockets, watching us. As I got closer, I could see his bottom lip trembling and noticed his eyes were already wet. He hugged me, didn't let go, and cried. Then he let me go; I looked into his glossy, wet eyes.

'I'm okay, Dad.'

He put his hand to his mouth and turned away. He and Mum talked quietly at the back of the car and then he got into the passenger seat, shutting the door. No goodbye, no conversation before the lack of goodbye. Was I that difficult to speak to? Was my life so abhorrent that he couldn't even ask about it?

We crossed the road and walked back into my street in silence.

'He loves you,' Mum said. 'This is difficult for him, but he's trying.'

'I haven't changed, I'm still me. What's so difficult about that for him?'

Her fingers dug into my arm. 'He's just found out what his son's been going through and simultaneously found out that he knew nothing about you. This' – she gestured down the street towards Martin's house – 'is very different to who he thought you were, and he's going to need time to adjust to that.'

A tear ran down my cheek. All I heard was, I was a disappointment to him for not being straight.

She let go of my arm and rubbed it. 'He just wants you to be safe and happy and grow up to have a beautiful life. We both want that. But the life you're living now scares him.'

'I want that too.'

'And you'll have that. You'll get there. We all will, together.

I should go back and take him home. I love you, okay? We both do.'

'I love you too.'

Oscar called and asked to postpone our date by a week because he had to work. I wasn't good at patience, and by the time the appointed day eventually arrived, I was beset with anxiety. I told myself I wasn't invested in the date with Oscar, but still I sat watching the clock, ready and waiting for his arrival. At six minutes past seven, he knocked on the door. He wore blue jeans that were too baggy to be stylish and not baggy enough to be fashionable. With the bunch of keys clipped to a belt loop of course. But his smile was inviting and the way his dirty blond hair flopped as he moved was endearing. He asked if I was ready to go.

'I'll fetch my jacket.'

In the kitchen Jo excitedly wished me luck.

Pulling the front door closed behind me, I said to Oscar, 'I've been meaning to ask, what's with all the keys?'

'Oh, you know how it is – all the locks for the house. All the locks for work and then the car and garage. It gets too much for a pocket and to carry a big bag for my keys seems daft. I think they look cool like this, too,' he said, flicking the bunch and making them jingle.

I laughed. 'Cute,' I said.

'Not how I'm normally described, but I think I like it.'

'Where did you park?' I asked, conscious of Tim's warning about not getting in his car.

'I walked. We're going this way.' He pointed down the street.

I made a comment about him being a man of mystery. He didn't reply. We walked away from the main street with its pubs and shops and into the quiet of the night. The roads he chose, lined with terraces of Victorian workers' cottages, had a peacefulness to them. He asked how I'd damaged my face. I'd told the story so many times it flowed easily. He was a good listener, and whenever there was a pause in the conversation, he always had a question to fill it. How were my family? Did they accept me? Did they support me? Did I see them much? Did I have siblings? When would I go back to school? Why had I stopped seeing my counsellor? Would I see him again? It was like I was being interviewed. 'I don't need a counsellor with you,' I said. 'Tell me about you.'

'Not much to tell, really. I'm not that interesting. I'm more interested in you.'

'Throw me a bone. How about where you live?'

'I'll show you. That's better than telling you.'

That seemed to be our date. No drink, just walking and talking. I liked how interested he was in me. Not like the other guys, who just wanted to feel me up and ask if I had plans for the night. Oscar really wanted to know about me.

We turned a corner, and he pointed to a house like Martin's: a mid-terrace, well presented. The small front yard had been turned into a garden, greenery brimming over the low brick front wall. It set it apart from the rest of the street.

'I love the garden. That must be a lot of work to keep it that nice?'

'She enjoys doing it.'

'Your mum?'

'She acts like my mum. Let's keep walking.'

'We aren't going in?'

'I'm enjoying the night air. Aren't you?'

So we kept walking and talking, for two hours, though somehow I couldn't bring myself to ask him directly who 'she' was. I imagined a blind aunt in a wheelchair, a disfigured, locked-away sister, or the dried-out mother in *Psycho*. Eventually, I realised we'd circled back round to his street again. 'I brought you here the long way earlier. You live less than ten minutes from here. I thought I'd show you the quick way as we walk back.'

When we got to my door, I unlocked it and stepped in, but he waited outside. 'Aren't you coming in?'

'I've got work in the morning. But I want to do this again.'

'You want to take me for a walk again?' I said, trying to bring a little innuendo to the phrase.

'Are you up for it?'

'Why not? Sounds good.'

'Great, I'll call you.' He turned to leave.

'No kiss goodbye?'

'Got to leave the girl wanting more.'

'You snooze you lose, is the phrase I'm thinking of.'

'Night, Richard. I'll call you soon,' he said, blowing me a kiss. The keys on his belt jangled as he walked away.

Jo was on the sofa waiting, looking like she was about to burst. 'How was it? Where did he take you? What did you do?'

I flumped down beside her, confused and deflated. 'I'm not sure how it was.'

'Oh. That's not good. Was he an arse?'

'No, not at all. A perfect gentleman, but we just walked about.'

'You just walked? How old is he?'

'Early twenties. He showed me his house, but we didn't go in. He seems really interested in me, but I don't know if I'm interested in him. He wants to do it again, which is nice, I guess.'

'Honey,' Jo said, her earlier excitement now gone. 'A woman answering his phone? Not letting you in his house?' She paused like she was waiting for me to cotton on. 'He's a closet case with a wife and kids, and you're auditioning to be the other woman.'

I'd seen it coming, but I hadn't expected her to put it quite that way. 'He's not,' I said, though I had no proof. 'He's just different. And I think I like him.' I put my head on one side and drew in what would become a sigh. 'I think.'

# 15

Mum came over two days later, just before 7pm. I assumed she wanted to see if I was going out on a Friday night, so I dressed casually to give the impression that I wasn't. I asked how things were at home. She told me the education welfare officer had been to see her and find out why I wasn't in school, and had visited without warning several times since.

'I'm not going back!' I said, panicking. 'I'll just wait until next year and start college a year early.'

'You realise they can take me to court? This isn't just about you.' I went to speak but she held a hand up to silence me. 'However, I'm looking into other options than Warneford for you.'

When I didn't ask what things, she steered the conversation to less volatile subjects. She only stayed about half an hour more. After she left, I changed into the outfit I'd already laid out on my bed and went off to the Cricks.

As I wormed my way through the crowd at the bar, I felt hands on my shoulders, and a voice whispered in my ear, 'Alfie tells me it was an actual date? Maybe you aren't like Ryan after all.'

I turned to see Tim's cheerful face. 'You're so mean,' I said, hugging him. 'Ryan loves you. Be kind to him.'

'Wow, someone has their serious panties on tonight. Let's get you a drink to loosen them up. You can tell me all about your date.'

We found a table and I told him all about it, and what Jo had said. Tim made a face. 'It does sound like he's got a beard.'

'He's clean-shaven,' I said. 'I wouldn't date someone with a beard – what if there was food stuck in it?'

When Tim stopped laughing, he said, 'Beard is gay for a woman a man uses to create the impression he's straight. Like a false identity. And a fake beard would make you look more butch.'

'A fake beard would just make me look ridiculous.'

I didn't know why Tim was so invested in my maybe date, but I felt a little rush from him caring about me. 'He hasn't called yet, though, so it can't have gone that well.'

'Give him time. He might just be waiting till his wife isn't around.'

I ignored this. 'He did say about leaving me wanting more.' I didn't mention he'd called me 'the girl'.

'You'll hear from him by Monday, I'm sure.'

It turned out to be sooner than that. At the club, later, once Alfie got tired of the dance floor and went to find beer, I danced with anyone fun. I was having a great time with a really hot guy who looked like a hair model and wore a fitted black t-shirt so tight his nipples looked at me while we danced. The DJ fumbled the track change, and for a moment we were all left off-beat and feeling awkward. He took the opportunity to pull me close and kiss me, one hand on the back of my head, the other in the small of my back. Ryan was instantly knocked off number one spot for best kisser. Then the hand on my back slid down into my trousers and squeezed one buttock. I pulled away, smiled, but with a look of 'no' on my face, and decided it was time for a break. Leaving the dance floor, I saw Oscar staring at me.

'Didn't think you'd be here tonight,' I said. 'Time for that drink now?'

Coolly he said, 'Obviously you didn't think I'd be here, or you wouldn't be doing that shit with him.'

'What? I did nothing. He did it to me and I left.'

'You think that makes it okay? I liked you. I thought we had a great time the other night and then I find you slutting it up on the dance floor.'

'Excuse you!' I said hotly. 'I was not slutting anything up, I was dancing and having a good time. *He* made a move, and if you were watching, which you always seem to be, then you saw me leave after he did!'

'Whatever. I thought you were different, but clearly you're not!' He stormed off.

'Fucking buzzkill,' I shouted after him, though I doubted he could hear me over the music.

Phil appeared from nowhere. 'Trouble in paradise?' How could a man so big move through a crowd so easily?

'He's a tosser! You should have heard how he just spoke to me. "Slutting it up on the dance floor". How dare he?'

'That guy's hot. I'd slut it up on the dance floor with him.'

That made me laugh. 'Don't you start. He's a good kisser, FYI.'

'Who's the angry little man anyway, and what's with those keys?'

'I know, right. The bloody keys!'

On Saturday afternoon, Jo shouted up the stairs to tell me I had a call.

'Who is it?' I said as I got to her.

'Oscar!'

I hadn't told her about the night before. She stopped doing the excited dance when I picked up the handset and greeted him with a flat 'What?'

'I'm sorry. Just listen. I'm sorry, I shouldn't have said those things. I just got jealous.' He sounded panicky. 'I'd had a bad day and I see the guy I think I have feelings for kissing another man. I reacted badly. I'm sorry.'

'You have feelings for me?' I wasn't expecting that.

'Let me make it up to you? I can come over on Thursday and cook for you. We can have a proper dinner. Please.'

'I don't eat fish.'

'Okay.'

'Or mushrooms.'

'Okay.'

'Or any meat with bones in.'

He laughed. 'Anything else?'

'That's about it. But. You treat me like that or speak to me like that again, and Jo will mess you up.'

'Yeah, I will!' she shouted from the sofa. All five foot of her bouncing up and down with pent-up energy.

'Who's Jo?' Oscar asked. Then, quickly: 'It doesn't matter, it won't happen again. I'll call in the week and we can plan properly; I need to get back to work now. Thank you, thank you for giving me another chance.'

'Catch you laters.' I hung up. 'Twat.'

'So do we hate him now?' Jo was excited again, a shark smelling gossip in the water.

'Oh god, I don't know. Is it too early for a drink?'

Martin came down after Jo and I had drunk enough vodka to be merry.

'Martin! Come out with us tonight?' I said, grabbing him in a hug.

'You just want me to buy you drinks.' My chest muffled his response.

'Drinks are just a bonus. You're the prize.'

He shoved me off him and I stumbled from the vodka. The mood changed. 'I'm going down my pub tonight. You guys do what you want.' He went to leave.

'Martin, I'm sorry. Come back.'

He didn't. The front door slammed.

Jo and I staggered home late, very drunk and needing something to eat before we went to bed. Jo hunted through the fridge, assembling possibilities to cook on the kitchen counter, while I provided the entertainment by caterwauling 'Dancing Queen' while dancing like a queen. Suddenly Martin appeared on the stairs.

'Shut the fuck up,' he said angrily. 'I get no respect here and it's my damned house!' Not waiting for my apology, he retreated upstairs.

After his outburst earlier, we both went into whisper mode. After a few minutes of doing that, our whispering became giggling. We had to remind ourselves to be quiet, and the whispering started again, building to laughter. A few more rounds of that and we decided we'd better go to bed with our plates of beans and ham on toast before our noise brought Martin down again.

Martin was up and out before I got up in the morning. He came back in the evening, but only to get changed and go straight out to his pub. He returned late, well past closing time, quite drunk, but in a much better mood. I made him a cup of tea and when I went back to the sitting room he'd put on

*Clive Anderson All Talk*. This was the name for the BBC's new version of the Channel 4 chat show *Clive Anderson Talks Back*. Martin thought the Channel 4 version had been much better and said so at length, making him sound more middle-aged than ever.

After a while of this, I interrupted and said, 'You're not angry with me, are you? If you want, give me a jobs list to do around the house.'

'No, no, of course not. You're special, Richard.' He put a hand on my thigh. Much as I wanted to, I didn't move it because I didn't want to do anything that would break his lighter mood.

'I was worried I'd upset you,' I hurried on. 'I meant it as a joke on Friday. We'd still want you to come out with us even if you were broke. I can get drinks for us; you've seen how easy it is for me.'

'You shouldn't do that. You're worth more than that. You're special,' he said again. He kept his hand on my thigh for the rest of the show, occasionally moving it to stroke my leg.

'I think it's time for my bed,' I said as the credits rolled. 'Would you like another tea before I go?' I started to get up.

'I have to tell you something.'

'What?' I said, sitting back down.

'I said you shouldn't get drinks like that, and I mean it. Those guys don't think of you the right way, they just want to fuck you. I get you drinks because I love you.'

'I love you too, Martin. Without you taking me in, I'd be living on the mean streets of London, sucking dick in King's Cross for cash,' I joked.

'No, you're not hearing me; I love you.' His big eyes intent on mine, he leant forward.

'Martin. You're great,' I said, putting my hand on his chest to stop his advance. 'I couldn't be more grateful for everything you do for me, but I just don't see you that way.'

He sat back. 'I know,' he said. 'I'm just an ugly old man.' He moved his hand off my thigh. 'And you're an angel. Look how easily you picked up that guy the other week. You just had to talk to him and he was yours. Why would you want me?'

'It's not that at all. It's just, I see you as a cool uncle and I can't say that would ever change to romance.'

'I understand,' he said heavily. 'I'm going to bed.' He got up and started to leave the room.

'You're special too, Martin.'

'Good night, my angel,' he said over his shoulder as he left.

# 16

On the Monday morning, I called Mum and asked if, next time she visited, she could bring some money so I could contribute to the household. Hopefully Martin would appreciate it. She didn't sound too happy, suggesting I come home to collect it and see her at the same time.

Despite the two long bus rides it took me, it was nice to be home again. As Mum put the permanently tea-stained cosy over the pot she'd just made, the doorbell rang. Our dog bounced and barked as I went to answer the door. Holding onto Skip's collar – he would go for strangers, jumping up at them in hope of treats or a pat – I opened the door to a small, old, bald man in a rumpled suit. He looked at me quizzically. There was some sort of photo ID on a lanyard round his thin neck. A picture of him on it looked like a happy turtle.

'You must be Richard.'

'Must I be? Who are you?'

'Mr Hogg, your education welfare officer. Your mother told me you'd left home and weren't living here.'

'She was right. This is called a visit. What d'you want?'

'I came to see you and your mother.'

'We're busy.' I shut the door on him and went back to the

kitchen. The doorbell rang again, sending Skip into a new frenzy. I told Mum it was Mr HogFace, and said if she let him in, I was leaving. She rushed to the door and a few minutes later came back looking flustered, but thankfully on her own.

'I see this time away hasn't affected your ability to make a first impression,' she said.

'He should be pleased I didn't just tell him to piss off. Was that some sort of set-up?'

'I told you they do unannounced visits to check situations out.'

'I definitely should have told him to piss off, then.'

'Well, thank you for not doing so!'

Once my hackles went down, the rest of our afternoon was pleasant. Just us catching up in our natural environment. There was something comforting about sitting talking with Mum over a cup of tea, at home, and I felt a sudden longing for my old life. But I'd made my decisions for good reasons, and those reasons hadn't changed. I took the opportunity to get more clothes from my room. Mum offered to drive me back to Martin's. Before I got out of the car, she gave me £70 and told me that £20 was for me and £50 for Martin.

'I know how much you eat, so this goes to him. Okay?'

I rolled my eyes at her, thanked her and we said we loved each other as a goodbye.

Martin was very happy with the contribution of £40 to the house. Ten pounds went to my drinking fund on the way to his pocket, sort of a drunk's finder's fee.

The rest of the week drifted by, with my normal routine of sitting about watching TV during the day, then hanging out with the others once they got home from work. One day the morning pack of cigarettes from Martin wasn't there; nor the next day either. That afternoon I went to the shop and got a pack of Benson & Hedges, some Rizlas and a pack of rolling tobacco. It was tempting to head down the Cricks, but I didn't, even though the leftover money was burning a hole in my pocket. I could get free drinks any time, but if I was going to have to buy cigarettes, I'd need to be careful with it.

As Thursday approached, my excitement built about dinner with Oscar.

He turned up on time with a smile and a carrier bag of goodies to prepare for our dinner. Jo and Wayne had already gone out for the night, to give us some space, and Martin had disappeared off to his pub before I could remind him, so we'd have the place to ourselves for several hours at least.

'I thought rather than just cook for you I could teach you, get you a bit more prepared for living on your own. Tonight will be good food on a budget.'

'Eugh, I have to do stuff?'

He turned from the kitchen counter, where he was unpacking, and when he saw me smiling he smiled back. 'I was a chef, so this is easy. You'll pick it up in no time.'

'You're a chef? That's cool, although my expectations just went way up.'

'Used to be. Tonight, we're having sausage pasta.'

'Sausage and pasta? Even I could do that.'

'A whole pasta dish. Simple student food, but good and healthy.'

To my relief, he did all the cooking. There was some demonstrating, but I didn't have to actually do anything. He put a tin of vegetable soup on to reduce, then went to great lengths showing me how to cook the single sausage he'd brought. I suggested just throwing it in the oven, but he gave me a withering look and a lengthy explanation as to why you should never prick the sausage before cooking, which, detailed as it was, I forgot before he'd even finished speaking.

I got a kick out of watching him work, though. I could see he was enjoying it and, despite getting carried away with whys and wherefores, he was an excellent teacher. Unlike on our other date, this time he talked endlessly, so I got glimpses into his life. He'd not spoken to his family since he'd come out, which gave the lie to everyone else's insistence that he was still in the closet and living with a beard. He'd trained as a chef but, needing to support himself, he'd got a job in a fulfilment centre. He then explained what a fulfilment centre was, which sounded remarkably like a warehouse.

Once the constituent parts of the dish were ready, he sliced the sausage up, added it to the reduced soup and poured that over the cooked pasta. It really surprised me how good it both looked and tasted. Had I not seen how he did it, I would have thought a lot more work had gone into making it.

He'd brought a bottle of wine with him, so we sat across the kitchen table with a glass each. Now he'd started talking, it was hard to shut him up. Just as he was telling me that if he had his time over, he'd train as a butcher, I heard the front door open and a moment later Martin came into the kitchen.

'Martin, this is Oscar. Look at what he made, and it was so simple. I'll make it for you over the weekend. You'll love it.'

'Uh-huh. I didn't know this was happening tonight.'

The way he was staring at Oscar made me uncomfortable, and I could see he was drunk. I suddenly felt very young again. I was the same height as Oscar, and taller than Martin, but it felt like these two grown men were towering over me. 'Sorry, I tried to tell you before you went out. It's okay, right? We can go to my room if you want the kitchen to yourself. I'll wash up as soon as we're done eating.'

Martin grunted, turned and left the house.

'Is he all right?' asked Oscar. 'He seemed like a jealous ex. I mean, you and him—'

'Oh, god no. No, never. He can get funny when he's been drinking. He'll probably just go back to the pub. He'll be fine in the morning.'

'Are you sure? I don't want to cause problems for you.'

'It's fine, I swear. What were you saying before he came in?'

Later on, when Oscar realised he'd been talking about himself most of the evening, he turned back to asking questions and we talked about me, about the new life I was building, and how, although I loved my family, I couldn't go back and live at home again. We spoke about my desire to be able to work, support myself and go to college to finish my education. Jo and Wayne came in part-way through, but Jo pushed Wayne up the stairs ahead of her, saying, 'We're not here. We're going upstairs. We'll have music on so we won't hear anything.'

'It's getting late,' Oscar said once their bedroom door had closed. 'I'll wash up and then go.'

'Don't be crazy. You did all the cooking, I'll wash up. I've really enjoyed myself.'

'So, I'm forgiven for the other night?' he said, looking happy and sweet.

'What happened the other night? Nothing happened the other night, did it?'

'Thank you.' He moved in close and put both arms around my waist to pull me into a kiss, slowly, passionately, expertly. 'See? Worth waiting for,' he said.

'Worth waiting for? I'm hard,' I said, laughing.

'Well, now you have something else to wait for,' he said with a devilish grin.

'Feed me, get me drunk and leave me hanging. I see what

your game is. What now? You'll call me, I suppose?'

'Good night, beautiful. Glad you had a good time.'

'It's been great, thank you.'

He kissed me again, and I showed him out. I went back to the kitchen with a spring in my step, until I saw the pile of washing-up in the sink. It was too late to call Alfie, and it was only a kiss, no matter how high I was feeling. While the sink was filling with bubbles, Martin came back in.

'Hey, you want tea?' I asked, reaching for the kettle.

'What the hell was that?' he said, swaying, wide-eyed and unblinking.

'What was what?'

'That!' he said, waving both arms at the kitchen table.

'Oscar wanted to cook dinner for me. It was kind of an apology, and our second date. It went better than the first. He seems really nice, don't you think?'

Martin's eyes darted about. 'And you thought that would be fine without asking me?'

I turned the tap off. 'Sorry, would you like me to ask before I have a guest over? I didn't realise. It won't happen again. I promise.' It was best to placate him when he was like this.

'He may as well have been fucking you across my table!'

'What? We just had dinner.'

'I went round the back of the house and watched you through the kitchen window. I saw everything! And it was disgusting.'

'Oh my god, are you for real?'

'Yes, I fucking am!' He came close to me. 'I saw what you were doing to each other. I saw how you were acting with him.'

'We had dinner and then he kissed me goodbye. You're acting crazy.' I moved away from him in the direction of the stairs.

'You were being a complete whore!'

My temper was rising. I said flatly, 'I'm going to bed. I'll talk to you tomorrow when you've sobered up. I'll do the washing-up then, too.' I turned my back on him and started up the stairs.

As I got to the turn in the stairs he grabbed my wrist and yanked on it. Trying to keep my footing I spun around, and he slammed me against the wall. The back of my head hit it so hard I lost focus. When I got it back, his hands were around my neck, his face in mine, red and distorted as he shouted, 'I saw you touching each other. Hands down each other's pants, playing with his cock at *my* table. After all I've done for you. You're just a WHORE, out for what you can get from everybody.'

I grabbed hold of his wrists but couldn't wrench his hands off my neck. He was too close for me to knee him in the groin, even if I'd dared to try.

'That didn't happen, we just had din...' My sentence was cut off as he moved his thumbs onto my throat and leaned in. I couldn't speak; I was just making gurgling noises. My thoughts raced faster than my pulse and settled on the idea that this was how I was going to die.

'YOU'RE A WHORE!' he screamed, his spittle spattering my face.

Jo and Wayne appeared at the top of the stairs and an instant later, Jo came rushing down to help.

'Get off him Martin, you're going to kill him!' She pulled frantically and ineffectually at his shoulders and clothing.

He loosened his grip, and with a gasping intake of air I wriggled free and pushed past them both, stumbling upstairs and into my room. Breathless and fuelled by adrenaline, I grabbed a bag and shoved as much of my stuff into it as I could fit. Wayne appeared at my door asking if I was okay, telling me to calm down. I could hear Jo downstairs shouting at Martin. With my overstuffed bag I pushed past Wayne and clomped back down the stairs. As I got to the bottom I saw Martin, sitting in a chair at the table, subdued and looking small and sad.

'Where are you going?' Jo called as I passed her.

I didn't respond.

'Richard! Stop!'

I didn't. I was out and onto the street before the door could close behind me. The cool night air in my lungs made me cough again. When I put my hand to my throat, it was tender to the touch.

'Richard, come back,' Jo called from the doorway. 'I don't have shoes on. I can't chase you.'

# 17

My mind was filled with the vision of Martin's face and the smell of Guinness and cigarettes on his breath; his hands on my throat; my windpipe forcibly closed; the abnormal warmth in my lungs as they panicked about not getting more air. If Jo hadn't been there, would he have killed me? I honestly thought yes; women get killed by men in a jealous rage every day. I began to feel the fear that the adrenaline had suppressed while the attack was taking place.

At the top of the empty, late-night street I looked around, my heavy, badly packed bag straining the wrist Martin had twisted. The back of my head began to throb. Could I have a fractured skull? A bleed on the brain? Should I go to A&E? But if I did, I'd have to tell them what happened, and I couldn't do that: doctors would become police, and then...

So where the hell was I going to go? I couldn't go back to the house; Martin might kill me in my sleep. There were no buses this late. Had I even picked up my wallet? Shit, it was still in my room. No cab, no coins for the phone box. I couldn't walk to Tim's from where I was; it would take all night. Mum? No, it would just prove to her that she'd been right about everything. Oscar! He'd only just left. Maybe I could catch up with him.

His place was in the other direction, which meant walking past the house again. Rather than do that, I went down the next street and cut through an alley. I found Oscar's street without difficulty and looked for the garden that made his house stand out from the others. *Please still be awake.* There was a downstairs light on. I knocked tentatively. He answered the door, looking concerned and confused when he saw me. The relief of seeing him, of being safe, turned my fear into shock and I started to cry.

Sitting in his tired but homely kitchen, looking into the surface of the tea I was holding as if it had answers for me, I told him what had happened after he left. The whole time I was speaking he sat facing me with his hands on my knees, telling me it was okay. By the time I'd got it all out I'd stopped crying and the shock had mostly passed.

After a pause, Oscar said, 'Do you want to go to the police? I can take you now if you do.'

'No. Tim told me the police won't help us. Anyway, if I go to them, they'll call my mum and make me go home.' Besides, what would I tell them? The old man I'd been living with and accepting money from got angry with me?

'Okay. Well, let me get you a towel. Have a shower, wash away some of the stress. Be quiet when you go upstairs, though. My landlady has already gone to bed.'

So it wasn't a wife, or a beard. It was a landlady. 'Okay. Thank you.'

He led me upstairs and unlocked his door. 'This is my room, number three. We don't want you wandering into the wrong one by accident.'

'You just have one room?' I'd thought this was his house. Though of course Jo and Wayne rented a room at Martin's. Just, Oscar had seemed somehow more...

'It's all I need,' he said flatly, stepping into the room and back out. 'Here's a towel, and the bathroom is just there.'

I looked at my throat in the bathroom mirror. No visible marks, but it was still tender. The shower was good, the water cleansing my mind and my body. After I dried off, I dressed again, not sure if Oscar would really let me stay. As I went into his room, he got up off the bed and said, 'My turn. Back in a minute.'

I looked round the small, chaotic room. Every surface – bedside table, chest of drawers, windowsill – was covered with stuff. Overflowing ashtrays filled with the butts of roll-ups that made them look like grey hedgehogs; tea-stained mugs, dirty plates and cutlery; so many items of clothing I couldn't tell where one started and the next ended. In, on and around all of this was literal rubbish: envelopes, packaging, crisp packets. I moved a pile of clothing with my foot and exposed the corner of a condom wrapper. It made me realise I hardly knew him. He only had a single bed, as narrow as the one I'd abandoned at Mum and Dad's, and it was the one article of furniture that wasn't covered with anything, except a crumpled duvet. I hoped he'd changed the sheets more recently than he'd cleaned his room. I found a place to put my clothes and towel, undressed to my underpants and got into bed. I'd used underwear as pyjamas for years, so at least that part of the experience felt normal. Now the panic had receded, tiredness came over me like a wave.

Oscar was in the room again. I must have drifted off. 'You look so tired. Let me get in and make you more comfortable.' He dropped his towel on the floor, got into bed naked and cuddled up to me. His body was hot. I turned to face him.

'Thank you for letting me stay.'

'You can't go back to that guy's house after this,' he said.

'He's nuts. Don't worry though; I'll look after you.' He brushed my hair away from my face, then kissed me on the lips.

I wanted to sleep, but being held and kissed woke me up. His hands caressed my body. This is what I'd wanted from James, and now I was getting it. It was worth the wait. He asked what I liked to do, and I was honest. 'I haven't done much, but I like blowjobs.'

A smile grew across his face and I couldn't stop myself from smiling back. We rolled so he was on top of me, and he kissed down my neck, torso, and to my thighs. Little sparks of electricity hit my nerves as his lips explored me, and when he sucked me it was so good my toes curled involuntarily. Although my throat was tender, my consciousness of the pain faded as I lost myself in Oscar. The warmth of his skin against mine, the sensation as I ran my hands down his back, over his butt, and encountered the hair on his thighs. The noises and movements he made as I explored and pleasured him. All the trauma of earlier melted away while I was in Oscar's arms.

'Have you done anal?' he asked quietly.

'Not yet,' I said, a little nervously.

'Would you like to try?'

'Yes,' I said breathlessly.

'Okay, the first time can be tricky. Your body wants to stay closed. You have to relax. If you tense up, it will hurt. It will hurt a little at the start, but just relax. Okay?'

'Yeah, okay.' I was nervous, but in a way that was giddy. This was really doing it.

'Turn over. Let me lube you up and relax you.'

I turned over, and he put on a condom, then I felt a cold liquid on my butt that made me flinch.

'That's lube. It makes everything easier. Okay, remember to relax.'

Sliding on top of me, he got between my legs, put a hand on the small of my back, and I felt his dick press against me. He put more weight on my back. 'Relax.' And he pushed into me.

There was a sudden burning pain. 'Argh! Stop! It hurts.' I turned my body away from him so I was on my side. His dick slipped out.

'Remember I said you have to relax – there'll be some pain at the start? Lie back down.'

I reluctantly did as he told me. He opened my legs wider with his knees, put his hand on my back between my shoulders, then leant on me. Then he was inside me. The pain it triggered made me try to move away again, but he leant on my back harder, and my legs were spread far enough apart that I couldn't escape him.

'Stop, stop. It hurts too much.'

His forearm smacked into my shoulder blades with enough force to take my breath away.

'Relax,' he whispered into my ear.

'No, it hurts. Take it out. ARGH!'

He pushed further in.

'Shhh, my landlady is asleep. Relax.'

'Please – take it out.'

With a last push, he was all the way in and with a groan of pleasure he sank down on top of me. His body weight pushed me into the mattress and I couldn't move. The searing pain in my butt grew and felt like I was being torn. He gripped my wrists and stretched my arms out.

'Please,' I sobbed. 'Please stop.'

'Just relax. It's fine.'

I twisted my head round, so we were face to face. 'Stop. You're hurting me. Please.'

For a moment he did stop. Then he moved his head to

behind mine again and I heard his breathy voice in my ear. 'Breathe. Relax.'

The pain started afresh as he began to move himself in and out of me again. I continued to cry out, begging him to stop.

'Shhhh, my landlady will hear. You'll get me chucked out.'

'Please stop,' I entreated him through my tears. 'It feels like you're ripping me.'

He pulled back and there was a brief respite from the pain. Maybe he was looking down to see if there was blood. Then he pushed back in again and I gasped. I begged again for him to stop, but he didn't.

I don't know how long it went on for. I went somewhere in my head that wasn't there. The pain didn't stop, I just became numb to it. My tears made the pillow damp against my cheek. His thrusts increased, each one making my breathing change, over and over, harder and harder, faster and faster. Then he gasped, and stopped. A dead weight, twitching slightly on top of me. He was still inside me, but not moving any more. Was he done? Was there more? He moved his legs from inside mine to outside.

'Roll with me.'

I didn't resist as he rolled my body to the side so we were spooning. He was still inside me. The pain was less, though.

'Can you take it out now?'

'Let me go limp first. It will hurt less coming out if I'm limp.'

I lay there, the safe place in my head not letting me enter. His chest and stomach were sweaty against my back. He started to pull out. No pain – more irritation, like it was fine sandpaper. There was a belching, farting sound that felt like the most obscene thing my body had ever done.

'I'm going to get rid of the condom and have a piss,' he said, as if everything was normal and fine. 'You want a shower?'

'No. I want to sleep.' I tried to sound normal too. It was over and I had nowhere to go. If I left now, I'd be on the streets for the night.

'Okay beautiful, put your underwear back on then, so you don't mess up the sheets.' He tossed my pants onto the bed. 'I'll just be a minute.'

I did as he told me and moved across the bed to get as close to the wall as I could. He came back in and sat on the bed, his back to me. He turned off the lamp. The darkness was like a blanket. I closed my eyes to let it cover me more. He slipped under the duvet and cuddled into me, spooning me again.

'That's it, right? I can sleep now?'

'You did great for a first time.' And he kissed the back of my neck. 'Sleep well, beautiful, I'll find you somewhere to live tomorrow.'

I didn't reply. I had nowhere to go. I listened to his breathing. Sometime after it changed, I fell asleep.

# 18

I woke from a dreamless sleep, startled by Oscar shaking my shoulder. My eyes focused on the dull magnolia wall facing which I'd fallen asleep.

'Morning, beautiful.' He leant over me and kissed the side of my face. 'You were sleeping so deeply it was hard to wake you. You looked so innocent.'

'I guess I needed it.' I didn't want to turn over and look at him.

'I need to make some calls,' he said. 'I didn't want you waking up and not knowing where I was. You know where the bathroom is, and I'll bring you up some tea once I'm done. My tobacco is on the side over there if you want a cigarette.'

I rolled over to see where he was pointing. It was hard to get my thoughts straight. I could feel where he'd been inside me, as if he was still there. But otherwise he was tender and caring, and I had nowhere else to go. I couldn't go home. Now the education welfare officer was involved, they would force me straight back to school. How could someone so nice act the way Oscar had? Maybe he hadn't heard me when I told him to stop? No. He told me to be quiet, so he did hear me. But he kissed me afterwards. Maybe he just couldn't control himself? Some men were supposed to be like that. If it was true of Oscar, could he do it again? Or maybe what he had done to me was supposed to be painful. Girls bled the first time, didn't they? Had it been like that for Ryan or Alfie?

The loop of thoughts and questions without answers continued while I showered. I pulled back the shower curtain and got out. I saw my reflection in the mirror. My throat was mottled from Martin's hands. This was the kind of bruise I'd wanted for my black eye. I would have shown that one with pride; this one was my badge of being a whore. Was that why Oscar did it? Because he could tell I'm a whore? Was it my fault?

Back in Oscar's room, I got dressed and made myself a lumpy cigarette. It had to be me. He just did to me what everyone else wanted to do. Like Martin said, I got all the drinks just because they all wanted to fuck me. And they wanted to do that because that's what I offered them: the way I flirted, the way I danced, letting them think they had a chance of doing that to me. It was me. It was my fault. That's why Oscar was nice again afterwards. He'd given me what I needed, and could go back to being himself.

He came bustling in, concentrating on not spilling the mugs of tea, on which he'd balanced some buttered toast.

'My landlady is up. I'm not supposed to have guests, so I told her you broke up with your girlfriend last night. If she asks, that's the story.'

'Sure,' I said, looking up from my puddle of thoughts.

'Oh my god, your neck! Can you swallow okay?'

I nodded.

'I could kill him for doing that to you. You must have been terrified.' The concern on his face seemed genuine.

'Do we tell your landlady my girlfriend did it?' I said flatly.

'Best to just wear a scarf. Let me see what I have. It's autumn, so no one will think anything.' As he hunted through his wardrobe, he told me he'd called his work and swapped his shift to the evening. Then he made some calls and found me a place to stay. His landlady had installed a payphone in the entrance hall, and Oscar made a comment about spending £1.70 on me. I knew my wallet was on my bed at Martin's, so instead of offering to pay, I just asked about the place he'd found for me to stay.

'This guy's been looking for someone for a while. He's one of us, so no need to worry about being yourself. On the downside, it's in Park South.' That was a run-down former council estate. 'Just don't go out too late on your own and don't talk to strangers, and you'll be fine. I told him you were seventeen. I didn't think a stranger would want to rent a room to a fifteen-year-old. I hope you're okay lying about that?'

'Yeah, I can pass for that age, anyway.'

'Great. It's £75 every two weeks, but your parents can afford that, right? I can pay today and you can pay me back.'

'Er yeah, I guess.' I hadn't thought about paying rent. Martin had never asked for any money. I'd need to figure something out fast. Maybe Mum... But I couldn't ask her until I was ready to say I'd moved. And why.

'That includes bills except the telephone, and he has Sky TV, which I thought you'd like.' He smiled, like he was proud of himself. 'We can go over at lunchtime. If you like it, it's yours. Oh, he has a dog. That's okay, right?'

'Yeah. We've always had dogs.'

We drove over to the house and although the area wasn't very good, the little cul-de-sac was a nice enough collection of detached houses that all looked cared for. Oscar had never met the owner, and I noticed him take a step backwards when the door opened. A short black man in his thirties – clean-shaven, wearing a check shirt and blue jeans – introduced himself as Lloyd. He was carrying some extra weight, with a little salt and pepper in his short hair, and he had a kind smile. When he was younger, he would have been cute. There was a hint of a Caribbean accent and he had a gentle way of speaking which was reassuring. First thing he did was introduce me to Zoe, his white Alsatian. He was starting to tell me not to worry because she was friendly, but he realised that wasn't necessary as I dropped to the floor and introduced myself to her.

'You like dogs then,' he said, pleased. 'My last tenant—'

'I grew up in the country,' I said. 'Unless it's a working dog, I introduce myself and let them know I'm not a threat.' I had to bob my head from side to side, to avoid her tongue going in my mouth when I spoke.

'That's enough, Zoe,' Lloyd said. 'You'll make Oscar jealous.' He pulled her away from me. 'Let me show you the room.'

It was much nicer than my room at Martin's. A good size, clean, and with sheets and bedding included. Lloyd had his own bathroom, so I wouldn't have to share unless he had guests or family staying. He said his aunt's jerk chicken and rice and peas, which she'd feed me until I burst, would make up for her monopolising the bathroom. The house was big, so we wouldn't be under each other's feet. He said he'd leave Oscar and me alone to talk, shutting the door behind him as he went down to the kitchen. Oscar gave me a hug and a kiss.

'I'm sorry,' he said. 'No one told me he was black. But the room is good, right? Do you like it?' He looked expectant.

Oscar's racism made me think of my father, who was prone to make the same sort of comment. I guessed addressing it with Oscar would be about as successful as it was with Dad, and in any case I needed Oscar to put down some rent money. 'Yeah, it's good, thank you.' I kissed him again.

'It's a bit far from me, but I can always drive over. There's plenty of room for me to park on the street.'

'I'll take it. You can pay the first rent, right?'

'I have the cash with me, so it can be yours now. I'll come back tonight and we can christen your new bed.'

I had a flashback to my face in the pillow and was suddenly conscious of the unpleasant ache inside me.

'What's wrong? If it's about him being black—'

'I was just thinking about last night and Martin. I don't know why it came to my mind.'

He kissed me again. 'If I see him again, I don't know if I'll be able to stop myself from clocking him. How could he do that to someone as sweet as you?'

I pulled away. 'He's not worth it. Let him be old and alone. That's his punishment.' I looked at my watch. 'He'll be at work now. If I call and see if Jo or Wayne are in, could you go round and get the rest of my things for me? Even my money is still there.'

'Let's tell Lloyd you'll take the room, then get your stuff out of the car and make the call.'

Wayne answered, and after checking I was okay, put Jo on the phone. They'd both called in sick to their jobs and stayed home in the hope I'd return. Jo was relieved to hear my voice and told me she'd come after me last night, but couldn't find me. I explained that I'd gone to Oscar's. She asked me to come back.

'Martin was so sad this morning.'

A pressure built in my chest. It felt like she was taking his side. 'Jo! You should see my neck. If you hadn't been there, I'd be dead, and now I have to wear this stupid bloody scarf until the bruises fade.' I adjusted the scarf and scratched the itch caused by its movement against my skin.

'He stopped as soon as I got to you. I didn't do anything.'

'You were tugging at his clothes and body! That's not him stopping, that's you stopping him. How could I sleep knowing he was in the same house? How can you sleep knowing he's in the same house? He's a psycho.'

She seemed to see my point and tried to change the subject, asking where I was now. That reminded me of the reason for the call, so I said Oscar was going round to get my stuff and asked her to bag it up for me.

'I'm so glad he was there for you. I can't believe I called him a dud. So how was it? You staying at his? Was he better than James?' They seemed like questions from another era, another planet. There'd been blood on the paper when I used the toilet that morning.

'I have to go,' I said. 'I'm on Lloyd's phone and calls aren't included in the rent. You have the number now, so we can catch up later. Oh, and if my mum calls, tell her I'm in the bath, or down the shop or whatever, and I'll call her back.'

I couldn't call Mum and say I'd moved. She'd want an explanation, and then she'd want to come round and see the new place, she'd ask why I was wearing a scarf, and I'd be dragged home via the police station. I'd get everyone in trouble – even Mum, for being a bad parent.

Oscar drove off to collect my stuff. Lloyd and I sat down with a cup of tea and a plate of biscuits.

'So why the scarf?' he asked, giving me a set of spare keys. 'Is that a new fashion thing? Is some band wearing scarves now?'

'You'll find out soon enough, I guess...' I took it off.

'My goodness! Are you okay? Did Oscar do this to you? I can stop him from coming in if he did.'

'No, not him. My landlord. He was in love with me. I guess I knew it, but I didn't do enough to stop it. I suppose this is one of those "If I can't have you, no one can" situations,' I added. Once more I was thinking about my own actions that had led to the attack. I wasn't the prince of anything, and thinking I was had led me here.

'Oh, my dear, I'm so sorry. That must have been terrifying.'

'I was a bit shaken up, but I'm okay now. I can swallow normally again, so I still might go out tonight. Can I make this look like a drag queen necklace, do you think?' I waved my fingers in front of the bruising.

'God! Swallowing and drag queens. I'm remembering why I don't go out any more,' Lloyd said, laughing.

That made me laugh too, enough to hurt my throat a bit. We pottered about together for the rest of the day. I wondered if I could introduce him to Alfie, whose boyfriend was never around unless he wanted sex. But no. Then Lloyd would find out how old I was.

Lloyd remarked that I hadn't brought any food, and I was suddenly frightened that he'd suggest a takeaway, expecting me to share the cost, but instead he offered me dinner. He took a large Tupperware container out the freezer asking if I liked brown stew, which I thought sounded like meat in Bisto. It turned out to be one of the best things I'd eaten in a long time. I told him how good a cook he was, and he explained that his aunt insisted on cooking the entire time she was there and filling the freezer for when she wasn't. I wondered if she knew he was gay, but didn't ask. We ate in front of the TV, which I always liked to do. Zoe looked up at us hopefully as we ate. At around 9pm, I said I was going to get ready to head out.

'Isn't Oscar coming round to see you?'

'It's late already. I guess something came up.'

'You be careful, yeah. And with bruises like that, no deep throat.'

# 19

I pulled my few clothes out of the bag I'd stuffed them into less than twenty-four hours earlier and piled them on the bed. This was my home now. I put them away in the chest of drawers and wardrobe. I kept out a white t-shirt as my outfit for the night. Hopefully, the creases would fall out on the walk into town. The crispness of the white accented the rawness of the colour on my neck. I couldn't hide it, so why not brazenly highlight it?

Parts of Park South were quite nice, but there were also parts that really were not. I got to the main through-road as quickly as I could, avoiding alleyways and dark recesses. This meant going out of my way, but it was better than stumbling into the wrong kind of people and adding to my woes. Not that I had anything to steal.

The walk took longer than I expected. It was nearly 10pm by the time I reached the town centre, so I went straight to the club. Hopefully Tim would be along soon, in case I couldn't blag drinks from strangers.

In the lobby Eddie, wearing his grey security jacket, pointed a sausage finger at my neck.

'What's this?' he asked.

'You don't think it's fetching?'

He put a hand on my shoulder and pushed me sideways, steering me into the ladies' toilet. The door swung shut behind us.

'Who did this?' No part of his body moved except for his mouth.

'Dragging me in here like this will make people talk.'

'If *you* don't start talking, I'll get Phil.'

'Why are you making such a big deal about this?'

He looked at me.

I sighed, realising I'd literally no way out of this. 'Martin. My landlord.'

'Did he do anything else to you?'

'Oh my god, can you just drop this?'

'No! What happened?'

When I first met Eddie, I was terrified of him. He looked like he was from Middle Earth. But as I'd got to know him, I realised he was more of a teddy bear, albeit a teddy bear who'd told me how to disable an attacker with a biro. At the moment, though, he was being half-policeman, half-dad, and I wanted neither. Reluctantly, I told him what had happened, everything from the dinner onwards, but I stopped the story once I got out of the house.

'You want to go to the police? You won't be in trouble.'

I pushed myself up so I was sitting on the sink counter. If I was going to be there a while, I might as well get comfortable. 'Yeah, that would be great. Should I explain to them that I'm legally a child, and my mum wants me to move back home?'

'You have a complicated life,' he said. 'So what, then? Just life as normal. What if he comes in here?' The way I stiffened told him all he needed to know. 'He won't be coming in here, then. I'll call the Cricketers and let them know the situation, too.'

'Thank you.' I jumped off the counter to hug him. Well, the half of him I could get my arms around. I wasn't scared of Martin, or I told myself I wasn't. But knowing he wouldn't be appearing behind me at the bar was reassuring.

'I'm still going to tell Phil.'

'He loves me. He won't be angry with me.'

'He'll be angry. Not with you, but he'll be angry.'

The neck bruise got me very different looks to the black-eye: concern, uneasy double-takes, the occasional look that felt judgemental. I had to tell some version of the story to each person I talked to, and each time it got shorter and I got more deadened to it. As the evening wore on, I eventually boiled it down to, 'That mole man that comes in here with me decided if I wouldn't fuck him, he'd kill me. You know how crazy people are.'

There was no talking on the dance floor, so I danced. The beat pounded through me, and the music filled my ears and blew out the cobwebs in my mind. I got closer and closer to the speakers until I could feel the bass thrumming in my bones. I peeled off my shirt and tucked it into my waistband. My chest fur always got me attention. It was neat: not much really, but full for my age. Martin, Oscar and everyone else receded from my mind.

I was busy getting my groove on when the guy in front of me was moved sideways, to be replaced by a furrow-browed Phil. He leant forward, tugged the shirt out of my trousers and said, 'Follow me.' He didn't check to see if I was obeying – just walked away, expecting me to come behind. I did. We got to the cellar. He opened the door, tossed my shirt onto the barrels at the far end of the room, and said, 'In!'

'You're a grump tonight,' I said, trying to be cute as I slunk past him.

'Let me look at you,' he said, closing the door, cutting out the music. He took hold of my shoulders, looked at my neck. He touched the bruise, pressing gently. I winced.

'What the buggery bollocks, Richard?'

'I was asking the same question myself.' I crossed my arms, partly in defiance, but mostly because it was cold.

'Put your shirt back on.' He pointed to where he'd thrown it. As I turned to get it something caught his eye. 'What's that one?'

'What one what?'

'You have a big bruise across your left shoulder blade.'

My mind went back to Oscar's forearm, holding me down. Oscar's weight. 'I don't know. I can't see my back, can I?'

'You have a bloody great bruise across your back, and you don't know where you got it?'

'Must have been where I hit the wall as he gave me this one,' I said, pointing at my throat.

Phil just stood there not speaking, then rolled one hand to indicate I should carry on talking.

'I don't fucking know! Perhaps it's you or Eddie or some other twat that keeps grabbing me and telling me what to do with my life.'

He looked pained. 'I'm not telling you what to do with your life, and neither is Eddie. He wanted to call the police, but I told him that was your choice to make.'

'No police,' I said, sinking down onto a barrel, my anger fading into sulking.

'They'll be on your side, and I can be with you the whole time, so you won't be on your own.'

'They'll make me go home.'

'Sweetie,' he said gently, sitting down beside me, 'is home

that bad? At least you won't get strangled there.'

'No, I'll be suffocated,' I said bitterly, but even as I spoke it felt trivial and pitiful. 'My dad couldn't even talk to me when I saw him – I disgust him that much. I won't be allowed here any more; just some bloody youth group.'

He looked sad. 'I'm worried about you.'

I looked at him sitting there, all big and kind and safe, and felt bad that I was making him sad. If there was anyone I could speak to openly, it was Phil. I wanted to ask him about Oscar. Ask if it was normal. I wanted him to tell me it wasn't, but I couldn't get the words out. It was my fault, and I couldn't have Phil thinking I was a whore like Martin did. He couldn't change what had happened anyway. Instead I cried, releasing the tears that had been trapped in me since Oscar did what he did.

We stayed in the cellar until I was done crying, then went back out, and Phil got me a drink. 'Take it easy tonight,' he said. 'I'm here for you, any time, about anything. Okay?'

'Thank you.' And he gave me a big hug.

I thought I might see Alfie or Tim, but they weren't there. Feeling lighter after crying with Phil, it wasn't hard to find other people to entertain me. And then Oscar appeared, his face stony like he'd just met Medusa. 'What the hell are you doing here?' he said.

'I needed to blow off some steam, and the dance floor was calling me.'

'You need to rest. We're leaving.' He grabbed my hand and went to walk off. I took my hand back.

'I'm having fun here.'

'You need to rest! Your body needs time to heal. I'm taking you home.' He reached for my wrist again, but I dodged him.

'I'm fine where I am,' I said, quite loudly.

He stepped forward and jabbed his finger in my chest. 'I went driving around town picking up your things today, and when I get to Lloyd's tonight, he tells me you've gone out. Do you know how disrespected that makes me feel? Like you don't care about me at all.'

'Of course I care but I—'

'No buts. If you want to be with me, then you'll listen to me. I'm taking you home. You can unpack your stuff, then get the rest that you need.' He took my wrist again. This time I didn't fight it.

As he led me through the club, I wished Phil would pop up and stop him, but he didn't. At the entrance, Eddie looked at me.

'You okay, Richard?'

I don't know why but I responded with a dull, 'Yeah.'

'Phil's just popped over to the Flag. You want to wait and say goodbye?'

'Tell him I love him,' I said, trying not to choke on the words as I was taken outside.

On the drive back to Lloyd's, we were quiet. Once we were there, I offered to make tea. Lloyd had gone to bed.

'It's late already,' Oscar said. 'I have to be up early. Have a shower. You stink of smoke.'

Again, I did as I was told. By the time I was done showering, Oscar was already in bed.

'Better,' he said, folding back the duvet cover for me to get in.

I got under the duvet, and he cuddled up to me and started stroking my body, kissing me.

'I thought you said you were tired.'

'I've always got time for you, beautiful.'

I should have said that I was too tired and needed sleep, or at least tried that; but instead I let his hands roam and his lips lock onto mine. Lying on my back with my eyes closed I could remove myself just a little: see the club, the dance floor, recall the feeling in my body when I was in front of the speaker.

'Turn over,' he said, moving off me to fetch the lube he'd brought from beside the bed.

'No. I'm still sore from yesterday.'

'You have to do it more to get used to it. Practice makes perfect.'

'But I hurt already. I think you tore me.'

'Don't be daft. I would have seen blood on the condom if I had. Turn over.' He gripped my shoulder in an effort to pull me round onto my front.

'I want to sleep.' I pulled my shoulder back from him.

'I paid for this place, remember. I'm trying to help you. Now turn over.' I looked into his eyes, which seemed darker than earlier. I turned over. My boxers were already half off my butt, he pulled at them and the elastic scratched down my thighs as he irritatedly yanked them off me. He got between my legs again and I felt the lube, cold on my sore asshole.

'Relax.' The hand was placed on my back. He leant on me and pushed his way in. It hurt less this time, or maybe I was more used to the pain. I didn't fight it, so he didn't need to pin me down with his bodyweight as he had last time. My submission meant both his hands went on the mattress, bracing him up, rather than holding me in place. I was free to move, but I just lay there. Sometimes I gasped, sometimes I winced, then with a thrill of dread I remembered...

'What about a condom? You didn't put one on.'

'We don't need them. I'm clean and you haven't done it

enough to worry.'

'But we should—'

'It's better without. Relax.'

He finished, and like the night before, rolled us onto our sides so we were spooning. He kissed the back of my neck. 'See? Wasn't that better than yesterday?'

'Can you take it out now?'

'I'll let it go limp, let the last of the cum out. I don't want my dick dribbling on the clean sheets.'

We lay there with him still inside me. Less pain this time; that's something, I thought. He pulled himself out, still a bit like sandpaper, but less. He kissed the back of my neck again.

'Goodnight, beautiful.'

I heard my name being called by a voice that sent alert signals to every muscle of my rigid body. My eyes snapped open. Oscar's face was inches away from mine. He was crouched beside the bed, smiling at me.

'Didn't mean to make you jump.' He kissed my nose. 'I have to go to work. I'll come by afterwards with some food for the cupboards and cook for you.'

'I was going to see my friends tonight. They weren't there last night.'

'Go where?'

'Just the pub. Maybe the club.'

'What if Martin comes down? You don't want to bump into him. You should stay home.'

'He's been banned from both places after this.' I gestured at my throat.

He stood up, thinking. 'I didn't know you were so well connected,' he said, with an odd expression. 'But no, stay in and recover. I'll be back around seven and I'll bring the things for dinner.'

As he went to leave I sat up and said, 'But what about my friends? They'll be worried about me. They'll have heard all about it by now.'

'Call them. They'll understand that you want to stay home after what you've been through.' He placed his hand on the door handle and added, not looking at me, 'Go back to sleep, beautiful. I'll see you at seven.'

I rolled onto my back and touched my throat. It felt better now but probably still looked nasty. It would go blue and black soon, I thought. I bet someone had spoken to Tim by now. I'd need to talk to him before he called Mum again. I *could* stay home. And I did need food, as Lloyd would get annoyed if I kept eating his. I turned over and went back to sleep.

I woke to the sound of Lloyd gently knocking on the door, speaking through it softly. He said there was a call for me. My brain blurred from sleep, I quickly pulled on my boxers and wandered downstairs. 'Did they say who it was?'

'A woman called Jo.'

The phone was in the sitting room. Lloyd put the TV on mute as I picked up the handset. 'Hey Jo. What time is it? I don't have my watch on.'

'Nearly noon, hon. Your mum just called. I said you were in the bath.'

'Thanks sweetie. You're a lifesaver. Thanks for getting my stuff to Oscar too.'

'I'm so glad he's looking after you. He's such a nice guy.'

A chasm opened silently between us, though she didn't realise it. 'What did Mum say?'

'She just asked for you. How's the new place?'

'It's good. Much nicer room, and Lloyd is... Zoe, get off me. Sorry, Lloyd is just lovely. Definitely not the kind of person to try and kill me for having dinner with someone.' I blew him a kiss. He smiled.

'Who's Zoe? Have you replaced me already?'

'Zoe is blonde, beautiful, and always happy to see me. But she has terrible breath, and this morning keeps sticking her face in my crotch. She's also an Alsatian.'

'Oh, I wish I had a dog. Maybe we'll get one when we get our own place. It's good you like Lloyd, too.'

'He's lovely,' I repeated.

'Martin's so sad. He still can't believe what happened.'

I didn't say anything.

'He's really sorry. He wants you to know that.'

'He can shove his apologies right up where no one wants to put their dick! And you keep passing messages from him and I'll stop taking your calls.'

'Okay, okay.'

'You don't get to just say sorry when you nearly killed someone with your bare hands.'

'I hear you. I won't say anything from him again, I promise. He did say next time we're out and see you, he wants to say sorry himself.'

'Tell him, good luck with that. He's been banned from both places.'

'You had him banned?'

'He banned *himself* by trying to kill me. Why are you even still there? You can't tell me you honestly feel safe.'

'Wayne has said we should move,' Jo agreed vaguely. 'We haven't started looking yet, though.'

I softened my voice. 'I'll be the first one at the housewarming, hopefully soon. Honey, I should go. I need to call Mum.'

'Okay. Glad you're safe. Say hi to Oscar for me. And Lloyd.'

'Call anytime. I'm not sure I want to call the house in case

Martin answers.'

As I hung up, I looked at Lloyd. He smiled whimsically and I suddenly felt self-conscious about him having witnessed my outburst. 'If I was still an artist,' he said, 'I'd want to paint those colours.'

I looked down and realised I was stood there in just my boxers. 'They're just red.'

He laughed. 'Not those, you idiot – your bruise. It's becoming the most amazing range of colours.'

I hadn't seen it yet. 'I'd take some pictures, but I'm not sure I want to keep the memories. I'm going to put the kettle on. Okay if I steal a tea bag?'

'Of course, my dear. Help yourself. But put some trousers on, will you? It's distracting...for Zoe,' he added with a giggle, looking down at her and fondling her ears.

While the kettle heated, I went upstairs and pulled on some trousers. The house was warm, so I didn't put a top on. I didn't think Lloyd would object, and the fact that he liked the look of me could only be a plus. God, I was becoming Ryan. I made the tea and returned Mum's call. As I waited for her to answer, I ran through the excuses I could use for why she couldn't come over. She just wanted to chat, which was a relief until she said it would be easier to talk in person. I told her I had a busy weekend planned, and I'd go round and see her next week. Oscar couldn't object to that. After a moment's pause, she went back to chit-chat about my sister. Then I called Tim's house, got Alfie, gave him my new number, told him to call me straight back and hung up.

Knowing it would be him, I answered the phone on the first ring. 'You won't believe what Eddie did last night.'

'You won't believe what I heard about you. Oh, maybe you will!' It was Tim.

I knew a lecture was coming, and my voice betrayed my lack of interest in hearing one. 'I was going to tell you after I spoke to Alfie.'

'So you didn't think calling me yesterday would have been nice?'

'I had a lot going on,' I said with an eye-roll that must have been audible.

'I came looking for you last night. Eddie told me you got dragged out of the place by Oscar.'

'God, they're all being so dramatic.'

'I'm worried about you. Your mother is going to completely lose her shit.'

'Don't you dare tell her! She doesn't need to know.'

'She doesn't need to know her child's been strangled and done a moonlight flit? Where are you? I want to come and check you out for myself.'

'I'm not falling for that twice, prick; you'll be on the phone to Mum the moment I hang up. You have my number and that's all you're getting for now, and please, for the love of god, don't give it to her this time. Jo is forwarding any messages to me, so Mum doesn't need the number yet. I'll tell her I've moved once the bruising's gone and she can see me without asking questions.'

'Eddie said you haven't been to the doctor or the police.'

'You said yourself the police won't help, and I don't need a doctor. Other than a very colourful neck, I'm fine, okay?'

'I'll see for myself tonight.'

'I don't think I'm coming out tonight.'

'You say you're fine and then you say you're not coming out on a Saturday night. Those two things don't fit together.'

'Jesus. I'm fine. All right? You aren't my parent, and you need to start bloody trusting me. I. Am. Fine.'

'When can I see you?'

'I'll come over next week.'

'How about tomorrow? Come for a roast. I'll do one specially for you.'

'I'll ask Oscar if it's okay. I don't know if he has plans for us or not.'

There was a long silence. I could hear Tim's breathing. 'Okay. Well, let me know. Still want to speak to Alfie?'

Alfie and I talked for ages, me hashing over Martin's craziness and Alfie his latest dramas with Tim, which he grudgingly admitted were minor compared with mine. He loved the way Eddie had turned out to be my protector. '*So* romantic.' I think he even meant it. He asked about Oscar, but I changed the subject. If I started talking, I might not stop.

Lloyd called up the stairs that Oscar had arrived. I came down, still with no top on, and heard Oscar saying, 'Tell me you haven't eaten yet? I bought enough for three.' Okay, he wasn't trying to push Lloyd out of the picture. Good.

'Not too much for me,' Lloyd demurred, sighing. 'Now I have such a skinny lodger, I'm seeing how fat I've got.'

Coming into the kitchen I said, 'You're not fat; you're cuddly.' And I gave him a hug.

'That's just politically correct for fat,' he said, hugging me back.

'Stop mauling him,' Oscar said to me tartly. 'I'm sure he doesn't want you draping yourself over him. And put a shirt on. You'll get cold.'

'Sorry,' I said, going to get a shirt.

'He's fine,' Lloyd said amiably. I noticed him give Oscar a look as I reached the doorway. 'I've really enjoyed his company.'

'Uh-huh. So tonight we're having marinated pork – only it's

a quick marinade as I don't have time for a proper one.'

Dinner was really good. It was the first time I'd really eaten that day, as I hadn't had much appetite earlier, and I hadn't wanted to be caught raiding Lloyd's fridge. Oscar dominated the conversation. He seemed to want to know all about Lloyd. I mainly just listened. Lloyd had had a surprisingly interesting life, studying fine art at the Slade and experimenting with a style he called Afro-futurism. I thought of robots and space stations, but one of his paintings hung in the dining room, and it reminded me more of a Picasso, except it referenced Caribbean things — an angular fisherman stripped to the waist pulling on a net, and nearby a beach bar with rows of rum bottles. Then Lloyd had lost his parents in a car accident, which put an end to his drive to create. That was why he had such a big house and only worked part-time: they'd left it to him. He took in lodgers for the company, so was glad to have found me. That gave me hopes that he might be lax about the rent I couldn't afford to pay. I was just about to thank him again for welcoming me when Oscar changed the subject. 'Are you going to wash up?' he said to me, gesturing at the dirty plates and dishes.

'Happy to.' I jumped up and started clearing the table.

'Let me help,' Lloyd said.

'No. He's fine. Least he can do. You haven't said much about work. What is it you do?'

After I finished clearing up, Oscar and I went upstairs. As soon as I closed the door, he got close to me and said in a low voice, 'I don't like the way he looks at you.'

'How do you mean?'

'He wants you. I saw it when you hugged him earlier. You can't do that any more. Make sure you're dressed properly when around him or even just coming out the bathroom.'

'I think you're worrying about nothing. He's so sweet.

Nothing's going to happen.'

'Now you know what I'm thinking?'

'I meant he's a good guy – he's not another Martin. He's kind and gentle and sweet.'

'Wake up. I need to shower before bed.'

'Bed? I've barely been awake ten hours.'

'And that's my fault, is it? I need to work early again.'

Picking exactly the wrong time to ask, I mentioned being invited to Tim's for dinner the next day.

'He invited both of us?' Oscar asked sourly.

'Well, no, it was just for me, but I can ask if I can bring you, if you like.'

'I just bought you all this food, and you still haven't paid me back for the rent advance.'

'Tim's doing a roast. That can be a bit of payback, can't it?'

Oscar looked at me blankly. 'We can eat here tomorrow night; I don't have much food at my place now.'

He left to shower and when he came back, his mood seemed better.

'What's that you're reading?' he asked.

'*Jurassic Park*. I didn't know it was a book. Lloyd lent it to me. It's scarier than the movie.'

'Come here. Give me a hug.'

'Let me just finish my chapter.'

He took the book out of my hands. 'The words will still be there tomorrow, but I have to be up early.' He dropped the book to the floor by the bed and started kissing me.

'I'm not in the mood tonight,' I said experimentally. 'Can we just cuddle?'

'This is how you know I love you.' He kissed me again.

I guess what he'd said about practice makes perfect was true. That night, him fucking me hardly hurt at all after the start. I didn't get why Ryan raved about it, though. He made it sound like it was this amazing thing that felt brilliant. For me, it was uncomfortable and boring.

When he was done, Oscar rolled me onto my side, then fell asleep still inside me. Once I was sure his breathing was slow enough that he was asleep, I adjusted myself, and the slug inside me was gone. Lying there in the dark, not remotely sleepy, I tried counting sheep. My mind was still active enough that some sheep caught their legs on the fence and tumbled in comedic ways, but eventually I fell asleep.

# 20

The next day I knew Tim would call about dinner, so I asked Lloyd if he could say I'd gone out. I didn't want to have to say no to Tim. He'd start nagging about when he could see me again and I just didn't need that.

Oscar arrived in the evening and cooked for us again. Lloyd tried to include me in the conversation between him and Oscar, but Oscar answered for me or changed the subject. After I washed up, Oscar took me to bed and fucked me. That was pretty much how every night of the week went. The only variation was sometimes he woke me as he positioned my body or applied lube to my butt in the morning as well. He said it was so I was satisfied during the day and wouldn't miss him and want to go out.

Being fucked got easy. There wasn't any pain any more; all I had to do was lie there while he did the work. I tried moaning, as it felt like something I should do, and I thought Oscar would like it, but he said it sounded like I was in a bad porn movie, so I didn't do it again. Sometimes I served myself when he'd gone, to prove to myself I could still cum, but the urge wasn't there. It was more out of habit than any sort of need like it used to be.

Tim and Alfie began to call more frequently, and it got

harder and harder to dodge them. I knew I had to speak to them at some point, before Lloyd got annoyed with being my answering service. When I called them back, they demanded I come out that night, both of them talking at the same time. I pictured them with their heads together, the receiver wedged between them, and the idea made me smile. They wouldn't take no for an answer, saying that if I didn't, they'd file a missing person report. Oscar was working a late shift, so I agreed.

'Great,' said Tim. 'What's your address? We'll come and get you later.'

'I ain't stupid.' I wasn't going to give him my address until I was ready for Mum to know I'd moved. 'Pick me up at the bus stop on Whitbourne Road, near the shops.'

I was only waiting a few minutes before they arrived, Alfie in the front with Tim, Ryan in the back hanging out of one of the windows and calling out to me in a high-camp voice. Already feeling like an absconder from a remand centre, I'd been doing my best to avoid eye contact with the other people at the stop, and now here Ryan was, hair flapping in the breeze like the world's gayest dog. 'The best rent-boy in Swindon,' he announced to the bus queue. 'Do you do group discounts?'

'Shut the hell up,' I said through clenched teeth, feeling my face burn. I got in quickly and slammed the door behind me, jarring my elbow. 'I have to walk these streets at night.'

'I knew you'd become a streetwalker, spending so much time with Ryan,' Tim said. 'Seatbelt.'

'Very fetching,' said Ryan, his fingers dancing over my neck as I reached round to pull the belt across. 'Not sure the colour matches your eyes, though. We should get you some green contacts. That would be fabulous.'

Alfie looked back at us. He had a smile that said so much and nothing at all. But he was pleased to see me; I could see that. It was good to be around them again. My smiles, my laughs, were real. We had so much fun at the Cricks that evening, it was almost like nothing bad had happened. Everything was right and normal again.

'Time to go to the club,' Tim said.

'Drive us there?' I implored. 'Ryan is so gay tonight, if we walk, he might dislocate a hip from mincing.'

Nothing had changed at the club: it had only been a week, after all; it just felt like so much longer. Tim went straight to the bar, but I needed to dance, so I didn't wait for my drink. Instead I dragged Alfie onto the dance floor. It was hard to talk out there, but we managed it. Shouting in my ear, he told me how worried Tim had been about me and how good it was to see me. Considering how infatuated I'd been with Alfie, looking at him now, he felt more like a brother, or maybe a cousin who I was really close to and secretly thought was hot, but obviously nothing would ever happen.

Here with him and a club full of happy people, I felt like I was a soldier home after a tour of duty; they were my family and they were happy to see me. Tim appeared with drinks for us. Then, once his hands were unburdened, he ruffled my hair.

'Don't!' I complained, clutching my bottle of Hooch. 'Jesus, dickhead.'

He laughed with delight. 'There's the Richard I know and love.'

I danced, first with Alfie then, after he was tired out, on my own. Later I found him and Tim sitting at a table while Ryan danced in the walkway between the table and the bar. He looked so free and unburdened, I thought he was dancing for himself, but then I noticed the guys watching him, and caught the glances he was throwing them. Ignoring Ryan, I sat down beside Tim. 'More please,' I said, banging my empty bottle down with a cheeky grin.

'I should've left you at home. I'd forgotten how much work you are.'

'But you missed me, right?'

'How could I not?'

'Then show me how much you missed me by getting me really drunk.'

Ryan bounced himself across the upholstered pew until he was close enough to share body heat. From the look on his face I knew he had mischief in mind. Looking around, he flashed a little bottle and suggested we get high and put another show on for everyone. 'High?' I asked.

He shook the bottle at me.

'What is it?'

'Poppers, obviously.'

I vaguely imagined those party things that exploded glitter.

'You know, that thing you see the guys sniffing on the dance floor,' he explained. 'It gets you all spaced and relaxed for a bit. Let's do it. Come on!' He took my hand and dragged me towards the dance floor, leaving Tim and Alfie behind.

The feeling the poppers gave me was odd. My heart raced, but my body relaxed. There was a smell like damp socks and furniture polish. Ryan jammed the bottle up one of my nostrils, I took another hit and my mind cleared. The music was my world and we danced, and then we kissed. There was no romance: we both knew that our kissing was for others not ourselves. It reminded me of an American teen-drama, when two girls kiss and the boys watch, jealous and fascinated, knowing we're doing it to turn them on.

I took my top off, and we continued to dance. Ryan playfully bit one of my nipples and I tipped my head back in mock ecstasy. We heard an 'Oi' over the music and turned to see Tim faking a frown and wagging a finger at us. Ryan and I laughed, looked at each other, back at Tim, and kissed again. The more I knew I was being observed, the further I wanted to go. As we got more daring, the crowd on the dance floor seemed to split. Part of it watching us and urging us on, the other part doing their best to make it known they weren't interested, and dancing more wildly to try and be noticed themselves. Whenever we stopped dancing and kissed, I felt hands on me that weren't Ryan's: they moved differently, there was a purpose to them. They would go too far and then Ryan and I would break away and dance some more. During one lengthy, very enjoyable kiss, hands gripped my arm tightly, and jerked me away from him.

'What the fuck is this?' Oscar's dark blue eyes blazed out against the red flush of his skin.

'Hey, it's okay,' Ryan said drunkenly. 'We're just friends.'

I could see Oscar's fists ball.

'I'm Ryan. I'm like nearly his oldest friend. You're Oscar, right? He talks about you a lot.'

Oscar looked at him suspiciously. 'I need to talk to him for a moment,' he said, after a long pause, during which I guess he decided Ryan hadn't said anything bad. 'But nice to meet you.'

Oscar led me to a corner of the dance floor. He pushed me into the corner and leant into the wall, one hand gripping my shoulder. 'After all I do for you, this is what you do the moment I turn my back?'

'He's just a friend. It doesn't mean anything.'

'Doesn't look like a friend. It looks like you're being a slut.'

'I'm not. I swear. I've never been attracted to Ryan, and he isn't into me either. It's just fun. It means nothing.'

'Everything all right?' It was Tim. He sounded fatherly and

stern. He pulled my shirt from my waistband and passed it to me.

'Everything is good,' I said, awkwardly putting my shirt on. 'This is Oscar.'

'His boyfriend,' Oscar said.

Tim gave him a long look. 'I've heard a lot about you.' He extended a hand to him like it was a business meeting.

'Sorry to bust up the party,' Oscar said, shaking Tim's hand. 'But we had plans tonight.'

'You're here now, so come and join us. We have a table over there,' Tim gestured, his eyes still on Oscar's.

'Thanks, but we're going to go. You know how it is.'

'I don't. Come and join us. Let us know. Be good to know more about Richard's boyfriend. He's special to me.'

'Thanks, but we're going to leave now.' He gripped my arm again and went to leave, but Tim grabbed his wrist. Oscar froze.

'One second,' Tim said coolly. 'I just need a word with him before he goes.'

Oscar's face twitched. 'Anything you need to say to him, you can say in front of me.'

'Actually, no. It's about his mum and it's private. He'll come and find you when we're done.'

Oscar's hand loosened on my arm. He let go and broke eye contact with Tim to look at me. 'Don't take too long,' he said. He moved away to a spot at the edge of the dance floor, and watched us balefully.

Tim took my shoulders. 'I do not like him.'

'You're not seeing him right. He's done so much for me, and he takes care of me. He's just upset that I forgot the plans we had,' I said quickly.

'The way I've just seen him treat you is not right. Just say the word and I'll have him removed from here.'

'No, please don't,' I blurted. 'You'll make him angry.' Even as I said it, I caught my breath.

'And what happens when he gets angry, ay?'

'Nothing. Please don't do this. I need to go. I'll call you tomorrow.'

'Tell me you're okay. I need to hear it and believe it.'

'I'm okay. I'm fine. Nothing is wrong. I just need to go.'

'Call me. Doesn't matter if it's the middle of the night, you call me if you need me.'

'I will. I promise.'

I went over to Oscar without looking back. I knew Tim and probably Alfie and Ryan would be watching. Oscar led me through the club, past Eddie, who just looked at me, whether out of concern or because he was being judgemental, I couldn't tell.

Oscar drove in silence, his hands gripping the top of the steering wheel, knuckles glowing white in the dim light of the car. Once home he ordered me upstairs and told me to shower. I obeyed, then got into bed with him.

'You make it so hard to love you sometimes,' he said to the ceiling, not even looking at me.

'I just wanted a night out with my friends.'

'Acting like sluts on the dance floor for everyone to see. That Tim guy trying to get you away from me. What's that about?'

'He's just worried about me.'

'Worried! About what? All I do is try to love you and look after you.'

'I know. I told him that. I swear.' He was scaring me.

'Turn over.'

'What?'

'You heard me – turn over.'

'But, I...'

He cut me off. 'I'm not in the mood either, but you need to be taught that I love you. Now turn over!' I did as I was told. He got between my legs and pushed a knee into each of my thighs to open them up. I felt the bed moving, wobbling. 'Give me a minute to get hard. Jesus, if I didn't love you I just wouldn't bother.' I heard him spitting, and then he pulled my cheeks apart and spat on my butt. He started trying to force his dick into me. The pain radiated out through my whole body.

'Arghahgh! No. You didn't put any lube on.'

He put a hand on the back of my head and pushed it down and into the pillow. 'Quiet. Lloyd will hear you.'

I opened my mouth to speak, and it was filled with pillow. 'Please,' I mumbled. 'I need lube.'

'I said shut up.' He put more weight on my head, my neck felt like it was bending two different ways. 'Sluts use spit. You behave like a slut, then I'm going to fuck you like a slut.' With that, he forced himself into me. I screamed into the muffling pillow.

He moved a hand over my mouth. He was heavy on top of me. My breathing was fast and laboured and dampened his fingers on my face. My arse was screaming. He was motionless on top of me, in me. I was frozen underneath him, the pain and fear holding me down more than he did. He started to fuck me and the pain was a new world. I felt raw, each tiny movement sending blades through my nerve endings. I gasped into his fingers. There was a knock at the door. Oscar froze.

'Everything okay?' Lloyd's hesitant voice came through the door.

'Tell him you're fine,' Oscar whispered into my ear as he moved his hand from my mouth.

'I'm fine,' I said thickly.

'What happened? It sounded bad.'

'You kicked the bed,' whispered Oscar, his body on top of mine.

'I kicked the bed frame,' I said, sounding a bit clearer. 'Too much beer.'

'Okay. I was worried.' A long pause. 'Well. Night then.'

We heard his bedroom door shut and Oscar's hand slapped back over my mouth, pulling my head back as he thrust again. My scream was muffled well this time. He kept on, his rhythm like a metronome: thrust pause thrust pause. I deadened to the pain, but it was still live through all of me. My body tried to stop recognising it, but couldn't. His pace quickened. Finally he grunted, and the thrusting became twitching. He rolled me onto my side and as his hot breaths on the back of my head slowed, he kissed my neck.

'Goodnight, beautiful.'

My tears came without sobs. My body didn't move but my pillow got wet as I lay there in his arms, him still inside me, the pain fading, only to be replaced by dread.

I didn't leave the bed or the room until after Oscar had gone to work the next morning. Lloyd was watching TV with Zoe when I came down. On the screen a tiny frog looked up from a dew-filled rainforest flower. I made some tea and brought the mugs through to join him on the sofa.

'How's your toe?' he asked.

'What?'

'Your toe. You said last night you kicked the bed?'

'Oh, right. It's fine thanks. What's the show?'

'David Attenborough. I like the animal shows. Zoe does too.' He looked at me. 'You know, if you ever want to talk to me about something, you can?'

For a moment I couldn't speak. He obviously realised

something was wrong, but how much had he figured out? Had he come back out of his room and listened to my muffled scream last night? What would Oscar do if he knew Lloyd knew? I had to pretend like everything was normal. 'Thank you, you're a lovely guy. You know that, right?'

He smiled gently. 'If only more guys that look like you thought that.' We both turned our attention back to the nature show.

A while later, I said, 'Lloyd?'

'Yes, lovely?'

'Tonight, when Oscar comes round, could you...could you tell him I'm sick and he can't come in?'

'Of course I can, my dear.'

Lloyd turned Oscar away three nights in a row, but on the fourth, ironically, I really was sick with flu. I woke to my door opening. It was Oscar. Lloyd hovered behind him, looking apologetic.

'You've been sick for so long, I had to come in and see that you were okay.'

'I'm fine. Just crappy. I'll call you when I'm better.'

Lloyd withdrew. Oscar closed the door. He sat on the bed and felt my forehead.

'God, you're so hot.'

'I feel cold. I just want to sleep.'

'Let me get in and keep you warm.'

It was the last thing I wanted. But he got undressed and shuffled under the covers to spoon me. Any part of his body that touched mine made my clammy skin feel hotter. I felt his hard-on push against me.

'Please, I feel so bad. Not now.'

'I can't help it. Even sick, you're beautiful.'

'But I just need to sleep, please.'

There was a whining edge to my voice. He rolled away from me and I thought I'd finally get to rest, but he rolled back and put lube on me. 'It will help you sleep. I promise.' He rolled me onto my front, and fucked me. I made no protest. I just wanted it done so I could go back to sleep. Next time I woke up he'd gone, and the next day I felt just about well enough to wash and have some food. That evening, he came back and cooked for me, 'to get my strength back', and then fucked me.

Lying there underneath him while he humped, I thought about the night before. I was so sick I could barely stay conscious, and he still had to fuck me. This wasn't going to stop. He wasn't going to stop. I was just something for him to cum in. Didn't matter if I was sexy and fresh out of the shower, or sweaty with a fever, I was just a place to put his dick. He grunted; I hadn't noticed he was getting close. He rolled us over and kissed the back of my neck. Only one way I could see out of this. I didn't want to do it, but it was the only way. The next morning I got up, got dressed, made tea, picked up the phone, punched in the number. *Pleeeeease, don't be at work.*

'Hello?'

'Mum?'

'Richard. I've been trying to reach you.'

'Mum?'

'Yes? What is it? Are you all right?'

'Can I come home, please?'

# 21

Mum had rules ready, of course. There was to be no clubbing, and I had to join the youth group. I was to start my counselling again. I wasn't going back to Warneford, but she had school options for me, and I would go to school. Reasonable bedtimes. No swearing. I let her get it all out. I was as desperate to be home, to be safe, not to be an object for other people any more, as I knew she was to have me back home.

'I'm still going clubbing,' I said, once she finally paused for breath.

'You're fifteen. You need to do things suitable for your age.'

'I also need to do things suitable for my life. I will still go clubbing.'

'We can talk about that when you're home.'

'I haven't said no to school or bedtime. I haven't even questioned trying to swear less. But I'm going clubbing.'

'I said no swearing.'

'Deal. No swearing, and I still get to go out on weekends.'

'I'll come and get you.'

'Mum?' I said hesitantly.

'Yes?'

'I'm not at Martin's.' I held my breath.

'Okay... Where are you?' I gave her the address. 'I can come over now.'

'Can you give me a couple of hours to pack and sort things out?'

'I'll see you in *one* hour.'

'And Mum? Can you bring your cheque book? I owe a bit of rent money.'

Packing was easy; I barely had any stuff. The hard bit was telling Lloyd. He wasn't surprised that I was going.

'I had a feeling you weren't happy here.'

'No, it's not that at all. I love it here. You're delightful. It's just, I just need to go home. Oscar...' I struggled to find the right words.

'You can come back any time. If you ever need somewhere to stay, then come here,' Lloyd said simply.

'Thank you. Can I ask one last favour?'

'Anything.'

'Oscar paid my rent when I moved in, and I still owe him. Is it okay if my mum gives you a cheque for £150 and then you give Oscar the £75 I owe him?'

'Of course, and you don't need to pay the next two weeks; that's fine.'

'I want to, and Mum'll pay anyway,' I said, managing a laugh.

I stripped my bed and loaded the washing machine. Lloyd remarked that it was little things like that that meant I was welcome back any time. Mum arrived nearly twenty minutes early. She was trying to look stern, but was obviously happy.

'I've told Dad already. He suggested getting Chinese for dinner. But that isn't a reward, it's a welcome back.'

'You want tea? Lloyd, this is my Mum, Mandy.'

They shook hands briefly. We all sat and talked, and the frosty tone Mum had when she first met Lloyd melted quickly. He was so gentle that you couldn't be angry with him, even when you were trying to find someone to be angry at. She brought up the rent, and I explained that I'd already been there two weeks and, as I was letting Lloyd down with no warning, the next two were owed. Mum sat holding her cheque book like Rodin's *Thinker*, except grumpy. Then she opened it on the coffee table and wrote out the cheque. Passing it to Lloyd, she said, 'Well, that's sorted. It's time to get him home. Thank you for looking after him.'

'He's welcome back any time. He's so thoughtful and sweet.'

Raising an eyebrow, she turned to me. 'Are you sure you've been staying here?'

I rolled my eyes at her. 'Can you take my bag out? I just want to say goodbye to Lloyd.'

She struggled down the hallway with my overstuffed bag, but made it out of the front door, leaving it open behind her. I turned back to Lloyd and said, 'I wanted to say thank you properly. You might not know it, but the meals, and even just watching TV with me, have meant a lot. Some normal in a crazy world.'

'You're going to be okay?' he asked. 'Sometimes you were so quiet I was worried, and other times your laugh brought the house to life.'

'I'll be okay.' I gestured towards the front of the house. 'She'll look after me.'

'And Oscar?'

Of course he'd worked out what was going on with Oscar, or most of it, anyway. I looked away awkwardly. 'He doesn't know I'm leaving. I just can't have that conver—'

'Don't worry about it,' Lloyd said, hugging me. 'I used to

box, you know.'

'Really?'

He smiled. 'Look, we all have to date a bad boy. They make the good guys that come later look better. I'll tell him you've moved out. Do you want me to pass any message along?'

A malicious smile grew on my face as a thought grew in my mind. 'Tell him you know I'm fifteen. Tell him if he tries to find me, I'll tell all the lesbians at the club what he's been doing, and lastly tell him to fuck off or you'll call the police and tell them yourself.'

Lloyd looked genuinely surprised. 'You're fifteen?'

'Yeah. Sorry. He lied to you and told me to go along with it.'

'It's not that. You're a child! And the things I've been thinking while you parade about in your underwear.' He shook his head. 'My goodness, how can I get bleach into my brain? Fifteen!'

I laughed. 'Thank you,' I said, getting ready to go.

'When you're old enough, come back,' he said. 'Even just to help me eat Auntie's food. Fifteen! Lord have mercy!'

'I look good for my age, right?'

'You don't look like anything but a child. Jesus, get out already. Go back to Mum. She's got sweeties for you.' He waved a hand, dismissing me.

'Bye Lloyd, and thank you again.'


Mum was quiet in the car but in a contented way. Eventually she broke the silence and told me that she and Dad had tidied my room. That made me anxious about what they'd found: the pot-pourri I told kids in year 7 was dope and kept behind some textbooks; the pair of Antony's underwear I stole when I slept over at his, kept in the cupboard beside my bed; all the things that could be considered gay that I'd stashed on a secret shelf behind my desk which I'd made by taping a strip of cardboard between it and the wall? But Mum and Dad knew I was gay, so what did it matter? She explained she'd done it so she could feel closer to me while I wasn't there. After another pause, she said, 'So, are you going to tell me why you were at Lloyd's, not Martin's?'

'It just wasn't working out with Martin. I loved being with Jo and Wayne, but you saw the room. It was kinda nasty.'

'And you were at Lloyd's for two weeks? That's why I haven't seen you in this time?'

'I didn't know how you'd react – if you'd try to bring me home.'

'I've been trying to get you home since you left.'

'I'm not going back to Warneford.'

'We can talk about that once we're actually home. There's a lot to go over.'

We were the only ones there when we got back. The familiar smell of the house calmed me, like the first cigarette after an argument. Skip sniffed my bag excitedly. I tried to get his attention, but other than a cursory face-lick, he didn't seem impressed by my return. He loved Mum because she fed him and walked him. I shirked walking him, and now he was paying me back. 'Zoe liked me,' I said, stroking his head. He licked my hand and then went back to sniffing my bag.

'Can I go to my room and watch TV?'

'I like this new polite you. Maybe Lloyd was a good influence on you. Give me your laundry first.'

I took my bag to the breakfast room and loaded the washing machine. When I was done, I saw her watching me from the kitchen door. Smiling, she said, 'New rule: you do your own laundry from now on.'

'Easy. And if I do my own, then I know my clubbing

outfits will be clean when I want them,' I said, smiling back. Checkmate, lady.

From the top of the stairs, I saw my bedroom door was wide open, when normally I shut it, both for privacy and to hide the chaos I enjoyed living in. I went in as if I was a stranger, a cop inspecting the room of a murdered or abducted child. I don't think it had ever been as tidy as it was now; even the shelves by the door that displayed my crystal and rock collection were completely dust-free. Right in the centre of my desk, leant up against the wall like the centrepiece of an altar, was my Boys Boys Boys folder. I was mortified. After all the things that had happened in the last couple of months, this little collection of pictures of pop stars, actors and underwear models suddenly seemed painfully childish and stupid. Picking it up, I wanted to throw it out, but I had nowhere to throw it.

'Dad didn't open it.' Mum's sudden and silent appearance startled me.

'Did you?' I said with a good amount of side-eye.

'It reminded me of the pictures I used to cut out and stick in my diary. Adam Ant,' she said dreamily. 'He was such a heartthrob.'

'Eww! Can we not talk about antique popstars in such ways please.' I looked back at the folder. 'This seems so dumb now.'

'But you obviously loved it. You've taken such care arranging all the pictures.'

'It's childish, and these people aren't real, anyway. I think I'll throw it away.' I turned a page and there was the picture Sarah had given me of Shane Lynch in his overstuffed underwear.

'I don't know if that's real,' Mum said. 'But if it is, there isn't much you can do with it.' She stifled a laugh.

'MOTHER! No! That's more disgusting than you fancying AntMan! Get out. Get out of my room!'

'Wait! Before you throw it out,' she said, once I'd manhandled her to the door, 'don't be so quick to throw away your childish things. You can't get them back once they're gone.'

'Get out, you dirty old lady!' But I was smiling as I shut the door on her and went back to the folder. I guessed it was kind of cute in its way. The years of boy bands and underwear ads looked back at me. I put them in a drawer.

Later I heard Jenny and then Dad get home. I was still in my room, watching TV. Maybe they'd hear it and know I was back. No one came upstairs though, and I was too apprehensive to go down. Eventually Mum knocked and stuck her head in.

'Dinner is here, and so is your family,' she said with a smile.

I went down with her, and things were strange and strained, but polite. Everyone was trying hard to be normal, so of course everyone was awkward. Jenny was the most normal: a bit grumpy and glaring at me when she thought Mum and Dad weren't looking. She'd probably enjoyed the space and not having to share a bathroom with me. Dad tried to make conversation with me and he was doing a reasonable job, but it wasn't easy. I felt like I'd changed so much. He couldn't or wouldn't ask anything about the time I'd been away. He couldn't ask about school. But we all struggled on. I accidentally let a swear word slip out at one point and I didn't get told off. That wouldn't last.

We started planning the weekend. I said I'd be going out on Saturday night and Dad looked at Mum as if to say, you answer that one. Eventually we agreed we could all eat together a little early, and I'd go out a little late, with Mum insisting on taking me. After dinner, I went back to my room and just sat on my bed. I didn't turn on the TV. I didn't think or stress. I just breathed.

# 22

Dad was in the kitchen most of Saturday afternoon, experimenting with a French beef-and-wine stew and some weird potato recipe, half cooked in stock and half cooked in the oven. Eating a proper meal cooked by him was nice though. I hadn't realised his cooking was one of the things I'd missed.

I could tell there was some sadness – or perhaps fear – in him once I was getting ready to go out.

'See you tomorrow. I'll be back by lunchtime,' I said.

'You'll be back tonight,' Mum corrected me.

'I'll stay with Tim or Phil. It's easier.'

'We want you to come home.'

'The taxis don't run at that time of night, so I'd need to hope a private hire is available and then get into a car with a stranger at 2am, hoping I don't get kidnapped and sold into international slavery.'

'Then you'll get to see the world, and they'll send you back in a couple of weeks when they realise how little you do,' Mum said, with a mocking tone but a serious face.

'Tomorrow, before lunch. I'll call your mobile before I go to bed tonight and leave a message to let you know I'm safe.'

'It's an acceptable compromise,' she said, 'but you'll have to compromise sometimes too.'

We pulled up outside the Cricks and Mum blurted out, 'I'd like to meet Phil and the other friends you talk so much about.'

'I can hardly invite them round for tea and cake with Dad to talk cricket.' Actually, for all I knew, Phil and the others liked cricket.

'No need for that tone,' Mum said, 'and don't be rude about your father. He's come a long way in a short time.' I hung my head; she was right. 'And you know these kinds of places.' She gestured at the Cricks. 'They don't just let teenagers in; old people like me can come in too.'

'You have got to be bloody kidding me!'

'I am not.'

'You want to come into *my* pub?'

'Your pub now, is it? But no, I was thinking the club at the start of the night, before it's busy.'

'You're joking, right? You want me to take you clubbing? My mother? With me? In a club?'

'I was young and out late at night once, too.'

'Yes, but that was like a hundred years ago...'

'If you're not careful, I'll tell them how you used to run around tugging on your penis like you were trying to pull it off.'

'MOTHER!'

'So next weekend then, whichever day works best for your friends. I'll only stay for one drink.'

'Fine! See – look at me, compromising. I'll see you tomorrow,' I said as I got out of the car.

'Love you,' she called through the window.

'Love you too.'

As I waved over my shoulder, a guy standing outside the pub

with a friend said, 'Ahh! He loves his mummy...'

I looked them up and down with scorn. 'You don't love yours? She must be a right twat.' And I quickly went inside.

At the club door, a scowling Eddie looked me up and down. I knew I looked good, my t-shirt was tight, my jeans had the cute turn-ups that everyone was wearing, and my hair had so much spray in it, it was bomb-proof.

'Oscar was looking for you last night,' he said.

The world closed in on me.

While Tim was getting the drinks in, he asked, 'What's the deal with Oscar?'

'No deal, and I don't want to talk about it.'

Tim shrugged. But I couldn't get Oscar out of my head. I went to the lobby to find Eddie. 'Can I have a word?'

'Can it wait? We're just about to get busy.'

'It's important.'

He looked into my pleading eyes, and sighed. 'Come outside – I need a smoke anyway.' Leaving Graham on the door he led me to a bench at the edge of the car park away from the entrance, sat and lit a cigarette, passed it to me, then lit his own. 'What's up?'

'You said Oscar came looking for me?'

'Last night, around eleven. He didn't believe me when I said you weren't here. Did you two break up?'

'Did he say if he was coming back?'

'What's going on, little man?' Eddie's tone had changed from big and gruff to teddy bear.

'He. We...' I stopped.

'Just between you and me.'

'I really, really don't want to see him again.' I wiped away a tear I hadn't even felt building up.

'Was he the one who put those bruises on your neck?' he asked in a very serious tone.

'No. Those were Martin.'

'Which ones did he give you?'

'I. He. I can't.' He put his arm around me and rubbed my back. 'He hurt me,' I said thickly. 'He...he gave me the ones on my back.' Eddie's hand stopped moving.

The silence felt like it went on forever, then, 'Did he hold you down?'

How did he know? Was I that much of a slag it was obvious? I replied with some uh-huh noises through my tears.

'It's not your fault, little man,' he said, squeezing me tight.

'But I let him. I didn't stop him. I had nowhere to go.' It was a relief to say that to someone, but I began to panic. I knew I could trust Eddie, but could I trust him with this?

He took hold of my shoulders and looked me in the eye. 'You listen to me. This is not your fault. You did nothing wrong. I just need to be clear that I'm understanding you. I believe you. I just need to be clear. He raped you?'

The word made the hair on my arms stand up. I'd stopped thinking of it as that. It had just become sex. My eyes blurred with fresh tears. 'I had nowhere to go.' *But I could've gone home. Why didn't I just go home?*

'It's okay. It won't happen again.'

I pulled away from him. 'You can't tell anyone! I didn't stop him. I stayed with him.'

'You did nothing wrong. You stayed as safe as you could. He did this to you. You didn't do anything. You understand me?'

'But...'

'No buts. You are not to blame for this. Come here.' He pulled me back into him.

I heard Phil's voice. 'What are you two up to?'

'This one needs some cellar time,' Eddie said getting up off the bench with a grunt. He pulled me to my feet and hugged me again, whispering in my ear, 'He won't be coming in. He won't be coming near you again. I'll sort this, I promise.'

'Hugs from Eddie, that's rarer than a sober virgin round here. Come on, let's get you in the cellar.'

'I need five minutes to make some calls,' Eddie said, making his way purposefully across the car park. A big part of me was hoping he'd call all his friends from Middle Earth to come guard the club.

In the cellar, Phil comforted me and chatted until my tears dried up, then asked me what was going on.

'It's complicated,' I said.

'Sure must be. So, you want to tell me?'

'Can I just say it's a nasty breakup and we leave it at that?'

'You and Key Guy?'

'Yeah.'

'Never bloody liked him. Rolls his own cigarettes in a club, for fuck's sake.' That made me laugh. 'You done getting chilly? Want to join the warm people and get a drink?'

'If you're buying?'

'Jesus, when aren't I buying with you?'

He opened the cellar door. As I followed him into the lobby, I heard a shout.

'Richard! Where the fuck have you been?' It was Oscar, looking furious.

My heart sank.

'HEY! I want a word with you!' Eddie came forward and got between me and Oscar. 'We need to have a little chat!'

Phil moved me towards the club, and Oscar tried to get round Eddie. 'No, you don't,' Phil said. 'You're done talking to him.'

Phil pushed me through the club doors. I turned back and through the glass saw Oscar shoving Eddie hard in the chest. Eddie barely moved an inch. *Good,* I thought. *Let them see him lose control.*

'You shouldn't be seeing this,' said Phil, blocking my view with his body.

'Yeah, I should,' I said, getting round him. Eddie had Oscar by the neck at arm's length, a finger in his face and both their mouths looked like they were shouting. Seeing him like that revealed something to me. Oscar had become so big in my mind, but really he was just a little man being held by his throat by a real-sized man.

'Break his neck!' I shouted. Then: 'Shit! Get off me!' I was moving through the air and picked my legs up just in time as Phil lifted me over the bar onto the staff side.

'Put him in the cellar,' he shouted to the barman.

I slipped away and was through the cellar and into the lobby just in time to see Oscar going out of the door backwards, Eddie's hand still attached to his neck.

'How did I know you'd do that?' Phil asked. 'Go to the cellar and STAY there. Please!'

'Fine.' I went and sat on a barrel.

Time passed slowly. I got cold. Eventually Phil came back in, looking exasperated. 'Well, whatever the hell that was, it's now sorted,' he said while lighting a cigarette and tossing me the pack.

'Did Eddie kill him?' I asked hopefully.

'Of course he didn't. He just took him round the back for a little chat about the facts of life.' He sat down beside me.

'A chat?'

'Where there aren't any cameras... Someone needs to tell me why at some point, mind you.'

I imagined blood spatter and scattered teeth. 'Can we go see?'

'No, you little freak. What's wrong with you?'

'Nothing – now.'

'This is feeling like a pattern. You getting hurt, us in here, trying to think what to do,' he said.

'No pattern; just a bad few months.'

'Are you going to tell me about them?'

'Nothing to tell at the moment.' I opened my eyes wide in the hope that the cold air would keep them from crying. 'Is Eddie back or are they still "chatting"?' I made massive air quotes.

'You think people chat for long with Eddie?'

'Can I speak to him? Then I'll come and find you. I promise I'll be quick.'

'I'll get him. Take as long as you want.'

After a moment on my own, the giant teddy bear manoeuvred himself through the door and I asked, 'Are you okay?'

'Not a scratch on me,' he said, looking thoughtfully at his hand. He was back to being a man of few words.

'Thank you,' I said, getting up. 'I really mean it.'

I hugged the part of him I could get my arms around. 'Don't go hugging me out there,' he grumbled. 'I don't need those cunts thinking I'm a hugger.'

'Thank you, my teddy.' I hugged him again.

'Oh Jesus,' he said, prising me off him.

'Drink time?' I asked.

'I'll have a whisky and Coke. Graham will just have a Coke.'

'What's Graham's deal? Why doesn't he speak?'

'Tell him *Star Trek* is better than *Star Wars*, then he'll never shut up.' He stopped with his hand on the cellar door. 'That,' he motioned to outside, 'won't happen again, because you're going to bring problems to me or Phil before they get there.'

'I hear you, and I thank you, and I need a wee. It's freezing in here.'

He laughed. 'Go wee, and wash your hands before getting my drink.'

I found Phil stood at the bar, sneaked up behind him to tweak his nipple.

'What have I told you about my nipples?'

'You said they were cute because they are attached to you. Can I stay with you tonight?'

He told me about all the things that wouldn't happen if I stayed, but after he'd finished his speech, he agreed. I thanked him and gave him Eddie and Graham's drinks order.

# 23

Phil was right: the lock-in was the best part of the night. Tonight it included Harry, who was Finlay's boyfriend and also worked at Gay Men's Health Project. He was fun, even though he was old, although he didn't dress like he was old. He looked like someone had put the head of a skinny granddad on the body of a raver. He had an unnerving ability to pinpoint my nipple through my t-shirt and twist it. The first time I was shocked, but everyone else laughed and then he started doing it to them too, so I guessed it must just be his thing. He did it to me every time I was cheeky, and soon had me giggling. I learned to put my hands over both nipples before I said something. Once the novelty wore off, he started getting all sex education on me. Normal boring shit that I'd heard before. Gonorrhoea, syphilis, discharge, warts, chlamydia. All the stuff you don't want to talk about while having fun. He checked I'd had the hepatitis B jab, which Alfie and I had already got at the Health Project. I brushed off the whole consent part of the conversation. Apparently, I could withdraw consent at any point I liked and the other person had to stop.

Then he said, 'And then there's rimming.'

'Rimming? What's that?'

Listening in, both Phil and Finlay looked awkward.

'What?' I said. 'What's rimming?'

'It's like a special kind of kissing,' Phil said.

I looked at him suspiciously. 'Why are you being odd?'

'Because you don't kiss on the mouth,' Finlay said dryly.

'If this is a gross foot thing, I don't want to know,' I said.

Harry leant in and said conspiratorially, 'Not feet. North a bit.'

'Like a blowjob?' I asked.

'Right area, wrong side,' Phil said, exhaling a short plume of smoke.

'What are you on about?' I asked crossly. Harry leant into me again and whispered into my ear. 'Shut. The. Fuck. Up!' I said. 'That's not true.'

'Oh, it's true all right. It's quite good if it's done right,' Phil said, chuckling.

'Like a dog! You all just go around licking each other's arses?' I was stunned. 'You're all lying. How stupid do you think I am?'

'No. It's a thing,' Finlay insisted. 'Normally it's the top doing it to the bottom.'

'Licking his arse?'

'Just make sure he washes well before you do it.'

'That's disgusting,' I said.

'All the best things are, darling,' Harry said, getting my nipple again. I wriggled away from him.

Finlay put an arm around my shoulders, pulling me into him. 'Leave the poor boy alone,' he said to Harry.

'Well, I will not be doing that, ever.'

'Tell us that in a year,' Phil said.

Back at Phil's, we sat with our baked potatoes and watched

some of his tapes. He introduced me to *Absolutely Fabulous* – or *Ab Fab*, as he called it – saying it was a modern classic. It was actually quite funny. Later, as we got into bed, I asked him if they were joking about rimming.

'No, not at all.'

'But why?' I asked.

'Because it feels good to both – well, or at least one of the people involved.'

'So, sex doesn't have to feel good for both people?'

'Sometimes you do things you're not that into because your partner really enjoys them. What's this fourth degree about?'

'Doesn't matter.'

'You want to tell me why Eddie was so pissed off with Oscar?'

'No.'

'You know you can, right?'

I cuddled into him, 'I do. I just don't want to talk about it. That's okay too, right?'

'Of course, as long as you know you can.' He put his arm around me. 'Face full of sodding hair again. Why did I say you could stay?'

When I got home the next day I stretched the phone through to the garage for privacy and called Alfie. The first thing I did was check with him that the others hadn't been winding me up about rimming. He confirmed it was true. He told me it helped relax the 'area'. 'Wait till you have it done to you; it's great.'

'But what if they want to kiss me afterwards?' I asked, repelled.

'That's why you should always make sure you're clean. Ryan can teach you how to douche.' He laughed. 'Maybe he'll even show you.'

My sister's voice broke in suddenly on the line. 'Are you

going to be much longer? I need to call Vicky.'

Adrenaline flowed through me. How much had she heard from the extension? 'Get off the phone!' I shouted. 'You've only got one friend, and she can't be missing you!'

Jenny started arguing so I opened the garage door and screamed into the house. 'Mum! Tell her to get off the phone! She's spying on me because she's so pathetic.'

Mum's glaring face appeared from the kitchen. She turned her head to shout for Jenny to hang up the phone, then told me not to screech or call my sister pathetic.

I slammed the garage door, and Alfie and I laid into how sad Jenny was, just in case she was still listening.

Over lunch, which was just me and Mum, she reminded me about going to the youth group, which I'd agreed to when I came home. I groaned and said, 'Let's talk about something else.'

'Okay. So: school options...'

'I'm not going back to Warneford.'

'I've already told you that you won't be. There are other schools within driving distance. Faringdon? Your friends from primary school go there.'

'Next option,' I said quickly.

'There's Stratton Education Centre. It's a pupil referral unit, for children with needs that don't fit standard education.'

'The place they put the kids too dumb or violent to be allowed around normal people?'

'After what you've been through, I'd have thought you'd have a little compassion for the problems of others.'

'Next option.'

She blinked slowly and took a deep breath. 'Sanford House.'

'Sounds like a military camp.'

'It's similar to Stratton, but it's for those with greater

emotional needs and school-refusers.'

'Can I be a school-refuser? "Greater emotional needs" makes me sound like a retard.'

She gave me a warning look, so I decided not to push my luck any further. 'Which one do you think is the best?'

'Honestly, I think probably Sanford House. It's one of the only education centres in the country trying to get school-refusers an education outside the normal school environment. Mr Hogg can tell us about it when he comes next.'

'The grumpy turtle man?'

'The education welfare officer. I know you don't like him—'

'He called you a liar for saying I wasn't living here. He threatened you with court. Now suddenly he wants to actually help me?'

Mum sighed. 'We need him on side. So you will be here, and you will be nice.'

The day arrived for Mr Hogg's visit. Mum brought him through to the dining room, and he took the seat at the head of the table. I pushed my chair back, got up and moved round to the opposite head of the table. Mr Hogg gave me a look, then began to explain at length what his role was. Whenever I glanced at Mum, she had a pleading look in her eyes, so I sat and listened. Eventually he got to the end of his monologue, looked over his glasses at me and said, 'First things first. How do you feel about going back to Warneford?'

I looked back at him and calmly said, 'Never gonna bloody happen.'

Pursing his lips, Mr Hogg made a note. I tried to read it upside down, but couldn't.

'Richard has made his feelings very clear about returning to Warneford,' Mum said, 'and I have to agree with him.'

'How does Richard feel about Sanford House?'

'Richard is right here,' I said. 'But if Richard isn't required, Richard can piss off and watch TV.'

'Richard!' Mum said. 'Mr Hogg is trying to help.'

I slouched in my chair and folded my arms.

'Mr Hogg, can you tell us more about Sanford House?'

Unpursing his lips, Mr Hogg explained that the school had two classes, junior and senior, and I could complete my GCSEs there. There would be just one teacher, and a small class. It operated from 9.30am to 12.30pm from Monday to Friday and was soon to relocate from a building in the centre of Swindon to a newly refurbished building on Drove Road.

I had to admit it sounded okay, not least because of the half-day timetable, and agreed to give Sanford House a try. Mr Hogg told us I could go along for a trial day and he'd be in touch with a date.

After Mum showed him out, she said, 'I want to thank you for not going further, but I'm not exactly happy with how you behaved.'

'I thought I showed restraint,' I said. My tone was more arrogant than the comedic one I was aiming for.

'Don't fall out with me over this. I'm the one going in to bat for you.'

'Can I watch TV now?'

'After we talk about the youth group.'

'I have friends my age. Alfie and Ryan.' I picked up the cordless phone from the computer desk in the corner of the room. 'Who I'm now going to call.'

Mum heaved a sigh and left the room.

Ryan answered and quite soon into the conversation offered to teach me about rimming by letting me do it to him. 'It's like cunnilingus but for guys.' I told him he was disgusting, he laughed, and we made plans for the weekend. With me going back to school, clubbing might become more difficult, so I decided to make the most of it while I could. Ryan told me that Finlay would bring something special that I'd love, but he wouldn't say what.

By the time the weekend rolled around, I'd forgotten all about Ryan's little tease, until Finlay and Harry jogged my memory by walking into the club. Harry looked thinner and more tired than usual, but Finlay looked as cool as always. I was there with Alfie, Tim and Ryan, but skipped over to say hi. Harry was already very drunk and went straight for my nipples. Finlay stopped him and gave me a big, sincere hug.

'Ryan said you have something special for us,' I said. 'What is it?'

'I'll tell you once we're sat down.'

That made me even more eager to know what was going on. When we were seated in one of the booths I squeezed in next to him and asked again.

'It has to be a secret.'

'I have lots of secrets. I'm good with them.'

He smiled kindly at me. 'You know what whizz is?'

'I do not,' I said, like it was a fun guessing game.

'Speed?'

'Like the drug?' I said, a bit shocked.

'That's the one.'

'They told us about it in school – that it was dangerous.'

'You want to try it then?'

I stopped for a moment. I wasn't sure. But my teachers were wrong about so many other things, so they could be wrong about speed too. 'Do I need to pay? I don't have much money.'

'Not for you, baby; my treat.' He gave me a kiss. 'I'll hook you up later. For now, go and enjoy yourself.' And he shooed me away.

No one hot was in that night, but there were still plenty of people to dance with. Ryan came over to me with a drink.

'Let's get fucked up,' he said. 'Down in one.' We both downed our drinks. It had the burn of vodka but a bitterness at the back that stuck in my throat.

As the night went on, it got better. The music was speaking straight to my body, I got drunker and the guys became more interesting. One took my top off for me while we danced. I tucked it into my waistband. He was replaced by another, and another, and the wheel of the dance floor turned round and round. Ryan and I put on our normal show, and when we stopped we each got a new partner. Mine must have been in his thirties. He was muscular and strong with bulky arms and a big chest. I stroked his biceps and felt them tense as he lifted me up. He carried me across the dance floor and held me against the wall while we kissed. Being carried around was insanely hot, so I was disappointed when he put me down. My disappointment faded as he undid the top button of his trousers, took my hand and put it down them. I felt about. His dick was stiff and huge.

Looking into my eyes with a beautiful smile, he said, 'Want to come back to mine?'

'Fuck, yes!'

He took my hand and led me off the dance floor. As we made our way through the club, my heart was racing. The entire night was so exhilarating. By the door Finlay stopped us and whispered something to Big Dick, who let go of my hand. I was confused. What had he said? Finlay leant into my ear, 'Not tonight, baby. Come and talk to me.'

I should have been disappointed, but actually I didn't care:

Finlay was offering me another adventure. 'Are we having the whizz now?'

'You've been on the dance floor for two hours. I put it in your drink for you.'

'Really? That's what it does? Makes you dance more?'

'It makes you feel more; gives you more energy; makes you feel good.'

'That's why I feel so good tonight?'

'Yes baby, that's the whizz.'

'Can I have some more?'

He put his hands on my shoulders, 'You don't need any more. Go back and dance. But I'll be watching you. You're not going home with anyone tonight. You'll make bad choices.'

'I don't care.'

'Exactly. Drink some water first, then dance.'

The night felt like it went on forever, but it was also over in no time at all. When the music stopped, Ryan and I kept dancing anyway. The club emptied out and Finlay called us over. Phil was complaining to Finlay that I had too much energy already; the last thing I needed was speed. Tim stood watching like he didn't want to be involved in the conversation, and Phil didn't seem to want to include him.

I beamed at Phil, 'I'll be a good boy, I promise.'

'Christ on a cracker, when are you ever good? You have to sleep. I need to be up early for some bullshit staff-training.'

He turned to Tim and said, indicating Ryan, 'You take that one. This one's my problem.'

# 24

The previous night, any thought that entered my mind had been immediately vocalised. I had memories of demanding a dance party and Phil putting on David Bowie's 'Let's Dance'; the party becoming karaoke, where I just made up the words; and being told there was absolutely no way we were going downstairs to race each other to the train station to see if the café was open and have snacks. At the time, Phil had found it funny, but now, having had very little sleep, he clearly found it a lot less so. Eventually he had to start work, and I got to sleep properly for a while. I was woken next by Finlay. It was disorientating seeing him in Phil's bedroom. For a moment I wondered what was wrong, but he told me Phil had let him in to check on me, and that I looked like shit. I felt like shit too. I tried to rub life into myself through my eyes and asked him the time.

'Twelve-thirty. I brought lunch,' he said, holding up a pack of cigarettes. I groaned. 'That's the price you pay,' he said, getting onto the bed and sitting cross-legged. He put the ashtray between us, lit up a cigarette and tossed the pack to me.

'Price for too much booze?'

'No baby: the drugs. You remember how good you felt last

night?'

'Sooo good. Can I have more tonight?'

'No. It's a treat, not a regular thing. But the price you pay for feeling so good last night is you feel shit today. This is your come-down.'

He asked if I was coming out again tonight. I had no fresh clothes and knew Mum wouldn't be impressed. But the idea was appealing enough to try.

Mum's reaction was a flat cold no. I pleaded with her, not willing to accept her refusal, and there was a lengthy silence on the end of the line. I didn't break it, in the hope she was at least weighing up the options. When she spoke, the deal she proposed was that she'd come to the club to check on me and meet my friends. Reluctantly I said okay, and we made plans to meet in the car park of the Flag at 9pm. After she'd rung off I started thinking about how badly this could go.

Finlay took me out for the day. Seeing Swindon with him, it all looked drab and pedestrian. It had always been humdrum, but today it was humdrum squared. We spent hours trawling the clothes shops to find me a new outfit, settling on bright orange jeans that clung to my legs, butt and crotch like elastic, and a blue lycra t-shirt that was patterned like oil on water. Together they made me look like a sexy cocktail. As part of the package, Finlay tried to buy me a jockstrap, but I refused. I said that I didn't see the point in underwear that didn't cover all the areas that needed covering, and he smirked.

Once we'd shopped ourselves out, he took me to a café that he liked. They served hot chocolate with whipped cream, and they had some amazing-looking cookies by the till. We sat outside at a table on the pavement and I took the opportunity to ask Finlay about anal sex. I'd tried to ask Alfie and Ryan, but Ryan had said, 'Pain means he's got a big cock and you're a lucky bitch,' and started going on about how a small dick tickled rather than satisfied. And Alfie dismissed it, saying, 'We all go through this shit; it's just your turn.' Finlay was always making jokes about sex, but spoke more earnestly if I asked a question seriously.

'If it hurts, your top is shit,' he said dismissively.

'He said it showed he loved me, but it wasn't good for me.'

'Did you tell him that?' he asked, more kindly.

'Yeah, but he said we had to do it because it was a love thing. He said I needed it.'

'Is this the guy Eddie "fixed"?'

'Yeah,' I said, looking down at the drooping whipped cream.

'Baby, look at me. Sex is supposed to be amazing, and love is thinking about the other person's feelings. If this guy wasn't doing that, then he's a shit.'

'So it isn't supposed to hurt? It's not just because I haven't done it enough?'

'No baby, it's not supposed to hurt.' He took my hand. 'You'll find that special person. You'll find many people that can make you feel as special as you are.'

'I'm kinda scared to, now.'

He sighed. 'Some guys are twats. It's like anything else in life, some people only think about themselves and want to spoil it for the rest of us. Don't let them steal your happiness.'

'I'm happy most of the time. I just don't want to do anal again.'

'Practise at home. You probably can't have a dildo, but use a carrot or a courgette and a bit of butter or marge. Just don't put it back in the fridge. Nobody wants arse vegetables on their plate. Oh, and make sure you take it out the fridge a good hour before—'

I cut him off. 'I don't have to do it, right?'

'Here's a rule for you to live by... Your body: your rules.'

'What do you mean?'

'If you don't want to do something, don't do it. If they aren't happy with that or they try to pressure you, just move on: there are plenty of others who will respect your wishes.'

'And if they ignore what I want?' I could feel the burn in my eyes as tears started to form.

He stubbed out his cigarette. 'Don't cry for a man. You'll be dehydrated your whole life.' He glanced about us. 'Have you tried topping?'

'No one's ever asked. They all just want to top me.'

He rolled his eyes and went into a long speech about the sexual stereotypes of the less-evolved gay male. As he did so, I realised I looked at men the same way. If they were camp, I saw them as a bottom, maybe someone to be friends with, but the butch guys were potential sexual partners. I wasn't as camp as Finlay, but I wasn't butch either. Was I looking for the opposite of myself? Older, muscular, butch, dominating? Although that last one was more about my shyness. I could dance and show off as well as anyone, but making the first move came with the dread of rejection, so I'd just wait for them to do it.

My mind drifted off as he continued talking about how tacky it was to assume that young guys only wanted to bottom. Until now, I'd only thought about being a man with men. Two dicks, two sets of pecs, stubble and chest hair. My fantasies had always been about the things that were undeniably male: boxers, bulges, I'd even put some thought into armpits. The idea of the manly scent of a guy at the end of the day – that mixture of deodorant, sweat and pheromones. I quickly changed my mind the first time I worked up the courage to stick my face in a guy's armpit, and it smelt like a wet dog wearing a two-day-old t-shirt. I'd spent no time thinking about being a top, and the idea didn't appeal. It made me feel dirty and a little disgusted. I couldn't separate the idea of butt from poop. I felt the same about my butt, though less so, as my butt seemed to be so desired, and being desired made a thing okay, didn't it?

Alfie, Ryan and I arrived at the club to meet Mum a bit before nine. Tim had told us not to mention Ryan being his boyfriend to Mum. Some people don't understand the age gap in a relationship, he'd said. Mum was standing by her grey Mini Metro in the car park and smiled a sideways smile, looking me up and down. I was suddenly aware how tight my top was. She looked at Alfie, all of whose clothing was also very close-fitting, then back at me again.

'You borrowed these clothes from Alfie?' she asked.

'I was going to, but then my friend Finlay offered to get me these.'

'That's very generous of him,' she said. 'I don't remember you mentioning him before.'

'You'll meet him soon. He's amazing.'

'Where's Tim?' she asked.

'He'll be along later. Come on, let's go in. It's cold standing around out here.'

We went in and I introduced her to Eddie and Graham. I'd never seen them look so bashful, but it was a delight to watch. Especially when Mum started asking about their tattoos and what they meant. Who knew these two mountain-sized men could be intimidated by one middle-aged woman.

The club was unusually busy for the time of night but, looking around, I realised I knew every single person there. Phil bounced up to us, dragging Finlay behind him, hugged me, and introduced himself to Mum. While hugging me, he whispered, 'I called this lot to come and meet your Mum! I thought it would be fun.'

Such an arsehole.

Phil turned to Mum and asked, 'Mandy, what would you like to drink? It's on me.'

'Just a Coke please, I'm driving. I didn't know it would be so loud in here. It's been a few years since I was in a club.'

'Barry!' Phil yelled across the bar. 'Tell Robert to turn it down for a bit.'

'You have got to be fucking kidding me!' I protested.

'Watch your language around your mother,' snapped Phil. I stood open-mouthed, stunned into silence.

'That's impressive,' Mum said. 'You'll have to teach me how you do that.'

In no time at all, she was sitting on a bar stool with a crowd around her. I sat at a table a distance away, watching and not amused. It seemed like everyone wanted to talk to her, all asking for stories about me from when I was a kid. Saying how nice she was. Saying that she wasn't what they'd expected. I was terrified that they might start to trade anecdotes and try to one-up her with revelations of my drunk and disorderly antics.

Once she'd met pretty much everyone I'd ever mentioned, except, thank god, Martin and Oscar, she said she should go. Everyone pleaded with her to stay, but thankfully she didn't. I walked her out to the car.

In the relative quiet of the car park, I asked, 'So?'

'They're lovely. I can see why you like them all so much.'

'So you'll stop worrying about me?'

'I'll never stop worrying about you. You're my baby boy.' She brought her hand up to my face.

'Thank you for not saying that in there.'

'I can see why you like Finlay, too. He has a wonderful spirit.' She looked at me oddly.

I looked back oddly. 'We're just friends!'

'Okay. I'm just saying that if you were to bring a guy like that home for dinner, I wouldn't be upset at all...'

'Didn't you say you had to go?'

She laughed, and we said our goodbyes.

When I went back into the club, the music was turned back up, and all night I had to hear shouted praise about my amazing mum. How was my mother more popular than me? Soon, however, I got drunk enough to enjoy myself and have my usual great time.

I slept in Phil's bed that night, waking briefly when he got up early and went downstairs, dozing and then waking again to find Finlay pulling back the curtains.

'Where's Phil?' I asked, squinting in the bright daylight.

'Working,' Finlay said. 'He said you were sleeping the sleep of the damned when he went down.'

'Do you have any cigarettes? I can't remember where I put mine.'

He threw his pack onto the bed. And started pacing the room with expansive gestures. He was going on about garbage cans and cages, needing to scram like a stray cat, and people not belonging to each other. After a while I interrupted him. 'What the hell are you talking about?'

'It's time I blew this popsicle stand,' he said in a bad American accent.

'Are you high?'

'*Breakfast at Tiffany's...*? It's iconic.'

'You're taking me for breakfast?'

He jumped onto the bed and crossed his legs. 'Nooo, it's a movie. From a book by Truman Capote. Truman Capote? Sweet baby Jesus, this is why I don't do baby gays.'

'There's a movie about some bitch making breakfast?'

Without warning his cigarette was pointing at the centre of my face. 'You take that back right now. Audrey Hepburn is a heroine, a diva, a dame, not "some bitch"' – he spat the word at me – '"making breakfast".'

I lay down again. 'It's too early for this.'

Finlay got off the bed. 'I'm leaving.'

'Good. I'm going back to sleep.'

His voice lost all its drama. 'On a train, in thirty minutes.'

'This is the movie still?'

'Nope. Bye, boy,' he said walking towards the bedroom door.

'Wait. What? Where?'

'London's calling. This town, these people – it's all too small for me.'

'What about Harry?'

'He's partying too much and drinking too much. He's not the guy I fell in love with and it's hurting me to watch.' He sat on the bed and slouched.

'But what about me?'

'You have people to look after you here. All those people talking to your mum last night? That's because they love you. You'll forget me soon enough.'

'I will not!' I said tearfully. 'I'll never forget you. I want to come with you.'

He smiled sadly. 'When you're older, if you're in Islington, come and find me. Ask for me in any bar on Upper Street. They'll know.'

'So, you're really going?'

'That's why I wanted you to come out last night. One last night to watch you loving your life on the dance floor, and this time in the fancy new clothes you have to remember me by.' He gestured to the pile of clothes on the floor that he'd bought me. I wished I'd folded them up and put them on a chair.

'I don't want you to go.'

'I can't stay and watch Harry self-destruct, and I can't help him get better.' We both wiped tears from our eyes. 'This is love. This is the feeling. Remember that.'

'Come back and visit?'

'I don't know. If I can, I will.' He stood up. 'Hug goodbye?'

I flew out of bed and hugged him. He held me tight, we said goodbye again, and then he was gone.

Ten minutes later, Phil came in with a cup of tea for me. He was sad too. We talked and smoked for a while, then he told me to stop lying around like a trollop and fuck off home. Normal life resumed.

# 25

I got home in time to join my family for a roast chicken lunch, after which Mum brought up the subject of the youth group again. I didn't want to talk about it, so I asked about Sanford House. The bait and switch worked: it turned out my trial day was the following week.

'The week Auntie and Uncle will be here?'

'Yes. I hope that's okay.'

It was. Uncle Eric and Auntie Yvonne were Mum's big brother and sister-in-law, and they were hands down my favourite relatives. Hell, Auntie was one of my favourite humans. We didn't get to see them as much as I'd like, but whenever we did, it was amazing.

They had a smallholding in Devon, which may not sound like somewhere a teenager would be keen to spend much time, but to me their home was liberating. Eric was an artist. He favoured pen and ink or watercolour paint on paper, but was creative in all aspects of his life – especially in taking the piss and making you laugh at yourself. Auntie's passions were gardening and animals. Humans on the whole held little interest for her, but animals were a different story. You could always find chickens foraging in the garden, and for a few years she had a goat which Uncle Eric named Psycho on account of its bad temper. And for a fortnight one summer she had a sheep, until the farmer whose flock it had escaped from came to her, apologised, and promised to look after it better in the future.

'Do they know about me?' I asked.

Jenny appeared from the sitting room. 'No one cares that you're gay. It doesn't make you special and it doesn't make you interesting.'

'The only interesting thing about you is your delusions and puking up every meal.'

Jenny screamed and stomped upstairs as Mum called after her, then whirled on me with such speed that I thought she might actually hit me. 'You cross that line again and...and I don't know what the consequences will be, but they will be big...'

It was a low blow. I knew Jenny was struggling, which was why I'd thrown the comment at her. But seeing Mum that angry, I begrudgingly agreed to go and apologise.

On Saturday afternoon, Auntie Yvonne and Uncle Eric arrived with Patches, who was their dog that could travel. They had another one that had to stay home as it didn't mix well or like changes to its routine. After the chaos of Skip and Patches racing around the house, reaffirming their bond, we all settled down, and the house was alive and vibrant.

After dinner, I went out with Auntie Yvonne to walk the dogs. She had an amazing ability to roll a cigarette one-handed. She passed what she made to me.

'Don't tell your dad,' she said with a wink, and made another for herself. 'How do you feel about starting your new school on Wednesday?'

'I don't see why I can't just wait and go to college.'

'Some things in life just have to be done, my dear. And you can't let your brain go off the boil. It'll congeal. Your mum's scared, you know.'

'I felt bad leaving, but I just couldn't stay there.'

She fumbled with a lighter. 'You're not going to do that again, are you dear? I'm not sure she'd cope with it.'

A small part of my brain was thinking I wanted to go to London and find Finlay, but a bigger part knew he'd bring me straight home, so I shook my head. My aunt and I walked in silence for a bit, then I asked, 'What do you think the other kids will be like?'

'I would think they'd be nice.'

'Why?'

'If you've suffered pain yourself, you can understand each other's pain.'

I wasn't sure that was true, but I didn't say anything.

'She also tells me there's a youth group that you're resisting going to.'

'I have friends and I have places to go. Why do I need to go there?'

'What if there are more friends? What if it's a new place for you to have?'

I didn't have an answer to that, except: 'A youth group feels so childish. I don't mean to sound like a twat, but it just feels beneath me, you know?'

She smiled. 'But you know you are still a child?' I started to say something, but she cut across me: 'A big one, with more experience than you wanted, perhaps, but still a child.'

'I guess.'

'So, you'll try the youth group then? I think it meets this Tuesday.'

'Fine, but if it's shit, I'm blaming you.'

'If it's shit, I'll let you blame me. Patches!' she called suddenly. 'Patches, leave that! Don't scavenge!'

One short dog walk and she'd worked some kind of magic. I even felt like it was my decision. I wasn't going on my own, though: if I had to suffer, I was doing it with some company. I rang Alfie and told him he had to come with me.

I met Alfie down the road from the Health Project, as we'd agreed, and we smoked a quick cigarette before going in. I was dressed nearly well enough to go out clubbing: I wanted to make an impression, to show I wasn't some kid. Alfie had on his usual blue jeans and white t-shirt. I was nervous, for reasons I couldn't pin down.

The youth group met downstairs. There were two youth workers: one woman of about forty with a buzz cut and a happy face, and one man, probably thirty, kinda hot in a nerdy way. His shirt collar showed over the neckline of his jumper, and I thought the excess of fabric probably hid a half-decent body. Ten or twelve young people stood, sat or loitered in two rooms and a mini-kitchen. They were mostly guys, but one of the three women stood out as she was tall, wore men's clothes, had a shaved head and looked really aggressive. I was surprised at how old they all looked – there was a chance I was the youngest – and yet I only recognised two from the Cricks and the club. I could see why, though, as they dressed like a bunch of school friends hanging out at the park. A couple of the guys would be hot if they put more effort in, but the location, combined with their dress sense, just made them look young, rather than the grown men I was into.

The atmosphere was very casual and the lead youth worker, Lyn, was lovely, holding out an arm to hug me saying, 'Sideways hugs,' while stepping crabwise towards me. Sideways hugs meant that bodies weren't pressed together but it was still a hug. That was the idea, anyway. We awkwardly put an arm around each other's shoulders, which wasn't actually a hug at all and felt stupid. Down the Cricks we'd kiss each other hello, hug properly, and when Tim got drunk he'd sometimes grab my butt while he hugged me. Lyn was nice, but I thought she was a bit of a prude. She offered us tea and said we could help ourselves to more whenever we wanted. I nodded hello to one of the guys I recognised from the Cricks. If there were people here I knew that were older than me, maybe it wouldn't be as bad as I thought.

Everyone was nice except the angry lesbian, and our conversation wasn't as structured or managed as I'd expected, although at one point Lyn spoke up and stopped a chat between me and a nineteen-year-old called Rob. I'd asked him why he came to a youth group and didn't go down the Cricks. He said something about an over-sexualised environment, then looked at me and said, 'Life isn't all booze and sex.'

His comment felt so pointed, I replied, 'You're right; it's also about the drugs and blowjobs.'

Lyn and Terence, the male youth worker, called everyone together saying, 'It's time for our group discussion.' And we were all told to sit around in a circle. I got the sofa and beckoned Alfie over to sit next to me. Terence stood in the middle of the circle, slowly turning to look at everyone as he spoke.

'What do you think, Richard?' he asked, looking at me expectantly.

'Sorry. Think about what? I wasn't listening.' I heard Rob laugh falsely and saw him lean into the guy next to him to whisper. No wonder Rob didn't come down the pub. He was such a little bitch, no one would want him there.

'What do you think about age gaps in a relationship?'

Terence asked me.

I hadn't really thought about it. 'It's up to them, isn't it? If they're happy then they can do what they like.'

Rob's nasal voice filled the room. 'Except when one guy is underage. Then it's abuse.'

'What?! When I hook up, it's my choice. It's not abuse.'

Rob said in a patronising tone, 'Except you're a kid, so he's a paedo.'

'Are you jealous that no one wants you?'

Terence interrupted loudly, saying we all needed to respect each other, and changed the subject.

In my peripheral vision, I could see that Rob kept looking over at me. Who the hell did he think he was, saying things like that about guys he didn't even know? I didn't say anything more in the discussion, or to Rob.

At the end of the evening, Alfie, Lukas and Owen, the two guys I knew from the Cricks, made plans to go for a drink. I wished I could go with them — I really wanted to hear what Alfie had made of the group, and what Rob had said — but it was the last dinner with my aunt and uncle before they left, and tomorrow was my first day at a new school. After giving Alfie a proper hug goodbye, with a kiss on the lips, I went to the car park to find Mum. Auntie was in the passenger seat: Mum must have wanted to bring the big guns along in case the youth group had gone badly.

'So, how was it?' she asked as I got in.

'Okay, I guess,' I said, putting on my seatbelt.

'That's all we're going to get?'

'They had a big bowl of condoms and lube in little individual packets that we could help ourselves to.'

Mum tutted. Auntie, who'd been a teenager in the sixties, said, 'Sexual health is important, Mandy.'

I would rather have spent my evening with a drink in my hand at the Cricks. But if going to a stupid youth group once a week was going to make Mum happy, then I'd go. Although if Rob spoke to me like that again, I'd have more to say.

In the morning everyone was trying to be upbeat. Lots of tea was drunk, and they all asked me questions to keep me distracted from the prospect of the day ahead. Eventually we set off – a whole carful. Mum would drop me off, then she, Auntie and Uncle were going to do some shopping in town; afterwards they'd come back to pick me up. Jenny refused to come with us, even though it meant a lift into college. She said I was grandstanding and sucking up all the attention as usual. Dad had left for work already.

My aunt sat in the back with me and took my hand. I thought about what it would feel like to be doing this journey on a daily basis. Mum wasn't going to drive me from Highworth to Swindon every day. I'd need to get the bus each morning. There were no changes, but it would take an hour. Still, if I got the 8am bus or earlier, then I was unlikely to bump into anyone from my old school.

I wondered why Mum was staying in town rather than going home and coming back. Perhaps it was the length of the journey, but I decided it was more likely she was worried I might decide the school wasn't right for me and walk out.

She parked in the bus station car park 'so we can see what the walk from here is like,' she said. I lit up a cigarette as soon as we got out of the car park. She didn't say anything. We walked past Dad's office, which made me wonder if he might drive me in each day. I imagined the strain of trying to keep the conversation going five mornings a week. We passed Tesco on the main parade and walked down a wide alley that brought us to an imposing, dark brick building. It was typical of the older buildings in Swindon, built in the heyday of the railways in late Victorian times. It had tall, skinny windows with broad lintels that looked like monobrows for unattractive eyes. It was three storeys tall and its grey slate roof towered over us, giving a sense of foreboding mixed in with hints of Gothic former grandeur.

Standing on the disabled access ramp at the front entrance was a small woman of somewhere between forty and fifty, in a cardigan and sensible skirt. A photo ID hung on a borough council lanyard, and as she saw us she raised a hand and waved a bit of folded paper at us. My aunt and uncle hugged me and wished me luck, then Mum and I went over to the waiting woman.

'Are you Richard?' she asked in a too-cheerful voice.

'Yeah.'

'I'm Suzanne, your new teacher. You'll need to finish that before we go in,' she added, pointing at my cigarette. 'And this is for you. Mandy, right?' She passed Mum the piece of paper. 'It's the number to reach us in case you need it.'

A teacher saying I needed to finish my cigarette, rather than telling me off for smoking in the first place? That was new to me.

'Thank you,' Mum said, taking the note. 'He's a bit nervous.'

'Piss off am I!'

Mum looked embarrassed. Suzanne smiled indulgently. 'It's fine. It's a big day; we've all had to do it before. New school, new job, whatever it is, it's always a challenge.'

No scolding for swearing. What was this place? What's the catch?

'So, I should be back here at twelve thirty to collect him?'

'That would be great.' Suzanne looked at me. 'Okay, Richard.

There's an ashtray behind you on the wall if you're ready to go in.'

After I stubbed out my cigarette and said goodbye to Mum, who had a fearful look in her eyes that made me suddenly wonder if this was all a front for something hideous, Suzanne led me inside, explaining as she did so that it was an old building, and we'd be moving to the new one soon, which was much bigger, and we'd have our own kitchen if we wanted to do cooking lessons. She was talking like it was a foregone conclusion that I'd be coming here, rather than a trial day to see what I thought about it.

'This is us,' she said, pointing at a door marked 4B. 'Easy to get to from the main entrance. If you need the toilet at any point, it's just down there on the right. Let's go in and meet the others.'

She opened the door on a surprisingly small room. There was a horseshoe table arrangement with just five other kids in there, and a spare seat for me. I was surprised to see that they all looked normal. I guess I was expecting a room full of freaks, but they were dressed like me – casual, like it was a social group rather than a school. Another woman with an ID badge, similar age to Suzanne but blonde and looking more confident, stood waiting for us.

Gesturing to me, Suzanne said, 'Everyone, this is Richard. He's going to be joining us for today. Richard, you can sit over there by Natalie, and you can put your coat up here.'

I didn't point out it was a jacket, not a coat. A woman wearing a heavy-knit cardigan wasn't going to care about the difference. I took the seat she'd indicated while avoiding eye contact with everyone as much as possible.

'Let's do some introductions. I'm Suzanne. I have a dog and two cats, and I'm hmaphtphumph years old.' She coughed into her sleeve as she said the number. 'Go round and tell us who you are and something about you, please. We can start with you, Liam.'

I looked at the boy she indicated. He was hot. Dark hair, dark eyes, a dark brooding nature. 'I'm Liam, and I won't have to be here by next summer.'

Suzanne let out a little sigh and said, 'Ben?'

Ben had untidy blond hair and as he smiled at me he revealed teeth that were even more untidy. 'I'm Ben, and unlike him' – he flicked a thumb at Liam – 'I like it here.'

'If we could have less about being here,' Suzanne said, sounding exasperated, 'and more about being you, that would be lovely. Becky?'

Becky wore glasses and a cheerful expression. Jake was a super-nerd, with pudding bowl haircut and a face full of zits. Natalie had so much dark, curly hair it could have been shared out with two other people, and she radiated confidence. After I introduced myself, the other lady with the name badge did her bit. She was the teaching assistant and was called Deborah.

'Who can tell Richard what we do here?' Suzanne asked, looking around at the five people who weren't me.

'As little as possible,' snarked Liam.

'Thank you, Liam, but that's just you. How about the rest of us?'

Did she just get bitchy with him? This had hints of the club and my friends: it wasn't like school at all.

Suzanne started with an English lesson, saying they were reading *Of Mice and Men*, but were only fifty pages in so I could catch up at home.

Ben interrupted her: 'Read it at bedtime if you can't sleep.'

'It might not be a popular choice with you, Ben, but it's also not a choice. Today, though, we'll work on Shakespeare's sonnets.'

Liam groaned. 'They don't even make sense.'

'They do when you study them,' said Suzanne, passing out photocopies.

Before I knew it, it was 11am, and time for break.

'Remember, guys,' Suzanne said, 'don't smoke by the entrance. We're getting complaints from other users of the building.'

'We don't,' said Natalie testily. 'We haven't since you told us not to.'

'Well, someone still has a bee in their bonnet about it, so if you could try to smoke as far away from the building as possible, that would be less work for me.'

All but one of us went out: nerd Jake didn't smoke, so he stayed in.

'Neither do I,' Becky said to me in an aside. 'I just don't want to hang about on my own with him.'

Jake seemed unpopular, but I hadn't seen anyone actually being nasty to him.

It was nice to have a bit of time with the others outside the classroom. They were all quite friendly and had lots of questions but no one asked why I was there. Natalie was confident, loud, and always talking, even when no one was listening. Becky was quiet, polite, and shyer outside class than she was in it. Liam was cool and dark but didn't speak much. That made it hard for me to look at him, which I really wanted to, as he was getting sexier by the minute. And Ben was a joker. He was always smiling, and his natural warmth made me look past his tombstone teeth and see his cuteness. As we went back in we were laughing, and Suzanne and Deborah shared a satisfied look, then settled us down for lessons again. This time the focus was on maths, which I'd never liked, but was good at.

*

I said goodbye to everyone at the entrance. Mum and my aunt and uncle were waiting for me across the road. Mum looked wary. I went over, trying not to smile as I got to them.

'Well?'

'Can we get something to eat? I'm starving.'

'Your friends are watching,' my uncle said.

I turned and saw them all standing there. They started waving enthusiastically. I waved back, my face burning. 'Can we go now before I die of embarrassment?'

My lifts to school stopped the next day. Mum knocked on my door at 7am to tell me I'd miss the bus if I didn't get up right away.

At the end of the day, my bus home stayed in the station for twenty minutes before pulling away. A few stops along, looking out of the window, I saw Rob from youth group, dressed like a young Tory, sat next to a chubby South Asian guy around the same age as him. The way they looked at each other, they were clearly into each other. Rob noticed me just as the bus was moving off. I scowled at him and pretended to scratch my nose with my middle finger extended.

I called Alfie as soon as I got home. 'I saw Rob with a fat Indian guy.'

'That's Imran, his boyfriend,' Alfie said, sounding bored.

'What?' Was that the reason he didn't go out on the gay scene and didn't like the hot guys that went out?

'It's less shocking than Graham and Eddie being a couple.'

'Are they?' I was speechless. I imagined Eddie's swollen naked body pressed up against Graham's, their tattoos squished into each other, two pairs of underwear the size of pillowcases on the floor. 'Ew!'

'Not everyone's into skinny chickens like you.'

His comment hit like a jab to the jaw. It struck me then that Alfie often hooked up with chubby guys. I'd thought he did it out of pity, not because he actually fancied them. Obviously I knew people found different things hot. But we were objectively hot. Young, thin, attractive. Every type of guy came on to us: old, young, fat, thin, muscled. It felt like the only ones that didn't were the ones that hated us because we were young and they weren't. I shook my head as the thought of Graham and Eddie rutting came back to my mind, and changed the subject.

Every week from Monday to Friday, I went to school in the mornings. After school, I helped Mum play *Tomb Raider*, watched TV and gossiped on the phone with Alfie or Jo, until Jenny chased me away so she could gossip with *her* friends. As the weeks became months, Jo and Wayne found a house of their own, still in Swindon, so I was able to visit them again, and they'd occasionally come out to the club, but not often. Most weekends I'd go out with Tim, Alfie and Ryan to the Cricketers and the club: my world.

I started taking a small backpack with me, containing a change of clothes and a toothbrush in case I stayed out two nights in a row. Mostly I stayed with Phil, as that meant I got to stay for the lock-in, then watch TV with him before bed. He moved into the bigger flat above the pub. It had a spare room which he said could be mine whenever I wanted it, but I still stayed in his bed. It wasn't unusual for Mum to ring him at the Flag and check I was where I'd said I'd be. At the club, I'd open the cellar door and sling my backpack on top of the barrels in the corner. Phil affectionately named it my 'slag bag', which I pretended not to find amusing. He mostly didn't know about the hook-ups I had. He'd made a comment about my safety, so I would tell him I was just staying at a friend's if he asked. I didn't see Oscar again, although once I thought I'd seen him in the lobby of the club and froze up for a moment.

I also noticed, on separate occasions, Eddie and Phil take men to one side and have stern-faced conversations with them. The hand gestures they made in my direction told me they were talking about me. Previously I might have been upset, but this felt protective.

Occasionally I'd go to the Cricketers during the week, mostly with Alfie or Tim or both of them, and at school the next day take a nap in the library corner. Deborah would wake me with a cup of tea once she or Suzanne felt I'd slept enough. But it didn't happen often.

Guys came and went. Mostly they went. After the conversation with Rob at the youth group, I noticed that all the guys who were keen on me were older than me, and made a point of not caring. If guys my age were immature pricks like Rob – kids, basically – then naturally I was only going to hook-up with real men. And they were just hook-ups. I didn't want a relationship.

When Remy appeared on the scene, a Parisian of Senegalese heritage who had somehow ended up in Swindon, he wanted a date before he'd even talk about sex, and kept asking me for dinner, but I didn't want that. Relationships came with control, and no one was going to control me. I was having too much fun. I had my friends, my places, my family; I was even enjoying school. A relationship would just be work. I had my pick of guys the nights I wanted them. Some were more memorable than others.

Mikey, twenty-seven, had a bright smile and a Manchester

accent which I thought was so sexy I even considered it becoming something more regular. I thought it was a lot less sexy when I called his house and had a pleasant chat with his boyfriend.

Tristan, twenty-one, was verging on albino and his appearance fascinated me, but personal hygiene was a serious issue which I unfortunately didn't find out about until we were in bed. We were in Phil's spare room, so I made an excuse of needing to pee, and went to share Phil's bed, leaving Tristan where he was.

Peter, nineteen, I met in the youth group. We did actually date briefly. He was nice, but it was hard to keep my attention, and 'nice' didn't cut it.

Matteo, twenty-four, wasted my time. He was an aspiring model and one of the most beautiful people I'd ever seen in real life, with the body to match. But as we kissed and undressed I mentioned my age, and he looked like I'd told him I eat babies. I stood there, in just my pants, while he told me I was too young. 'You think I'm some kind of kid?' I said angrily. 'I've probably had more sex than you.' He eventually said I could stay, which I assumed was him playing hard to get, so once in bed I cuddled into him and reached for his crotch. He pushed my hand away, got out of bed, and went to sleep on his sofa.

Mark, thirty-four, was unmemorable. Well, that's not true. I remember him because he was so drunk he fell asleep while I was sucking him. I didn't realise until it went soft and he started snoring. Twenty quid went 'missing' from his wallet to subsidise my cab back to the club, where I banged on the doors until Phil opened up and I joined the lock-in.

One after the other, they made my nights less boring, and they all played by my rules. I said I didn't do anal, and we didn't, even though some asked more than once if they could top me. Finlay was right. My body: my rules. I said it and they listened.

The weeks became months and the next thing I knew, we were talking about putting up the tree and discussing what we wanted for Christmas.

# 26

One day, Suzanne brought up the idea of a class Christmas party. It would take place on the last-but-one day of term (because there was various admin stuff to be got through on the last day). We'd have our normal morning lesson, then after our break we'd move into the kitchen and have the party. She wanted to make it educational for us, so we were to make a menu plan and cook (home economics), she would take us to the supermarket to buy everything (life skills) and, so that maths wasn't neglected, we'd work out a budget. She tried to add in a music lesson by suggesting we sing some Christmas carols, but that idea went nowhere.

Otherwise we loved it. Roles and responsibilities were discussed, and I knew exactly which job I wanted. 'Bagsy me doing the Christmas cake, and I'll do some chocolate truffles too. Nut-encrusted for normal people, coco-rolled for any weirdos who die if they eat nuts.'

Suzanne looked over her glasses at me. 'I've told you about calling people weirdos.'

'Hey, if the prescription footwear fits.'

Suzanne glowered at me. 'Moving on. Do you have recipes for the cake and truffles?'

'Truffles, yes. The cake, I can get my dad's recipe, but I'll need brandy.'

'It's a school party. You can't be drinking brandy.'

I gave her an exaggerated eye-roll. 'We won't be drinking it. I'll need to feed the cake, and it brings out the full flavour in the truffles.'

Natalie whispered, 'Nice one.'

'Okay, we can get a miniature, but I will supervise its use and be watching closely.'

At the end of the day the others congratulated me for getting Suzanne to agree to us having alcohol. Only Becky was surprised, as she'd thought I was telling the truth. 'It's a little bit true,' I said, 'but mostly I want to see if we can get Deborah drunk.'

When the time came for the shopping trip, Suzanne said she could only take two of us. The class instantly nominated Natalie and me. Despite our best efforts, Suzanne got us around the store without having a nervous breakdown and with only one trolley race. Mostly it involved her taking things out of the trolley, then having to listen to our wild reasoning as to why we absolutely needed whatever she'd taken out. Once she'd said no for the tenth time, we'd give up and move on to the next thing we couldn't live without. The biggest discussion was about the brandy. Suzanne took a miniature from the shelf.

'Are you kidding me?' I objected. 'They serve bigger ones on aeroplanes! How about this one?'

'One and a half litres? Put it back.'

We eventually settled on a 250ml bottle. Suzanne got us to write down what we thought the total spend would be. We were supposed to have kept track as we went around, but we hadn't. Suzanne watched me and Nat load the assorted bounty onto the conveyor belt.

'I'm their teacher. We're doing a home economics class,' she said to the uninterested checkout lady.

'Let's have some fun,' I whispered to Nat. 'MUM!'

'I'm not their mother,' Suzanne said hurriedly. 'Richard, what are you——?'

'Mum, we've told you before. It hurts us when you do this.'

'I'm their teacher, not their mother.' Suzanne was blushing furiously.

'We're adopted,' I said to the checkout lady. 'She thinks this is funny.'

Nat nodded, looking serious.

'You're not adopted. You both have parents who love you.' Suzanne turned to the checkout lady and in a panicked voice said, 'I'm their teacher. I need to be here for the alcohol. They're too young to buy it.'

'She needs the brandy to make living with us easier,' Nat said.

That inspired touch made me want to high-five her.

Aghast, the checkout lady stopped scanning our purchases.

Trying hard to make my eyes water, I said quietly, 'She beats us with a tennis racket when she has too much.'

Nat had to turn away quickly. Viewed from behind, her laughter looked like sobbing.

'Richard! That's enough.'

'Sometimes she uses a metre ruler.'

Natalie started roaring with laughter. I lost my composure and laughed as hard as she did.

'Five days a week, this is my life,' Suzanne said, throwing her hands up. Unsmiling, the checkout lady began to scan the rest of our things.

I don't remember who taught me to make chocolate truffles. It was either Grandma (on Dad's side) or my first home economics teacher, Miss Montgomery. It definitely wasn't Nana (on Mum's side). She was a brilliant grandparent, and when she was told that I was gay, she called her sister Joyce to proudly pass on the news. Joyce's response was, 'Oh goody, we've got one each now', as my cousin had, unbeknown to the rest of us, come out that summer too. Despite all that, she wouldn't have taught me to make something with alcohol in it.

But I had a recipe from somewhere, and all I had to do now was increase the proportion of brandy by a factor of ten.

'Why don't you put it on the stove and reduce it?' Suzanne suggested. 'It will intensify the flavour.'

I gave her a suitably withering look. 'It will also boil off the alcohol. You're our science teacher. You know we know this.'

I found the perfect balance of truffle to alcohol: they just about held their shape when deeply chilled. The cake was in a similarly sodden state.

Deborah said, 'Rather than being fed, you've sent it swimming.'

I couldn't disagree, and I crossed my fingers that it would all absorb overnight. By the morning I was pleased to find that it had, so I gave it the last of the bottle, put it back in the fridge, and we were ready for our little party.

The next day Suzanne struggled to keep us focused on our work. She had an air of relief when she said it was time for our break and we could start the party when we got back.

Deborah refused my solidified booze truffles after Suzanne tried one and gagged on the high alcohol content, which was disappointing but did mean there were more for us. We guzzled them all and followed with the drunken cake. By this time we were tipsy enough to agree to Suzanne's singalong after all, although she probably hadn't envisaged our rendition of Run-D.M.C.'s hip-hop 'It's Like That', to which Liam did some break-dancing and nearly broke the oven door with his head.

Once my school day was done, I couldn't let the buzz go to waste, so I went down the Cricks. At that hour it was virtually empty, and after a quick drink, I made my way to Tim's. No one wanted to come out, but they helped me keep my upbeat mood going with a few beers, and Alfie lent me a top to wear to the pub.

Tim drove me. 'Have fun and don't stay out too late,' he warned. 'You have school in the morning, remember?'

'Fuck off, Dad, but thanks for the lift,' I said with a wave.

The pub hadn't got much busier, but there were enough people to make it more interesting. I did a couple of laps of the premises, said hi to those I knew, and eventually settled on the centre table as my spot. It was too tall to sit at, so you had to stand, and I rested my elbows on it, arched my back and showed off my butt to the room.

It wasn't long before the tactic worked. Soon I was approached by suitors and the drinks started flowing. While talking to one guy, I felt another hovering behind me put his hand in my back pocket and squeeze my butt. I didn't break off from my conversation, so the owner of the hand moved in beside me and tapped me on the shoulder without removing his hand from my butt.

I turned my head to see an attractive face with a big smile and kind, deep eyes. His short, curly salt and pepper hair gave him a fatherly look, but I'd guess he was only mid-thirties.

'I'm Terry,' he said, pulling his hand out of my pocket and offering it to me to shake. His biceps strained against his t-shirt sleeves, sending a tingle down my spine.

I'd seen him around but had never spoken to him before.

'Nice to meet you. I'm Richard.'

He laughed. 'Everyone knows who you are. I've been trying to get your attention for a while, but you never seem to notice me.'

'Well, here you are and here's my attention.'

He flirted as we talked, rubbing my arm, putting a hand on my hip, staying close to me.

'Let's go sit down,' I said, and we moved to a corner table. Now he wasn't in competition with other guys, he flirted less but was funnier. He complained about greying early and how it made him look old, but I said it was sexy and made him look distinguished.

'You think I'm sexy?'

'I didn't say that, did I? I said your hair is sexy.'

'I'd better get you another drink then – see if we can make all of me sexy.' He held up my bottle. 'Same again?'

'Yes, please.'

Terry got back from the bar and sat down next to me, putting his hand on my thigh. 'So, is this a date?'

'I don't know. Is it?'

We got lost in conversation. He'd been in the army, but changed the subject when I asked if he'd shot anyone. He'd then qualified as a prison guard, and I resisted asking if he'd seen anyone get shanked. I asked what brought him to Swindon. 'Civvy Street needs a family, and mine's here,' he said.

Before we knew it, the music was being shut off and it was closing time. He suggested continuing the night and having a drink at his place. I was enjoying his company so agreed without hesitation. It was a chilly night but Terry's house was only a short walk away, and the alcohol helped keep me warm.

He turned out to live in a part of town where all the houses were in tightly packed terraces and the access alleys running behind them were famously popular with prostitutes.

As he ushered me through his front door he apologised for the state of the place, telling me, as he snapped on the hall light, that he was doing it up from top to bottom. He'd got the major building work completed, including the kitchen and bathroom, but was still doing the rest. I looked around and wondered what he was worried about, as everything was tidy and seemed in good order.

'I'm going to replace all the woodwork and radiators to make it more modern. Once that's done, I'll decorate.'

'It looks good. Hopefully, I'll get to see it when it's all done,' I said, taking my jacket off and trying to act casual as I stood there.

'What would you like to drink? I don't have any of that Hooch stuff, I'm afraid.'

'That's fine. Vodka?'

'That I can do. Coke or tonic?'

'Coke please.'

'Make yourself comfortable.'

I took a seat on a big, plush sofa. It was soft, and I sank into the rich fabric. Unlike most guys, Terry had bookshelves with more than just VHS tapes on them, and real art on the walls, not posters. I looked at the spines of the books and saw textbooks on politics, religion and fiction ranging from cloth-bound Dickens and the Brontës to brightly coloured modern paperbacks. Even *Of Mice and Men*, which I'd been studying at school. I didn't recognise the art on the walls but each piece was so distinctive, I was going to have to ask him about them. Factoring in that he was hot and funny, I was struggling to see why he was single and wishing I'd paid attention to him before.

He came back with our drinks and we both angled ourselves towards each other on the sofa. As the night went on, he replenished my glass whenever it got close to empty. He pulled my legs up and put them across his lap, gently massaging my calves and ankles while we chatted. We talked for hours without ever having a quiet or awkward moment, and he didn't make a move, which left me wondering about how interested in me he was. Or maybe he liked to do weird stuff in bed. Was the perpetual massaging of my lower legs working up to him asking to do something disgusting like suck my toes?

I was going on about why I preferred East 17 to Take That when, looking at his watch, he said, 'It's nearly two o'clock. D'you want to head upstairs?'

'I'd love to, but I should go. I've got school tomorrow' – there was the tiniest flicker of his eyes at the word "school" – 'and I haven't showered since this morning,' I said, though I was thinking about how I'd get a taxi at that time of night and if I had enough money to pay for it.

'We can shower together,' he said.

I'd never showered with anyone before other than in the school changing rooms, which was the opposite of sexy, and the thought made me feel shy. But he talked me into it.

The bathroom was amazing. It looked like it belonged in a posh hotel in some faraway city: gleaming white wall tiles, grey slate floor and, in place of a bath, an enormous glass-walled shower. He rummaged in the bathroom cabinet and triumphantly produced a toothbrush for me, still in its plastic packaging. After we'd both brushed our teeth and Terry turned the shower on to warm up, he pulled me into his arms and kissed me. It was so intense coming from this gentle giant, his powerful arms around my waist. Slowly his hands went up inside the back of my shirt and we stopped kissing while he pulled it over my head. Quickly he peeled off his own and tossed it to the side. I expected him to rush because it was so late, but he wasn't tired, and nor was I.

He removed the rest of our clothes and led me into the shower. There was ample room for both of us in there, and under the warm, flowing water we pressed our bodies together and kissed more. He squeezed out a glob of shower gel and lathered himself up, then put more in his hands and caressed my body with the bubbles. There was a strong smell of rosemary.

'Turn round. Let me do your back.'

I did so, and he lathered up my shoulders. His slow gentle strokes slid down my back, then he dropped down and covered my legs with bubbles. The entire experience was exhilarating: there was something so caring about him, that made me feel secure and under his protection. He stood up and unhooked the shower head to remove the suds from my skin. He washed off my front without asking me to turn around, his big chest against my back. Once he'd replaced the shower head he crouched down, put his hands between my legs, pulled my hips backwards and rimmed me. I was shocked at first, but it turned out everyone was right. It felt good.

Once our hands were crinkling he shut off the water and dried me with an outsize and wonderfully fluffy towel, then led the way to his bedroom. The décor was mismatched with the rest of the house. A metal bedframe straight out of *Bedknobs and Broomsticks*, with a sleek, white gloss wardrobe and matching bedside tables. But an important part of Terry's body was pointing straight at the crisp linen sheets, and I was in no mood to disobey. On the bed, we rolled around pleasuring each other for a while, and then he said, 'Turn over.'

Something about the use of those two words put me on edge. 'I don't do that.'

'Don't do what?'

'I don't fuck.'

He laughed and said, 'That's not what I heard. But I just want to rim you some more. Turn over.'

Reluctantly, I did so, and enjoyed the sensation he gave me. When he stopped, I felt him moving up the bed. I turned my head to see him getting condoms and a lube sachet out of the bedside table.

'I told you I don't do that — I don't fuck,' I said, turning onto my side.

'Okay. How about something else fun then? Blindfolds?'

'You or me?' I said with a laugh.

'You. It will heighten the sense of touch.'

Because I felt a bit guilty about refusing to be topped, I agreed, and he got a sleep mask out of the drawer and put it on me. His caress made me shiver. He held his lips just away from mine so I could feel the warmth of them, and held off kissing me. He gently took my wrists and held them above my head and lay on top of me, moving himself between my legs in a slow rhythmic motion.

'You want to get a bit more fun?' he said.

'Okay. What you thinking?'

'Let me cuff you,' he said, and kissed me before I could answer.

I heard the handcuffs rattle against the wood of the drawer and wondered what other delights were in there. 'Are these the fluffy ones from Ann Summers?'

'Much better. I got them from an Army friend of mine.' I felt the cold metal on my skin as he put a cuff round my first wrist. It rasped as he clicked it closed. 'Not too tight?'

'No, that's okay.'

He lifted my right arm above my head and brought the left up to join it. I heard the cuffs clink on the metal bed frame as he looped them round it to cuff my other wrist.

'Cuffed to the bed? This won't be like some cheap romance novel?'

'Not at all.'

We kissed some more. When he had me melting, he kissed his way down my body, opened my legs, put his hands under my knees to lift them, and rimmed me again. I gasped and sighed. Then he moved back up the bed, hooking my knees over his shoulders as he did. He kissed me again while rubbing himself against me.

'Now you're relaxed, we can fuck,' he said.

'No. I don't do that.'

'Yeah you do. I've seen all the guys you go home with.'

'I don't! I'm happy to do anything else, but not that.'

Something in his voice changed. 'So they all get to, but I don't?'

'They don't get to. I don't fuck!' I said, trying to move around underneath him.

'I've heard the stories. Everyone has.' His body weight moved to one side and when he moved back, I heard the tearing noise of him opening the lube sachet. I tried to move away from him, but he grabbed my hips and yanked me down the bed. The cuffs cut into my wrists as my arms were pulled to full extension.

'Fuck. Oww. That hurts.'

'Stop fighting me then, and it won't.'

A chill went through my skin. 'Please, I don't do this, I don't fuck.' I tried to haul my legs off his shoulders, but he caught them with his arms and put them back in place. I brought one leg forward and tried to push his shoulder with my foot, but he deflected it without much effort and put it back where it had been. Then his hand closed around my neck just below my jaw, crushing my larynx. Nothing but choking noises came out of the back of my throat as the air was cut off.

'Stop! Fighting me.' His voice had no hint of the kind, calm person he'd been earlier. It could have been a different person.

He released my neck. In a gasp of air, I said, 'But I don't do this.' My voice broke as I spoke. 'I don't fuck. Please, untie me.'

'All those other guys get to have you and I don't?' he repeated. 'I bet they didn't treat you half as good as I did.' He pushed his lubed finger into me.

'Please don't do this. I don't want this.' I tried to wriggle free again. His finger still in me, I felt the lube sachet land on my stomach and his hand went back to my neck to close off my airway again. *He's going to kill me.*

'I said don't fight me.'

The burning sensation was growing where the metal cuffs were cutting into the soft flesh of my wrists. He released my throat again, and the burning got worse. 'But I don't fuck,' I said through sudden tears. 'I don't do this. I've only done it with one guy and you're bigger than him. You'll hurt me. Please.' *Should I remind him I'm fifteen or will that make him worse?*

He moved himself forward, and I felt his dick press against me. 'I'll be gentle.'

I hadn't heard him open a condom, but I didn't want to ask him to use one, because that would sound like consent to what he was about to do. 'Please don't. I don't want this. Please.'

He took a handful of my hair and pulled my head back. I could feel his breath on my face. 'I'll be gentle,' he repeated, and kissed me. His mouth over mine muffled the noises I made as he pushed into me. I tried to push him back with my thighs as the pain grew, but he held me in place. He was still kissing me. My head was locked by the handful of hair, his tongue moving around my mouth, his dick boring its way into me.

Once his hips were pressed up against my butt, he stopped

pushing. The searing pain in my butt stopped growing, but it screamed relentlessly.

'See? Not so bad,' he said.

'It is. Please take it out,' I cried, my voice wobbling.

'After the night we've had, you want me to stop now?'

'Yes, yes, I want you to stop.'

'You think everyone doesn't know how you put it about? Everyone else has had a go. Now it's my turn.' He pulled his hips back and ground back into me. The pain started afresh and the scream it created was cut off along with my air as his hand crushed my neck. I just made gurgling noises again. 'Everyone likes a moaner, but you need to keep it down.'

He took the pressure off my throat. 'Please stop. Please. You're hurting me. Please.'

He gently placed his hand on my neck. 'I need you to talk less.' He thrust again, and I made as little noise as possible. 'That's better.' He leant in and tried to kiss me. I turned my head away, but a handful of my hair brought it back to him. 'I just want to enjoy you.'

He 'enjoyed' me for a long time. The pain in my butt eventually went from live to dull, but the burning in my wrists and shoulder sockets grew worse with each drive of his hips. He loosened his grip on my hair as his rhythm increased, and stopped kissing me to grunt as he came, each grunt a breath on my face. He lay there, the full weight of his chest on mine, his ear beside mine, then with no warning, he pulled out. The sudden removal of his dick made me gasp.

'Fuck! You weren't clean. I need to shower,' he said, getting off the bed. Now he'd said it, I could smell my own filth in the air, and the feeling of being disgusting brought fresh tears. He wouldn't be angry if he'd used a condom.

I heard the rush of water in the bathroom and moved my

body up the bed six inches to take the pressure off my wrists. The blood flowed back into my hands and they went cold, then prickly.

I heard him come back in, and flinched as he took hold of my wrists to unlock the cuffs. 'You can shower now. I need to change the sheets.' Still wearing the mask, I listened to him leave the room.

I took it off as I heard him go down the stairs, and blinked in the half-light coming from the landing. There was a dark smudge on the duvet that made me want to cry again. I left the bedroom. In the bright light of the bathroom, I was surprised to see there were no cuts on my wrists. The indentation from the cuffs was there, and they were red, but they hadn't broken the skin. No proof, then. My clothes had been kicked into a corner of the bathroom, my watch tossed on top of the pile. I showered, washing gently around my arse. It was tender and swollen. I grimaced as little bits of faeces circled the drain, then I returned to the bedroom. The bed was stripped. The room looked...normal. I went downstairs.

Through the kitchen door I could hear him pottering about. The washing machine was going.

'I'm gonna go,' I called out weakly.

'Probably best. I need to make the bed after you made a mess of it.'

I mumbled a 'sorry' as I let myself out.

# 27

I had no destination. I just needed to not be where I was. I walked away from the filth I'd left in that room, trying not to focus on the feeling in my wrists. As I walked, I began to leave behind the stupid, cocky, naïve little boy who thought he had power and could behave how he wanted without consequences. I thought of Alfie, and how we never really told each other the truth. I walked for long enough to have a couple of cigarettes, drawing on each one as if its noxious fumes could fix me, cure me, wall me off from the onslaught of wretched disgust. Although I needed to get away from the scene of what had just happened, my feet moved slowly. My eyes burned from the cold, blurred by tears that were as hard as glass.

Suddenly exhausted, I sat on a garden wall. A security light flicked on behind me. My shadow stretched out in front of me over the pavement and up the side of a parked car. Someone knocked on a window behind me. I looked round to see an old lady with curlers in her hair gesturing to me to move on. I stood up and walked again. A glance at my watch told me it was heading towards four o'clock. Could I get home before my parents got up? Where the hell was I, anyway? I looked for familiar street-names and tried to get my bearings. If I set a good pace, I should be able to make it back by six-thirty.

By luck I'd been ambling in the right direction since leaving Terry's, so I kept going, just more briskly. I hadn't eaten for... what? Ten, twelve hours? I felt lightheaded. Was this all I was good for? Everyone had heard the stories, everyone knew what I was like – that's what he'd said. Did everyone know I was Oscar's cock sock for all those weeks? Was that what he meant?

Why couldn't they just be obvious bastards? Why did they have to be so nice before they did this to me? Why make me believe I'd found someone nice, make me feel secure? Why didn't they just trick me into getting blind-drunk, use me, then throw me out like yesterday's cum rag? I stepped off the pavement into the road, nearly getting hit by the only vehicle out at that time of night. Its horn blared as its tyres bit and ripped on the tarmac. I heard a shout. I just walked around the back of it and kept going. What did it matter that one more person thought I was a dumb cunt? I needed to pay attention and not be such a stupid twat, though. Where was I? This way. *It's so cold. Walk quicker; it will keep you warm.*

I neared the edge of Swindon. The direct route to Highworth ran through the countryside, meaning there would be only verges and no pavement. Even though it was still early, it was a busy road and the first commuter traffic would build the whole way, increasing the chance that someone who knew me might see me. I saw a sign for South Marston, a little village between Swindon and Highworth. If I went that way, I could avoid the main roads and get to Highworth the back way. There'd be no streetlights, but less traffic. It was a longer route though, so pick up the pace.

I wondered if it had been easier for Terry once he had put the mask on me. Which was his real persona and which was the act? The sweet cheeky guy who massaged my legs while we laughed, or the guy whose voice said coldly, 'I need you to talk less.' The way he gently laid his hand on my neck was worse than when he suddenly pushed his hand into it, blocking my airway, letting me think that I'd get to breathe again soon if I just did what I was told, that maybe I'd die if I didn't. The gentle hand was a warning, a threat of what was to come. *I need you to talk less.* I only knew his calm, friendly face, the guy who was excited to get my attention in the pub. My brain wanted to put that face to those words, but words and images just cycled back round again. *Enjoy you like everyone else does... All the guys you go home with... I'll be gentle.* I could only see in my mind the sweet guy who'd made me smile, who'd made me shy. Maybe I should have gone into the kitchen and seen him one last time, as he really was.

I made it home around the time the sky was changing colour. Could I get to my room before Dad got up? I quietly stepped into the hall. The dog heard me and stuck his head around the door into the dining room, but no one else did. I could hear someone in the kitchen, so I closed the front door as quietly as possible. I stripped off my top and trousers and hung them up behind my jacket. I saw my wrists. The bruising was now pushing purple up through the red. I put the top back on so the sleeves would cover them, but not my trousers.

'Morning, Richie,' Dad said. 'You're awake early.'

'Just couldn't sleep.' It wasn't a lie.

'Interesting look you have this morning.'

I looked down at my bare legs. 'My dressing gown's in my laundry box.'

'You could have gone for both. Top and trousers. Or is this the latest fashion?'

I smiled weakly and went up to my room. I shut the door

and sat on my bed, holding my head in my hands. I closed my eyes, but the images of Terry's sweet face appeared, making my stomach twist. *I need you to talk less.* It was so polite, but it wasn't a request. Stop ruining my fun, or I'll stop you. I hoped against hope that I wouldn't have bruises on my neck; there was no way I could cover them up. Then I must have fallen asleep, as when Mum knocked and came in, my elbow slipped off my knee and I woke up to my head falling forward.

'I thought you might have gone back to sleep. Dad said you were up early. Come on now; get a wiggle on. I'll drive you in. You'll be late if you try to get the bus.'

When I took my top off in the bathroom, I could see my wrists clearly. Red, glowing, confessing. My butt felt odd. I sat on the toilet and pushed. A dribble of Terry's cum dropped out of me. I'd never had that with Oscar. I guess with him my body absorbed it overnight. I still felt like I was moving in quicksand. *Shower quickly dumb-arse; you're late.* I could smell Terry's shower gel on me, and I wanted rid of it.

I picked out the longest-sleeved top I had, excluding button-down shirts. The cuffs would cover the marks, but pretty much anyone who'd ever met me would ask why I was wearing it.

'Have I got time for a coffee before we go?' I asked Mum when I came down.

'Not really. Are you okay? You don't look well.'

'I'm fine. I just didn't sleep well.'

'Just this once you can bring the mug in the car. Don't overfill it though.'

I loaded in four sugars. I still hadn't eaten anything.

We listened to the radio on the way, which was a relief.

'Are you sure you're okay?' Mum asked. 'You're not normally this quiet.'

'I had weird dreams all night.'

'If you're this quiet, Suzanne is going to have a peaceful day.'

I managed a derisive snort, and we went back to listening to the radio. We got to school, and Mum reached into the back of the car for her handbag, gave me some money and said I should buy anything I liked at break.

Nat and the others were waiting outside the gates and I went to join them as they stubbed out their cigarettes.

'You okay, babe?' said Nat.

'Bad sleep,' I said.

She gave me a look, but didn't follow it up.

'You'll love it today, Richard,' Suzanne said, as I joined the others taking their seats. 'We're starting with maths.'

'Can I rest and warm up first?' I said, heading for the comfy chairs in the library corner.

'All right. Just for a bit, though.'

The library corner had waist-high bookshelves. They'd built out two of them to form a square with the corner cut off. Inside, there was a beanbag and some oversized cushions. I took off my jacket and got comfy in the beanbag. I fell asleep almost instantly.

I woke startled, hearing my name called. 'I brought you a tea. Maths is nearly over.' It was Deborah. 'You gently snored all the way through it.'

'I don't snore,' I said defensively, sitting up, my brain fried and disconnected from everything.

As I reached for my tea, she changed her tone. 'What's happened to your wrists?'

'Nothing!' I said, pulling at my sleeves to cover them.

'Show me.' When I didn't, she leant over me and grabbed my hands, pulling them towards her.

Something in me snapped. I yanked my arms back from her and stood up, screaming in an increasingly high pitch. 'GET OFF ME!!!' I was trapped in the reading corner and she was blocking the entrance. My head down, my eyes locked on her, I was snorting like a bull about to paw the ground.

'Deborah?' came Suzanne's voice softly and calmly. Deborah looked at Suzanne, then looked back at me and stepped back.

'Sorry, Richard, I shouldn't have touched you,' she said. 'Sit down and drink your tea. I'll leave you alone to get some peace.'

'Fuck this!' I said, grabbing my jacket from the floor and heading full-speed for the door. I was out of the class, out through the side doors, and into the car park. The cold tightened my lungs. Where were my fags? I fumbled them out of a pocket at the same time as trying to get my jacket on and marching towards the gate.

'Richard?' It was Suzanne, her voice plaintive. 'Richard, please stop. Richard?'

'What?' I shouted at her turning and coming to a stop.

'I just wanted to say it's really cold out here, and I wish I'd brought a coat like you did.' A little smile on her face.

I grunted at her. 'You're supposed to be the smart one.'

'I can't be right all the time,' she said.

'I'll remember that next time we do maths.'

'Hopefully in the next lesson we won't have snoring in the background the whole time,' she said gently.

I didn't know how she could do it. Less than a minute ago, I was ready to break things, possibly break people if they'd got too close to me, and now I was close to smiling. 'I don't snore.'

'Can we go back in? I'm freezing out here.'

'I want to finish this,' I said, lifting my cigarette up.

She nodded and hurried back in, rubbing her arms for warmth. I looked around the car park and sighed. I couldn't go around acting like a wingnut. It would make people ask more questions. I couldn't tell the truth. I'd let him cuff me. I was complicit in what had happened. So I had to lie to protect myself from the shame of that. But the more I lied, the greater the chance I would end up getting caught out. I had to show less anger and keep everything simple. I drew on my cigarette, using the breath to push down the feeling of wanting to run. Make a joke out of it. Deflect, disarm, deny.

Natalie came flying out of the doors, pulling her coat on. 'Bitch, you're crazy,' she said as she approached me. I shrugged.

Nat and I were both a bit broken, so we weren't shocked by each other's lives. Putting her cigarette in her mouth, she lifted my arm and pulled my sleeve back a bit. She looked at me, then back at my wrist.

'I just wore my watch too tight,' I said.

'That ex I told you about put a "watch" on my ankles once.'

We changed the subject and talked about normal life until Suzanne came out again.

'Time to come in, you two.'

'We'll just finish these,' I said.

'Now!'

'Jesus! Okay lady, keep your wig on!' We went back in and Nat went to her seat. I headed for the library corner. 'Just need to warm up a bit first.'

Deborah took me aside.

'Are you okay, Richard?' she asked.

'I'm fine. Just a...just an accident with my watch,' I said.

Deflect, disarm, deny. My new mantra. I settled in the beanbag, and she didn't push me any further.

# 28

After school I went home and straight to my room. I cobbled together a selection of watches, bracelets, snap bands and other assorted jewellery to cover my wrists with colour and texture. I then put on three necklaces – two beaded and one Robbie Williams-style dummy – to make it look like I was going for boyband chic. I went downstairs and raided the fridge and cupboards, taking armfuls of snacks and junk to the sofa to watch Mum play *Tomb Raider*.

'You working tonight?' I asked, dropping the crisp packets, snack bars and other things onto the sofa.

She gave me a judgemental look as I popped a bag of Wotsits. 'I am. We have normal sessions until the Christmas holidays.'

She'd qualified as a youth worker and worked two nights a week at Highworth youth centre, spending time with many of the arseholes who'd made my life so interesting months earlier. 'Feel free to tell them to go fuck themselves from me.'

'We've actually been doing a lot of work on lesbian and gay issues and acceptance.'

I grunted. 'So, what's this bit?' I asked, pointing a Wotsit at the TV screen. 'You were stuck here yesterday, weren't you?'

'Yeah. I can't get to the ship without running out of oxygen.'

Multiple tries later, we'd found the spare oxygen tank and made it into the sunken ship without Lara drowning, but we left getting to the room we needed without getting blown-up for another day. It was nice to sit there with her, my thoughts entirely occupied by saving the computer avatar. For that small amount of time, my life was normal again. I got up and cleared up my pile of snack rubbish.

'What time did you get home last night?' she asked casually.

'After you went to bed. Glad I didn't wake you.'

'I normally hear you come in. You're not very quiet. But I didn't hear anything until your door opened this morning when you went into your room.'

'I've been trying to be quieter. Making an effort and such.'

'You remember the rule that if you stay out, you leave a message on my mobile?'

'If I had my own phone, it would be a lot easier.'

'You're not getting a phone. You don't need one.'

'Sounds to me like you just made a brilliant argument for why I do.'

'You're not getting a phone. Anyway, I don't want you staying out on school nights. You need to be fresh for class. Or at least awake.'

'Oh my god, what a backstabber! It was only maths. I'm already ahead of everyone else.'

'That's not the point. You need to be home before ten o'clock on school nights.'

'Fine. It was just a Christmas thing, anyway.'

She asked if I had plans for the weekend, but the last thing I wanted to do was go out. God only knew what Terry would have told his friends about finally getting to enjoy the slut of Swindon.

'Dad's going to get the tree tomorrow. You could go with

him and help him pick one out.'

Despite the cold, I went tree shopping with Dad. It was quite fun roaming around what was normally a car park but had now become a festive forest. Once we made a mental shortlist, we had to remember which ones we liked. We wanted a fat one but not a fat one with a skinny top. Once our exhaustive search was finally done and the tree tied to the top of the car, we got chips from the on-site burger van and went home.

I let Jen and Mum decorate the tree and sat checking that the lights still worked. The phone rang. It was Alfie. He wanted to know what time I'd be out and if I was coming to his place first. When I said no, he moved on to the rumours of me leaving the Cricks with Terry on Thursday. I said nothing happened. If I told him, he'd tell Tim, and everyone would ask why I let it happen. Why I let him cuff me. Why I was so stupid. Then I'd not just be a slag, I'd be a joke. It was easier to just say it didn't happen. Terry wasn't one of the guys we said was creepy, or even one that people said was bad news. No one would believe me.

I did the room decorations with Dad – paper chains from the light fittings, big bells in the corners and strings of metallic snowflakes everywhere else. At one point Dad said that, with the amount of jewellery I wore, I could be a decoration myself.

'It's fashion,' I sighed. 'You wouldn't understand.'

But it meant my disguise for my wrists was working.

Otherwise I spent a lot of time in my bedroom. I liked being on my own: I didn't have to put on any pretence for anyone. But it gave me too much time with my thoughts. I sketched to keep my mind busy: flowers in the style of William Morris stained glass, lots of pages of colourful ropes all intertwined. I cleared my head of everything except the need to work out which angle to cast the light from, and which bits to accent.

By Thursday, however, I needed to get out of my self-isolation, so I called Alfie and made plans for Friday.

Getting ready to go out was nice. I felt sort of normal again, and by now I could wear less jewellery as my wrists were less obvious. I didn't want my skintight trousers and t-shirts, though. I decided on a kind of goth look: baggy black jeans which no doubt Alfie would hate, and a loose black t-shirt with 'You Have the Right to Remain Stupid' written on it.

After a week in my room, being at the Cricks felt like freedom, and I drank far too much. Actually I was drunk before we got to the club. It was more of a talking and laughing night than a dancing night, and with the alcohol obliterating all my worries it was great – until I saw him. Terry. I'd got up to get more drinks, when he walked in behind some friends, big smiles on all their faces; a train of people heading for the bar.

I froze to the spot, afraid I'd lose control of my bowels. He glanced at me for a split second and something – doubt maybe; I couldn't call it fear – flashed across his face. Then his smile was back and he walked right by me like I wasn't there.

I meant that little to him? He could do that to me and now I was nothing – less than nothing?

'I guess you really did get a taxi home then.' Tim's voice came out of nowhere.

'What?'

'The way he just blanked you. Must be because you left him hanging and went home.'

'I guess.'

'His loss, mate. Plenty more to pick from.'

I looked around. Suddenly they all seemed like pigs. They all knew what I was like; that's what Terry had said. Now they were all just waiting for me to let them have their turn. And if I didn't let them... I carried on drinking. Tim asked if I was going back to his, but I couldn't. I'd have to take my wrist coverings off at some point, so I replied, 'Don't know. Time to dance.'

More dancing and more drinks. The night became a blur, and the guys did too.

At around 7am my eyes opened, and I saw a bedside clock I didn't recognise. I turned over and wondered who the guy was and what we'd done. He wasn't a regular. He was still snoring though, so I showered, noted my butt was a bit sore and saw the condom in the bin under the sink, and left. Once home, I went to my bed and slept, then got ready to go out again.

That night was similar, only this time the guy woke up before me and insisted on making breakfast. He was lovely, but kinda ugly. I must have been out of my tree to go home with him. It was awkward over breakfast as I wanted to ask what we'd got up to, but that would've been rude, and who knew? Maybe this nice guy would get angry too.

As it was the Christmas season, the club was open on Sunday too. Mum objected as I got ready to go out. 'Three nights in a row? That's too much,' she said.

'It's the party season, and it's not like I have school tomorrow.'

'It's Christmas. It's a time for family. For spending time with family.'

'We have the entire week to spend time together,' I argued. 'One last night out and then it's family, family, family.'

I thought Sunday night would be quieter, but the club was rammed. It would've been hard not to get bought drinks when the ambience was so good. But Phil took me into the cellar, saying he wanted a word with me.

'What's wrong?' he said, as I wobbled a bit and sat down on a barrel.

'Nothing's wrong. I'm having a great night.'

'You're drinking too much and something is different about you.'

'I'm a merry little elf. You're imagining it.' I got up to leave. He blocked the door and gave me a look. 'I'm fine!' I snapped.

'Okay then. What was the name of the guy you went home with last night?'

I waved a hand dismissively. 'Pfff. His name was Makes Good Eggs Guy. Who cares?'

'You're staying with me tonight.'

'No, I'm not. I'm staying with that guy in the grey top who keeps buying me shots.'

'Richard, this isn't right. What's going on?'

'Just giving 'em what they want!' I tried to leave, but he pulled me into a hug.

'Get off me!'

He didn't.

'Phil, get off me,' I said, trying to hit him, but my arms just flapped about. 'Please!' My voice broke; I hugged him back and my tears made his shirt wet.

We stayed in the cellar for quite a while, and we talked a lot, but I didn't tell him. I couldn't. That would make it all real again, and I didn't want it to be real. However, he made me agree to stay at his, and promised me the best lock-in of the year.

We went back out to the club, where I did a few more shots, and then went home with the guy in the grey top when Phil wasn't looking.

# 29

I got home the next afternoon to find Dad busy in the kitchen, getting ready for a party he and Mum were having for their friends and neighbours that evening. There was another one planned the next day for Christmas Eve, but today's was for all the people who'd be seeing their own families then. There was a giant dead fish in the sink. The sink was full of water so the fish looked like it should be swimming, but it just stared back at me vacantly, its belly cut open. I sympathised with it.

'That's disgusting,' I said.

'Whole poached salmon. Delicious.' Dad waved an oddly shaped knife. 'Want to help cut the scales?'

'Ewwww!'

He laughed. 'Skin and slice the cucumber, then. I'll arrange them as scales once the fish is cooked and skinned.'

Later, when the guests arrived, I was able to hide in the crowd and sneak drinks to dull my senses, as well as hoover up the cheese and cocktail sausages. Everyone said the same things to me:

'You've got so big since I last saw you.'

'Wow, you eat so much but you're so skinny. I wish I was like that.'

'How's school?'

'Got a girlfriend yet?'

I tired of that quickly, so took a bag of cheese biscuits and went to my room. I only had to come down when I needed a fresh drink.

Christmas Eve was better. The leftover salmon was served up again, despite my warning that it would give everyone food poisoning. There were fewer people, and a higher proportion of them knew about me being gay and changing schools, so there were fewer dumb questions. Everyone wanted to hug me, like somehow I needed commiserations. It was as if they knew what else had happened to me, which was an uncomfortable thought. What I actually needed was for people I hadn't invited into my space to back off and not touch me.

Christmas Day came and went pleasantly. Boxing Day was leftovers and more sitting about watching TV and going on the PlayStation with Mum. On the 27th we went to see Dad's parents – a two and a half hour drive to Orpington – as that was Grandad's birthday.

Dad told me I couldn't wear my jewellery, but my wrists had recovered by then, so I didn't need to. I had to wear a button-down shirt, and managed to find one that still fitted. The fabric around my neck made me uncomfortable, so I refused to wear a tie or fasten the top button. Dad stopped the car down the street from Grandma and Grandad's house, and Mum and I had a cigarette before we went in. Dad's parents had never approved of her, so it didn't matter if she smelled of smoke. I, on the other hand, had been told I couldn't smoke once we got there.

Stepping through the door, we were assailed by the smells of baking: Grandma was hardcore WI, so she always had cakes and biscuits on the go – delicious, even after so much gorging over Christmas. But it was uncomfortable for me: they didn't know about me, and Dad didn't want them told. Thankfully, they were always more interested in Jenny.

I went outside to 'keep Mum company' on a cigarette break. Dad gave us both a disapproving look.

Standing on the doorstep with her, I casually said, 'Lying is bad, right?'

She looked at me suspiciously. 'Go on...'

'Well, we're all lying about me.'

She looked sad. 'They're from a different time, and your father thinks this is best.'

'Nana is from that time too, and she doesn't care.'

She sighed. 'They love you. That's all that matters.'

'How can they love me if they don't know me?'

She trod out her cigarette. 'Always be proud of who you are. If some people don't like it, that's their failing, not yours.'

I trod out mine. 'When can we go home?'

She laughed. 'When the day is done.'


After Friday at Grandma and Grandad's, I was in so much need of a dance that, on Saturday, it was all I could think about. I picked out some jewellery, so I didn't just go from lots to none without warning. Then I selected my tightest top and the jeans that made my butt look nicest.

The Cricks was quiet when I got there, so it was easy to find Tim and Alfie. No Ryan, as he was off visiting his family. We went to the club. It was quiet, so we settled down to catch up on Christmas stories and watch the crowd dribble in. When Phil showed up, he marched over and snatched my drink away.

'Hey, that's mine!'

'You promised me you'd stay at mine and then you disappeared!'

'Did you see that guy? He was so hot,' I said, trying to get my drink back.

'You disappeared. Pull shit like that again and I'll tell the bar staff not to serve you.'

I laughed at him. 'Come on – like that's the only way for me to get a drink.'

'And I'll also tell Eddie to take any drinks off you that aren't Coke.'

'You wouldn't!'

'Watch me.' He banged my drink back down in front of me.

Tim spoke before I had a chance to. 'I think you're being a bit hard on him.'

But Phil dismissed him without even taking his eyes off me. 'You're staying with me tonight,' Phil said, 'or I'm calling a taxi for you right now.'

'Oh my god! Fine. I swear. Jesus.'

Alfie made a joke about me having a new dad and received a look from Phil that was so sharp it could have cut him. Phil wasn't normally like that, so I took it seriously, and the club was quiet, so less fun anyway. Alfie said I should come home with him. It meant no baked potato for a bedtime snack, but it also meant I could catch up with him properly. I approached Phil with Tim, who confirmed that I was going back to his place. Then Eddie wouldn't let me go without Phil's express permission, so I had to go back and ask Phil to tell Eddie it was okay for me to leave. I hadn't even realised I was being held hostage until I tried to escape. I guessed I'd just have to be good for a few nights and hope things went back to normal soon enough.

Back at Tim's, we smoked a little hash and had a few beers. I melted into the sofa as my muscles remembered they could relax. Alfie went for a shower and Tim rolled another joint, passing it to me. 'So, matey, what's wrong?'

'I'm fine,' I said flatly

'Uh-huh. So what does this new attitude mean?'

I dragged angrily on the joint. Tim could piss off if he thought he was getting it back. 'It means I'm not the nice one. I'm just another slutty teenager. They all know it.'

'"They" who?'

'All of them. All the guys that paw at me.'

'Who? The guys on the dance floor?'

'Tim, stop this!' The hash, the kindly expression on his face, was making it all too real again.

'Tell me.'

I focused on the joint, watching a bit of the Rizla go black with a tiny grey fringe as it died. With my head still down, I mumbled, 'That was what he said. He said they all know what I'm like.'

'Who?'

'He said he'd be gentle.' And there, in the quiet of a safe place, with someone who'd become a father figure to me, the barrier holding back my tears broke.

I told him everything. Alfie came down halfway through. I didn't even realise he was there until he asked if everything was okay. I told him it was fine and Tim told him to give us some space. I continued to tell Tim all the sordid, shameful, disgusting details. I just kept going. If I stopped, he was going to tell me I was stupid for letting it happen. But eventually I ran out of things to say. He hugged me.

'It's not your fault. Let it out.'

'You can't tell anyone. They'll think it was my fault. I let him handcuff me.'

'No, don't think that. How would you know he would do that? And from what you say, if he hadn't cuffed you, he could've been a lot more violent.'

I looked down again as my mind filled with jumbled images of how it could have been worse. Part of me knew he was right, but a bigger part knew that my secret was out. I was stupid. I was a slag. Everyone else would think it was their turn now. 'You can't tell anyone, okay?' I said again.

'If that's what you want, I won't.'

'It's what I want, and you can't do anything to him either. I just want to be normal and left alone.'

'Oh, mate, you are normal. Well, you're a soggy, tear-stained mess, but that's normal for you.'

That made me laugh, which was a relief: everyone had been so serious about everything recently. We talked more, Tim telling me about his time in the Royal Air Force when he'd had to hide the fact that he was gay. I couldn't see the parallels to my situation, but I was high enough for the conversation to lift my mood.

Then he said, 'One more cigarette and it's time for bed. Ryan's away, so there's room in my bed, and it saves me having to set up the camp bed for you.'

I followed him upstairs.

'You're on the wall side,' he said as we went into his bedroom. 'I don't want to have to climb over you if I need a piss during the night.'

I laughed, as this made him sound so old. Both of us stripped down to our underwear and got into bed. It felt a bit odd, and I wondered what Ryan would think as we lay there, side by side. We talked a bit more, smoked another couple of cigarettes, then Tim leant over me and kissed me on the lips goodnight, and it was lights off.

'I'm sorry you had to go through that,' he said.

I turned to face the wall. 'Me too.'

I felt him moving around in the bed, and then his hand was on my butt. 'You just need someone to love you,' he said.

I couldn't move and I couldn't move his hand. He slid in closer and spooned me, his hand sliding onto my chest.

'You're special.' His stubble scratched my skin as he kissed the side of my neck.

I didn't say anything. My mind was racing, but my mouth and body were paralysed.

His hand moved down my body and started groping at my crotch through my underwear. 'Let me show you you're loved.'

The only bit of my body that responded was the one bit I didn't want to. I could feel it swelling as he pawed at it.

'I just want to sleep,' I finally managed to say.

He kept rubbing. 'Let me show you you're loved.'

'I'm not in the mood.'

'That's not what your dick's telling me.'

He moved back and pulled on my shoulder. My body, still not doing what I wanted, rolled so I was lying on my back. He put his hand into my pants and kissed me on the mouth. His stubble was rough, and he kissed hard. It was like someone was working my face with sandpaper. He pushed his tongue in. It still felt odd, the same as the first time he kissed me. He stopped kissing me to take my underwear off, then resumed playing with my dick while sandpapering my face.

He got on top of me, rubbing his body against mine. I wanted to shout out, or move, but I couldn't. I thought about Terry, and how well saying 'no' had gone with him. I wanted to say 'stop'. I wanted to say 'get off me'. I wanted to say 'your stubble is hurting my face', but all I could manage was a lame, 'I'm really tired.'

'Turn over,' he said.

'I don't want to fuck!' I said. Not him. Not this.

'We won't. Just a tit wank, but between your cheeks.'
'What?'
'A little lube on your butt, then I just rub myself between your cheeks.'
'You're not going to fuck me?'
'No, mate. Turn over.'

I figured if I did, it would get it over with quicker, and if I was face down, then at least he wouldn't be kissing me, so I turned over.

He applied the lube and positioned himself. His weight pressing down on me was the only nice thing. The pressure felt good for some reason, like a heavy blanket. I lay there while he humped. He put his legs between mine and opened them a bit with his knees. His hump strokes got longer. Part of my brain was screaming at me to get up and get out. This was all too familiar. His strokes continued to get longer. I felt his hand move in between my butt and his hips to adjust the position of his dick.

'No, I don't want—arh!' He was inside me.
'When it's a good guy, there's no pain,' he said as he pushed in fully.

I hadn't touched or seen Tim's dick before. Compared to the others, he was small. He kissed the back of my neck and it reminded me of Oscar after he'd cum. Something small inside me, not moving much. I didn't fight, I didn't plead. This was just how things were. They didn't listen if I pleaded. I got hurt if I fought, and he was right; I felt no pain. I mentally drifted off as he humped me: my safe room let me back in. I didn't really register anything until he said he was going to cum, and I suddenly thought about the lack of a condom. Somehow it seemed part of it. He rolled off me, panting a bit. I lay there, not sure what to do with myself.

'Did you want to cum? You can wank if you like,' he said as I heard the spark of his lighter. He said a few more things, like normal chit-chat, despite how far from normal the circumstances were. Then he kissed the side of my face and said goodnight.

The sun was breaking through the gaps in the curtains when I woke up. I looked around and Tim wasn't in bed. A relief. I lay there for a bit with my feelings, then pushed them down, threw off the duvet and pulled on my clothes. The smell of Tim and his bed was still in my nostrils. As I entered the kitchen, he said cheerily, 'Morning. Well, it's lunchtime actually. Tea?'

'Please.'

Alfie was sitting at the kitchen table. A knowing half-smile appeared on his face. I gave him a half-smile back. We didn't need words.

Tim took me home, acting like nothing had happened. I chatted to him while trying to work out why. Did I mean nothing to him? Once home, I ate the lunch I'd missed. Dad had left a plate for me to microwave. The soggy reheated roast potatoes summed up my mood perfectly. Then I went to my room.

I turned on the TV but I wasn't really watching. My mind could idly look at the pictures while it attempted to make sense of what had happened. I was still trying to make the pieces fit together. A man I loved, who in some ways had been more of a supportive father figure to me than my own dad, and who'd always been there for me... How he could be yet another man who only saw me as a piece of meat, a hole, just another notch on his bedpost?

I called Alfie during the week. We talked rubbish like we normally did, but there was a heavy undertone of awkwardness between us. After a while I bit the bullet and brought it to the surface.

'Is it just me, or is Tim's dick tiny?'

He laughed. 'One time when he got me really drunk, I had to ask if it was in yet.'

'Shit, what did he say?'

'He said I had a bucket arse. He sounded a bit hurt, though.'

'Ha! I bet it didn't stop him.'

'I think he tried to fuck me harder, but it was difficult to tell.'

We both laughed. It was like I was watching us, looking down somehow.

'If I stay again,' I said, 'can I share with you?'

'You're not still in love with me, are you?'

'Fuck off! I love you, but I'm not in love with you.'

We chatted for ages, and laughed a lot, the way I guess people do who've been through something together. We could normally be on the phone for an hour or more, but that day we talked for long enough to require several toilet breaks. I felt light for the first time in ages. Alfie wasn't telling me everything would be fine. He wasn't saying it wasn't my fault. He wasn't saying I could tell him anything. That wasn't what I needed. I needed not to be alone, and now I wasn't. Better than that, I was not-alone with my best friend.

No matter how wrong the situation was, we had each other, and what we'd been through was the price we needed to pay for our lives, our freedom. Sharing my secret with someone who really understood comforted me more than anything or anyone else ever could.

# 30

I stayed at home on New Year's Eve and sang 'Auld Lang Syne' with my family and their friends. Then it was January, so back to school. Spring came and went, summer started and life was...regular. I found a balance between being a drunk slut and a grounded, sober nun. It seemed to keep everyone happy.

I stayed with Phil a lot. He gave me an education in the classics such as *Ab Fab* and the works of David Bowie, as well as life lessons like how to make battered sausages. I thought they were disgusting, but they were his favourite, and watching him try to drunkenly lower a dripping sausage into a deep fat fryer had its funny side. I nearly always got my jacket potato before bed and, within the walls of his flat in the small hours of the morning, I could cry, knowing that I was truly safe. Not every time, but whenever I needed to. He would always ask me what was wrong, but I could never tell him. I just needed to let it out, and his arms were the place I didn't need to censor my tears.

Then one day I was standing at the bar waiting to be served, and Barry the Irish barman put a drink in front of me.

'Happy birthday,' he said with a smile that sang.

'My birthday isn't until September.'

He put a finger to his lips to hush me and went back to serving other customers. It took me a moment to understand what had just happened, but as I did, he looked back and saw me smiling. Why hadn't I paid attention to this tall, broad guy before, with his super-tight t-shirt and intense blue eyes?

That night we spent his break in the cellar, talking. He asked why we hadn't done this before, and I didn't have any sort of answer, so I just said it was good we were doing it now. I kept getting happy birthday drinks that night, and the next.

The next weekend he once more put a drink in front of me and said, 'Happy birthday.'

I called him back. 'Barry? I love the drinks, but will you ask me the hell out already?'

And he did. That, and the smile with which he did it, made me happy, so I answered, 'Let me think about it,' and walked away laughing.

He was so soft, so gentle, but so big. He made me feel secure. When we walked through dark streets to his home late at night, I had no fear. I'd missed that feeling. He didn't need to be told the rules. They never even needed to come up. Things just flowed.

He tried so hard to make everything fun and exciting. One night, he got up and left me in his room. 'Wait here, I've got something new to try.' He came back with ice cream.

'I know I'm skinny, but I'm not new to ice cream,' I said.

'Not just to eat. To eat during sex, like they do in the movies.'

'Like, off each other?'

'Yeah. Although now I say it out loud, it sounds silly.'

'It's cute, but it also sounds sticky and cold, and there's this.' I pulled at my chest hair.

'Yeah, It's dumb.' He was so disappointed, it was painful to see.

'We can still eat it, though, right?' I said.

He opened up the tub. 'I've only got one spoon.'

I smiled more and opened my mouth, and he was happy again. The room was bright with his smile as he fed me.

'Still kinda like the movies,' I said through a mouthful of ice cream. 'Only now we don't need to shower afterwards.'

Barry never told me I was special; instead, he showed me that I was. I was heartbroken when he told me he had to move back to Dublin. I spent the night crying in the club again, only this time in the ladies' toilets, not the cellar. I needed lesbians to comfort me for that kind of pain. It was my first real heartbreak.

Barry and I agreed to do the long-distance thing: to call, write and keep it going. He even left me his favourite jacket to bring back to him when I visited. It was far too big, and I looked like a child dressing up in his dad's clothes, but it smelled of him.

I screwed it up, of course. Four weeks after he left, I was so excited to tell Alfie about something that had happened at school that I went out, forgetting Barry was meant to be calling. He was disappointed not angry, but the letters stopped, and the calls became less frequent. It broke my heart a second time, and this time the pain was worse because I knew it was my fault.

With Suzanne's permission, I got a job at a shoe store. When I went into school wearing my dress shirt and black slacks because I had work after lessons, everyone laughed at me. They laughed less when I always had money to spend.

The last day of term came round. Leaving gifts were given out, and end-of-term ones to Suzanne and Deborah. After Suzanne had broken up a fight about which music to play by threatening to put Radio 4 on, we were all about to leave when she asked me to stay back for a word. I told the others I'd catch them up.

'I know it's been a tough year for you,' said Suzanne, when the two of us were alone together. 'Seeing you like this makes me happy.'

'Eugh, they get a leaving gift and I've got a terrible feeling all I'm going to get is a hug.'

She hugged me in her usual careful-not-to-overstep-the-bounds way. 'You've had us worried a few times this year.'

'I'm fine,' I said. I turned to go, then stopped. 'Screw that! I'm good.'

And I believed it when I said it. Without even being aware of it, I'd become good at knowing what people wanted to see in me and giving them exactly that.

I'd divided my life and personality into different sections for different people. Which personality was actually me? The one that came closest was the one that emerged when I was alone with Phil. With him, I didn't need to pretend.

But I did think I had to hide the truth from him. As a result, I started to see him less. Plus, Phil would always say if I was drinking too much, or comment if he saw me taking drugs, and especially if he saw me going home with guys. I didn't want to hear any of that. I thought I had the situation under control and was having fun.

I was still fifteen when I was first offered money for sex, by a guy called Jeremy.

At first I laughed in his face. 'You think I'm some cheap prossie?' I said, and walked off before he could answer.

An hour later, when he offered again, the sum he proposed suggested that he really didn't think I was cheap.

He was every bit the used-car salesman: his appearance; the way he spoke, with a disarming natural charm; the glint in his eye that was endearing and dangerous... So I relented and we started meeting on a semi-regular basis. I had to start finding places to hide my cash.

It wasn't long before he introduced me to other people. And I learned that very few people thought I was cheap. The sex, like the guys, was unremarkable, but the drugs on that circuit were top-notch and, for me, free. These men wanted a cute, dumb, easy boy, and that's who I gave them. The kind of boy who giggled when a group of middle-aged men wanted to do lines of coke off his dick.

Tony, a Londoner in his fifties who called himself Italian even though he had an East End accent, was the only one of them who looked past what I was showing and saw me. And I guess he saw the potential I'd been wasting in Swindon. Just before my sixteenth birthday, I found myself drinking champagne in a limo on my way to a high-profile client. Other similar bookings followed. Each client wanted something different, and for each of them I gave them the personality they ordered. The entry-level jobs I had by day became a front to explain how I always seemed to have money.

My actions and my choices were my own, and I won't make excuses for them, but I wonder how my life might have turned out if I hadn't been so effectively taught that my value and worth were intrinsically linked to my physical appeal.

Tim moved from Swindon to Bristol around the end of 1997, taking Alfie and Ryan with him. The following summer, he picked me up on the way to London for Gay Pride. When he dropped me back home in the small hours of the morning, I waved him goodbye for the last time in what would turn out to be more than twenty years.

Tim not being in my life, nor having any degree of control over it, allowed me to go further off the rails. Alcohol was my crutch of choice. I pretty much stopped going out on the gay scene, which meant I saw nothing at all of Phil, my anchor to reality. I finished school, not caring that I only got three Ds. What did my grades matter when I had a safety deposit box in London filled with possibilities? But then my client list started shrinking, as the 'classy young man' who could chameleon into any situation started showing up drunk and high.

I took it as a personal insult. They were taking away my means of validation, so I got on a train and showed up at one guy's office. I was sixteen going on seventeen and I walked into a London corporate lobby dressed like a tart. The fear on his face was worth every second of the embarrassment I suffered on the way there.

At first he didn't seem to take it too badly. My pager went off two hours later, booking me for that night. But it would prove to be my last job. I don't think I'll ever be able to say out loud what happened. Let's just say I came to in the early morning and attempted to hold my head high as I limped through Mayfair. My clothes were torn and my left eye was swollen shut. I went to the staff entrance of a hotel where the concierge liked me. He arranged for a doctor to look me over, gave me something less tattered to wear, and suggested it would be a good idea for me to stay away from London for a while.

I was blacklisted and my name and reputation were trash. I had no choice but to be 'normal', but not only did I not know how to do that, I no longer knew which of the various personalities I adopted was the real one. When I wasn't working those entry-level jobs, I drank. Being anaesthetised by alcohol felt like the truest available version of me.

At one stage I managed to get my drinking under control. I bought a selection of tailored dress shirts and got a job at the head office of Thames Water. I worked in a server room, selecting calls to be monitored or reviewed. On my third day, I bumped into a guy from the parties of my past and ended up in his office. He was a senior manager, with a photo of his wife and kids on his desk. After he'd fastened his belt, he took out his wallet and pushed a few banknotes towards me. I felt wretched taking them, but they weren't banknotes to me: they were vodka and maybe some speed.

As the new millennium dawned, I quit yet another job, only this time I didn't look for another one. I still had some stored cash, so I moved into a flat above my parents' garage and started rejecting the world. I turned down invitations to go out, and people stopped contacting me. I didn't care. I didn't want to be around other people. Swindon had one 24-hour grocery store, and every few weeks when my cupboards ran dry, I'd go out at 2am to refill them, knowing the shop would be empty and I wouldn't have to deal with other humans.

Spending time with Mum became my social life. In this tiny new world of mine, the thought of the real world beyond my little flat became a horrific prospect. One time I tried to cut my wrists in the bath, but I used a safety razor and couldn't make it work. My tears were washed away as I slid under the water, but I wasn't brave enough to inhale. However much I wanted a permanent silence, and even though I believed everyone would be better off without me, I just couldn't do it. I sat on the floor draped in a towel with my back to the bath. As my childhood cat, Tibbles, tried to lick my legs dry, I wailed. She cared more for me than I cared for myself. She was the reason I didn't go to the kitchen to get a knife, and instead went to find Mum.

My mother got on the phone while making a pot of tea, then drove me to the doctor's. She came into his room with me, just like she had when I was beaten up at school. We left shortly afterwards with a prescription for some little pills that would, apparently, fix my self-loathing. I took them, gradually upping my dose until I could convincingly say I no longer had intentions of killing myself.

With the pills numbing my anxiety, I tried going out on the gay scene again. The pub and club of a few years before had both gone, to be replaced by different versions. I mostly hung out and danced with the lesbians, but the lure of men looking at me stirred something inside me. I had the occasional hook-up, but it was unsatisfying. I couldn't fake it any more; I could no longer get the old gratification from their desire.

I moved on to internet chat rooms, where I made use of Mum's state-of-the-art digital camera – a whopping 1.3 megapixels – to develop a side-hustle selling pictures of my feet, as well as other body parts. Then one day, in a local chatroom, a window popped up asking how I was doing. I clicked on the associated profile and laughed at the guy's pictures. Objectively they were sexy, him lounging in various positions in different brands of underwear, but his expression was priceless. He was trying to look alluringly at the camera, but failing. In his last picture, he was in full Scottish dress.

'A Scotsman, aye? You're a bit far from home.'
'So far that I don't even have the accent any more.'
'LOL. How you doing?'
'Good but really hungover. You?'
'You know the best cure for a hangover?'
'I'm Scottish, remember. Irn-Bru.'
'Well, I was going to say a blowjob, but sure, you can have

some metal-flavoured fizzy pop.'

And that was it. The man who made me laugh at first sight, and who would go on to become my husband, came to pick me up. He was unlike anyone I'd ever met, and we spent all day sitting in his apartment chatting and sharing stories. By the time we went to bed, it was literally bedtime, and the next morning he woke me up to say he had to go to work.

'No, it's fine. Stay there,' he said, as I made to get up. 'Pull the door shut if you want to leave, or I'll be back around eight if you want to have dinner.'

By day three, I needed to go home, but as he drove me back, we arranged another meeting.

Something in the way he could instinctively read me was completely disarming. By that time, I hated people touching me. Whether it was knees touching, hand-holding, a shoulder rub or, worst of all, snuggling, I loathed it. But something in me still needed physical affirmation. The first time Jon and I sat watching TV together, I reached across the sofa, gently poked him in the shoulder and said, 'boop'.

An hour later he did it back to me, and by the time I moved in with him, that was our love language. We could even do it across a room at a party, just mime it to each other. I didn't need to explain myself or try and set a boundary; he just recognised it and accepted it. We laughed, we cried – well, I did – and we watched TV, which is my favourite pastime. I learned to cook more than just spag bol or lasagne, and no matter how much of an epic fail my attempts were, he was always supportive.

Our first row was a doozy and, like a lot of couples' rows, it was over something completely insignificant. When he got home the next day, I was packed and ready to leave. I just needed him to drive me, as I had so much stuff. I couldn't understand his shock and sadness. The row had been big; things had been said that couldn't be taken back; things were obviously over. But Jon had lived a different life to me, so that wasn't obvious to him.

A conversation and a gin and tonic later, I looked at my bags and said, 'So I packed for nothing?'

# 31

I trained as a youth worker. Ironically I ended up working at the new incarnation of the gay youth group I'd once fought so hard not to attend. I always kept a special eye on the young people who were too quiet or emotional, or who exhibited behaviours older than their years.

I was routinely given meds by a GP, and was seen by psychologists, counsellors, mental health nurses and a psychiatrist. I never told them about my past, only my present. I didn't understand my past, so how could I describe it? I accepted their diagnosis of anxiety and recurrent depressive disorder and, even though I hated the pills, I took them when I was told.

I continued to struggle with validation. It was obvious that Jon loved and appreciated me, but something in me needed to be an object not a person. I'd spend hours each day in different chat rooms flirting, exchanging pics, hoping to be adored by anyone who would pay me attention. I even made plans to meet some of them, but would always ghost or block them before the meet actually happened.

Jon and I moved from his flat to our first house, and I took up vegetable gardening. Domestic life suited me. I could potter about all day and when Jon came home I'd be able to provide a meal. Then one day a couple of artists came to work with the youth group to make costumes for a parade, and I ended up in their studio with a canvas and oil paints. I took to it with ease and passion. I not only started working with them delivering art projects, but also creating my own work in my spare time. So now I was an artist too.

Life was never completely settled. Jon kept getting promoted at work and, as he became more senior, he'd spend more time at the office. That made me look for attention elsewhere, and I remained as vulnerable as ever to flattery from manipulative men who wanted to possess and control me. In one disastrous episode, I ended up having an affair with a particular admirer and actually splitting up with Jon and moving out to my own place. But it ended appallingly, with the new admirer sharing me out for sex with his friends, and then screaming at me when I dared talk to a friend of my own in a bar.

That night, he locked me out of his flat. Rather than return to my own home, I realised I needed Jon. It was past 1am, but I still had keys to his house. I got in my car and drove over. When I climbed into bed, he turned and hugged me, the world went quiet, and I slept.

Jon and I got civil-partnered in 2013, ten years and countless rows after we first met. We'd said we wanted to wait until actual marriage was legalised, but we needed to be spouses for visas so we could move to the US. Jon had been offered a job in Delaware, halfway between New York and Washington DC.

I was now in my early thirties, and I was beginning to understand myself more. Importantly I had begun to understand how other people affected me. Over the ten years we'd been together, both of us had made mistakes, had conversations with third parties that were inappropriate, and been pursued by others. But we were now closer than ever. We also had a good standard of living, because Jon was well paid.

One day he came home from work and I could tell there was something on his mind. As the evening went on his silence grew, as did my unease. Eventually he said, 'Can we talk?'

Big red siren lights went off in the back of my mind, but I didn't show it.

He stumbled over his words, started and restarted his sentences, and eventually said, 'I've been offered a job in Ohio.'

As a result of both the emotional build-up and a strong desire to not live in a square state without an international airport, I burst into tears.

'Shit. Fuck. Sorry,' he said. 'It's Singapore, not Ohio. I thought that would be funny.'

I cried more, this time from relief. I also smacked him on the arm and called him a few names. Then, as my geography is terrible, I asked which part of China Singapore was in.

Singapore proved to be a different world. Everything was manicured, designed, perfect... Even the motorway verge was planted with flowering shrubs and trimmed to shape. People smiled, ambled between destinations having casual conversations with friends, and everyone seemed to know and appreciate the rules and laws, both societal and judicial. I like rules, especially ones that make sense. The structure they give me is a comfort.

After we were settled, my view of the country became more nuanced. We had one very close friend who encapsulated everything I thought I had seen in the society: he was generous with his time, interested in people and kind on a level that I just wasn't used to. However, I gradually realised that most other people behaved that way publicly, where they could be seen and judged, but not privately. While Jon and I built an amazing circle of real friends, it still felt like we were living in *The Truman Show*. Or we'd moved to Disneyland and were starting to learn that all the mascots had recording devices in them and the management was fond of using corporal punishment and the death penalty.

I'd always treat myself to some time away after Christmas, and simultaneously treat Jon to some time to himself. It was also a good way of exploring the region of the world that had become our home. In January 2020, I flew to Hanoi to spend a month in what I had come to consider as my food heaven. I'd arranged to meet my sister, who was flying out for a tour of Cambodia and would then join me in Vietnam.

I took her to a café I loved, which overlooked a road junction that was normally the most perfect organised chaos – a ballet performed by vehicles. Today, however, it seemed quieter.

'It's normally more chaotic than this,' I said. 'This flu that everyone's talking about is being taken really seriously here.'

I'd just arrived back home, at the end of January, when Singapore closed its borders. Then, one by one, Jon and I watched the other countries around us do the same. My visa was due to expire at the start of May, but surely the madness would be over by then.

Mum, Jen and I all kept in regular contact as the situation developed. (Dad wasn't really part of our lives by then.) We didn't have much else to do by March, as the entire world was told to stay indoors. I was on the phone to Mum one day, talking about someone who'd tried to make me feel inadequate. I heard myself saying things that sounded like it was someone else's life: 'I like my life, and I like who I am. Get on board or get the hell out of my way.' With all the isolation and time to think, I was turning a corner and accepting myself for who I was.

Mum had been in isolation since the start of the pandemic.

She had rheumatoid arthritis, which is an autoimmune disease. The medicines she took to control it meant she barely had an immune system. By April, she was in a Covid ward. After a few cheery photos from her hospital bed, the Facebook messages slowed, then became just a thumbs-up. I would send her a picture of the sunrise or sunset from my balcony on the other side of the world, and the 'read' icon was all I needed to see.

Compared to some other families, we were lucky: Jen was allowed onto the ward to be with her. One day, sensing the end was near, Mum told my sister, 'I'm not worried about Richard. Tell him I'm proud of him and I know he'll be fine.'

Later that night I got the call that she'd died. Mum was my one true constant – the person who had protected and fought for me all my life. Gone.

A month later, still reeling from the devastation and loss, I boarded a plane to the UK, leaving Jon, the cats and my home behind. I was living in Singapore on a tourist visa which had run out, so I needed to leave the country and then come back in again.

'It will just be for a month, maybe two. Worst case three, then you'll be home,' Jon had reassured me.

Jen picked me up from Heathrow and brought me back to her flat in Swindon. The plan was for me to stay in her spare room until the hotels re-opened. I'd had a blow-up mattress delivered, and she wedged it in between her desk and a bookcase, leaving just enough room for my suitcases.

The part of me that was an annoying little brother had never really grown up. Jen soon tired of me sitting on the sofa playing loud games on my phone. With all the subtlety of a big sister, she said, 'Why don't you do something creative, and stop just taking up space and making noises?'

I had no access to any art materials or space to make any

artwork. As Jen has a degree in creative writing, she suggested I open up a Word document and write something.

So I did.

Until I started writing my history, I hadn't realised quite how much I'd blocked out. More than two decades of saying, 'I'm fine; I've dealt with it; it's in the past.' But I hadn't dealt with it. All I'd done was put everything in boxes, closed them up, and put those boxes somewhere I thought they couldn't hurt me any more. As I started opening each of them, I understood how much they'd been festering in the dark.

Slowly the words I was writing stopped making me cry so much, or making my heart race. Laying everything out in a clear timeline for the first time allowed me to see what I'd always considered to be a series of separate incidents as a chain of events. I recognised the manipulation and abuse for what they'd been, not as I'd got used to telling them.

Over the years, I'd told Mum parts of what had happened to me. She knew I'd been assaulted, but not the details, and definitely not who by. How would that have made her feel? She had made the best decisions she could, and had made them thinking only of my welfare. I would have hated her to feel responsible or guilty if she knew everything that happened. I think that's why the first draft flowed relatively easily – because Mum was no longer there to read it.

In her stead, Jen was the perfect companion as emotions I thought to be long dead started to resurface. She never expressed platitudes like, 'It's not your fault,' or 'You're safe now.' She knew exactly where to put the blame and said 'keep going' whenever I started to clam up.

She was the first person who ever challenged me on what I was saying and made me look at things clearly. I didn't know, for example, that I shouldn't be saying things like, 'but he looked after us,' and 'Compared to the others, though...' to defend Tim. The layers of manipulation beneath which he had buried his actions were so effective that, twenty-four years later, I was still under his influence. As a result of my sister's honesty and directness, it all became clearer. Just because I had no physical injuries after Tim had used me, I shouldn't classify him as any less harmful than the others. He wasn't just a rapist, he was a predator, which actually made him more dangerous than the rest of them.

Jen listened, offered support and didn't allow me to continue shouldering the weight on my own. We discussed my options, including calling the police or other places of support, but in the end I turned to Alfie and Phil.

What Alfie and I had been through created a bond between us which I hope will never be broken. We lived it together and no one else can ever understand it the way we do. We drifted apart after Tim moved him to Bristol, about which I still feel hugely guilty. I was safe, I could try to move on, and although it wasn't a conscious thought, Alfie reminded me of times and actions I wanted to forget. We finally reconnected on Facebook in 2013, exchanging a few messages, but there remained a wall of unaskable questions between us.

Phil and I had kept in contact thanks to his determination. I'd change my phone number or move house and not mention it, but he always found me. In 2005 my phone rang with an unknown London number, and when I answered, it was a joy to hear his big cheery voice. We talked for hours and he kept asking about my health. I hadn't spoken to him since before my breakdown, and I assumed he was talking about my mental health. I told him I was doing well.

Now, in 2020, I revived both of those friendships and allowed them to flourish. With Alfie, I spoke properly for the first time about what had happened, starting with messages during lockdown, and eventually we met in person. Somewhere inside the gruff, fat bear he'd become, hid the young man I had loved at first sight. Twenty-four years of not saying the real words didn't make speaking about our past any easier, and I still wasn't brave enough to say sorry for leaving him with Tim. But he and I talked everything else out, using real language not euphemisms for the first time.

We spoke about what Tim might be up to, now the internet had become such a fertile ground for predators. At first, we ended up concluding it was all too late and we'd waited too long.

When I related all this to Phil, saying we'd decided not to call the police, I can't have been sure about that decision, because I added, 'I can't stop thinking about what's on his hard drive now.'

'You're not responsible for that,' said Phil. 'But why don't you google him? He was never that bright. If he kept on doing it, he'll have been caught at some point.'

That night, after Jen had gone to bed, I did what I'd actually done many times over the years: I typed the name 'Tim Darch' into Google. This time, however, because of how I now looked at my past, I added a third search term: 'paedophile'. I hit return, and the world stopped moving.

*Richard: 21:51 1st July 2020*

Link sent to Alfie. Article headline: 'Paedophile escapes justice'

This is him, right? Right age, right location, right sex of victims. But the name? Did he use his middle name with us?

*Richard: 22:21*
Alfie! Fuck! Look at your fucking phone!
*Alfie: 22:34*
Wide-eye emoji x 2. Yup, that's him. I forgot that Tim wasn't his first name, but that's him for sure.
*Richard 22:35*
fuck
*Richard 22:36*
I have to call the cops.

The article I'd found detailed the conviction of Julian Timothy Darch at Swindon magistrates' court in August 2017 for making and possessing illegal images of children. Some of the images were category A – the most severe type. Despite pleading guilty on ten counts, he had escaped with just a £250 fine, plus an entry on the sex offenders' register. I couldn't help but imagine the nameless, faceless boys, scared and alone with Tim and his camera. And part of me died, knowing my silence had allowed that to happen.

The article included a comment from Wiltshire Police, who said they encouraged anyone who had been a victim of sexual abuse in any form to contact the police, regardless of how much time had passed. They seemed to be talking directly to me, and I made up my mind. Almost exactly twenty-four years after I'd first met Tim, I committed the ultimate betrayal, as he would have seen it, and did what he always told me never to do. I gave his name to the law.

'They don't help people like us,' he'd said all those years ago. 'They leave us alone and we leave them alone.' He told me they victimise us, they don't believe us and even if they do, they don't want to help gay people. He'd said they couldn't be trusted and they'd find something to charge us with, even if it was just wasting their time.

But they believed me.

I was interviewed by CID, first at home, and then at the police station, where I put my testimony on video. In December of that year, Alfie did the same. By November 2021 the police had found Ryan and he was on record too. Other witness statements were taken, Tim was brought in for interviews and, in October 2022, he entered a plea of not guilty to multiple counts of rape of a child, indecent assault of a child, and also counts of rape and assault of an adult.

After a series of delays which added to the debilitating emotional turmoil, the case came to trial in February 2024. Jon and I had now moved to Malaysia, but I found myself back in Swindon, the place where all this had started, waiting in a witness room at the Crown Court.

I appeared in the witness box twice, for around two hours total. All the witnesses had been instructed not to communicate with each other, meaning that Alfie and I were each separated from the only other people in the world who really understood how we were feeling. As witnesses, none of us was allowed to be in the court unless we were testifying, so when the jury went out to deliberate, we had no idea what had happened other than when we were on the stand.

Two agonising days later, the police detective who'd looked after me since my first interview – my knight in shining off-the-peg suit who was fast becoming a proper friend – started to talk about the possibility of a hung jury and a retrial. The prospect of going through it all again totally floored me. I was still in tears when I received two more texts from him:

'Guilty on all eight counts.'

'Remanded until sentencing 28th March.'

On 28 March 2024, Timothy Herbert Darch – aka Julian Timothy Darch, aka Cllr Tim Darch, until recently a member of his local parish council – was sentenced to twenty-two years in prison.

On the other side of the world, at our flat in Kuala Lumpur, I felt a wave not of euphoria, but of grief and guilt. Tim had once been my protector, and I had done this to him, so what kind of monster did that make me? It was only gradually that I came to recognise my reaction as yet another result of Tim's manipulation. He had got inside my head at such an early age that I still felt somehow responsible for him, despite everything he had done to me.

The verdict also made me feel oddly disabled, not knowing what shape my life was any more. For four years, the investigation and trial had been all-consuming, and now it was all over.

It took me a few days to understand that I was free.

# 32

After the dust settled, I still felt like a shell. For four years I'd neglected friends because I couldn't focus on anything other than the case. Now I reached out to the world, and some of the world reached back. I made new friends, and one of them said something that really got my attention. 'Have you ever been assessed for autism?' he asked.

Not long afterwards, I found myself in a psychiatrist's office. And at the age of forty-two, I found out that my lifelong mental health struggles were actually symptoms. I was diagnosed with autism and attention deficit hyperactivity disorder (ADHD). In trying to cope with and mask my issues, I'd given myself obsessive compulsive disorder (OCD). As a result of my early trauma and my attempts to function in a world where I had tried to make myself fit in, I also needed treatment for post-traumatic stress disorder (PTSD) and its more complex version, CPTSD.

Jon was amazing, as he always is, discreetly watching videos and reading up on how to accommodate my conditions. He didn't need to change anything he was doing; he just changed how he delivered news or asked questions. One day, at around 5.30pm, he stuck his head into the room where I write and paint and said, 'It's fajitas tonight.' (That's a dish I always cook.) Would you like dinner at six-thirty, seven or seven-thirty?'

Normally I get instantly grumpy if I'm disturbed when working, especially if that disturbance involves a demand on me to do something. This time, I just cocked my head and said, 'Seven, I think. I'll be out in a moment when I've done this email.'

I didn't finish the email, as I remembered my psychiatrist saying that if I give myself options rather than demands I may find it easier to get things done.

'Did you just life-hack me?' I said as I came out of my office.

Jon laughed, and I told him I loved him and that he was a dick.

I had a lot of homework to do to prepare for the intensive trauma therapy I was about to start, and something clicked into place for me. I've always held shame for what happened, and although I would tell anyone else who had experienced assault that it wasn't their fault and they shouldn't blame themselves, I could never make myself believe it.

Despite its name, ADHD isn't really about attention or hyperactivity. It's actually a dopamine disorder. Dopamine is the chemical that most people's brains release as a reward on the completion of a task – the happy hormone. Our brains don't do that. We only get dopamine from things that stimulate and excite us. As a result, we end up repeating those particular actions. That's why around a third of young people with ADHD have problems with substance abuse, and a quarter of those who seek treatment for addiction also report having ADHD.

Autism, meanwhile, involves all sorts of differences in how we process stimulus and interaction. We're stereotyped as only being able to think in facts because of our tendency to take everything literally. We trust people and believe they are telling the truth if they say they are.

I felt like screaming through my tears. Without my knowing it, Tim had given me a constant dopamine trail: drugs, alcohol, friends, the pub, club, new experiences. And when he told me everything was fine and normal, I believed him.

*It wasn't my fault.*

That was the first time I had ever said it and believed it.

To call Tim 'manipulative' barely does justice to the deceptions he spun all around him. Those of us he raped were not his only victims.

In October 2020, before the case began, I met up for dinner with Phil and a few others from the old Swindon gay scene. By 1am, Phil and I were drinking in his hotel room. He was bitching about how there was only Budweiser left in the minibar, after I'd taken the vodka and red wine, but we also talked properly for the first time. He obviously had questions that he couldn't find the words for, and as his tears became snotty and ugly, I asked what was wrong.

'Let me ask you this,' he said through his sniffing. 'Are you HIV-positive?'

The question came so far out of left field that I laughed, whereupon he called me a twat.

Looking back, it's a minor miracle that I'm negative. But I couldn't understand why, of all things, that's what Phil wanted to ask. Until he told me.

All the way back in 1996, Tim had approached Phil and asked to bring another young person to the club. Phil had never wanted to allow Alfie and Ryan in, and he definitely didn't want a third. But Tim told him this 'young man' had been abused and now had HIV, so he wasn't going to live for very long. (HIV was still a death sentence back then.) 'So let him come here and live what's left of his life,' he urged. Then I showed up at the club.

It took a while before this sank in and I understood what it meant. And not only did *I* then ugly-cry, it made me love Phil all the more.

That was why my having bruises wasn't unusual. That was why I got away with murder in the club and Phil protected me no matter what. That was why he never pushed me to say what was wrong. That was why he always found me when I vanished from his life. And that was why he wasn't confused about me crying so much. Because he thought he knew why.

Suddenly the abuse I'd experienced, which had until that point been so personal to me, was bigger. The ripples of Tim's words hadn't just affected me, they'd flowed out to other people and across the decades. I was left with a question I will never have an answer to: what had he said to my mum?

I've thanked Phil many times over the years. But until now I've never thanked him for just letting me cry. He means the world to me. I often think how different things could have been if I had told him everything back then. I guess I didn't because his flat and his time were somehow separate from the real world. A special, safe place where the world was shut out, the noise was turned off and I could always get a baked potato and a cuddle.

Not long after that revelatory hotel-room conversation with Phil, I got to know the staff at the Swindon and Wiltshire Sexual Assault Referral Centre.

In the middle of a pandemic, I could only deal with them by phone, but that was a massive help nonetheless. I was able to say things out loud, in detail, which I'd never told a stranger before. I heard the word 'rapist' used to describe the man I was telling them about. Usually, trying to be tactful, people say 'attacker', or 'the guy that did that to you'. And one simple question shook me for a couple of days: 'Was it violent?'

I genuinely didn't think of what had happened to me that way. In my mind, violent rape involved someone being dragged off into a bush by an unknown assailant and ending up in a hospital. I now know better, of course. I've seen statistics that say one in three women are raped, one in six children, and one in eighteen men.

Let those figures sink in and look around the room you're in.

If not you, then who?

We're never alone. We're just silent.

# Some parting thoughts from me

I'd like to start by thanking Simon Edge and Dan Hiscocks at Eye Books. The day Simon's email popped up on my phone asking for further information, I leapt off the sofa with such enthusiasm, I pulled a muscle in my leg. And although I was limping, I still managed to run to my office to reply. I know Dan took longer to come around. Until he spoke to me, I don't think he understood that the arsehole I was two and a half decades ago is not who I grew up to be. I understand his hesitation: I don't think I would like fifteen-year-old me. But I took it as a compliment that I'd written myself as I truly was.

My publishers haven't just allowed me to get my words into print. They have also given me faith that I could achieve something that somebody else might value or recognise. I have a long way to go with self-belief and self-worth, but they have helped me on that journey in ways they may not understand.

There are a lot of real people in these pages, even if they aren't all identified by their real names. They all played a significant role in my life – some positive, many negative. All of them made me who I am and changed me forever. I'm no longer angry at those who harmed me. To those who've helped me, stood by me and fostered the good traits within me, thank you.

In earlier drafts, I disguised the name of the Swindon Gay Men's Health Project because I didn't want to vilify anyone who worked there at the time; I don't believe they actually knew what was going on. But obviously they should have done. 'Safeguarding' wasn't a word we heard so much back then, but my story shows why it matters. Allowing Tim to operate within the organisation required a level of institutional naivety. The project was not to blame for Tim's actions, but I should never have been introduced to him. I hope that lesson will be learned by anyone in a similar role today.

If you're wondering whether there were links between Tim, Oscar and Terry, you're not alone: the police wondered exactly the same. I'm certain there was no link between Tim and Oscar, but I can't say the same for Tim and Terry. What happened with the pair of them could just have been a coincidence, but it's crossed my mind that it was more. I wouldn't put it past Tim to have arranged it like that, to see if I kept rapists' secrets.

When the police found Ryan and asked if he was willing to help with their investigation, I talked to him briefly on the phone. It was the first time we'd spoken in more than two decades. We were never really friends. Alfie was my friend, and Ryan came as part of that deal. Tragically, not long after Ryan made his statement to the police, he was diagnosed with cancer. I'm very glad he made that statement and I'm thankful that he was able to see Tim convicted before his own untimely death. I hope the outcome of the case brought him some peace.

I worked with or was supported by a range of people and organisations during the investigation and trial. I'd like to say I'm grateful to all of them, and that's nearly true, but I don't have warm feelings about the Crown Prosecution Service. From my point of view, as one of the victims and the main complainant, it felt like the conviction was achieved in spite of, not because of, them. I could bore you with my thoughts on this for the length of a whole other book, but I'll confine myself to this: I was shocked to find how badly the system is weighted in favour of the defendant.

I'm thankful for the dedication of Ross Duff, the police detective who held the case together and got it across the line. Swindon and Wiltshire Police are lucky to have someone like him working for them, and I'm eternally grateful that he was on shift when I had my first interview. He's the man I told there were monsters under my bed; when he found one, he didn't stop fighting until he beat it. We're still in touch and I was proud when I heard him call me a friend.

So many people helped me learn how to write a book and offered various kinds of support, from providers of cookies, to those with a sympathetic ear when I wanted to talk about the events I was reliving. I know the process took its toll on some of them. At one stage, I started work with a professional editor who had to regretfully back away because they had suffered something similar and found my story triggering; there really are a lot of us around. After that I found John, a friend of a friend, who offered to help me with basic editing, but then gave me an education and a skill-set I can use for the rest of my life. I'm immensely grateful.

And of course there is my sister, Jen (the aforementioned provider of cookies). Her strength and resilience are just what a little brother needs as a role model. Her support is, and always will be, a treasure to me. She's also the proud recipient of the Best Response award after I started telling people I was diagnosed with ADHD.

'Hey, guess what? I'm not annoying, I just have ADHD.'

'You're still annoying, you just also have ADHD.'

To go back in time for a moment, thank you to Nerdy

Prefect Oliver and to Chris. You might not even remember me, but I remember you, and always will. Thank you to Deborah and Suzanne for my education and for letting me be myself. I was difficult, I know, but you accepted me, which was what I needed at that point in my life. To all other teachers, especially English teachers, after all the berating, the putting me down and saying dyslexia isn't an excuse, all the times you said I wasn't trying and all the different ways you made me utterly hate writing and reading, I say this with all my heart: bite me.

If you've known me at any point during my life, perhaps this will help you understand me a bit more. Why I was so angry and volatile for so long. Why I react to some things more than I should. Why trust is one of the most important things in my life. And to one person, why you have scars from my fingernails in the back of your hands after you woke me up with a hug.

Thank you/sorry (delete as appropriate) to John, Diriye, Mel, Phil, Pennii, Alfie, Lee, Jane, Mic, Sarah, Andrew, Mark, assorted Campbells, Toni, Gordon and a lifetime of friends, family, lovers and opponents. The list could go on. I haven't forgotten you or left you out; I just can't be arsed to keep typing.

I've saved Jon, my husband, to last. How he's put up with me for twenty years, I have no clue, but he's more than my rock. He's my mountain, my world. I can't imagine my life without him, and I dread to think where I'd be if he hadn't entered it.

He met me in my 'prime', at twenty-one years old, and somehow tamed me. Well, mostly. He's the kindest, most generous, most forgiving person I've ever met. For so many years I was unable to go into the detail of my story to his face, which is why I wouldn't let him into the court when I was testifying. He'd have been so hurt not to have protected me from it, even though he didn't know me at that time. Each year I'm with him, I'm a little bit more fixed, and that's his doing.

I said I was saving Jon till last, but actually I want the last person to be you, the person who got to the end of this book despite my teenage selfishness, my antics and attitude, my foul language and filthy past. Thank you for staying with me until I grew up, and for letting me get all of this out. Sometimes all we need is that one person to listen, and that person is you.

### THE END

Or, finally, a beginning?

If you have enjoyed or been moved by *I'm Fine*, do please help us spread the word – by putting a review online; by posting something on social media; or in the old-fashioned way by simply telling your friends or family about it.

Book publishing is a very competitive business these days, in a saturated market, and small independent publishers such as ourselves are often crowded out by the big houses. Support from readers like you can make all the difference to a book's success.

Many thanks.

Dan Hiscocks
Founder, Eye Books